OLMSTED'S AMERICA

OLMSTED'S AMERICA

An "Unpractical" Man
and His
Vision of Civilization

Lee Hall

A Bulfinch Press Book

Little, Brown and Company

Boston • New York • Toronto • London

Frontispiece/title-page spread: The Boston Common and Public Garden contained some of the features Olmsted believed important to a rural park in an urban setting: curved walkways to encourage strolling, shade to provide places to rest, and water for its aesthetic and recreational properties.

First Edition

Library of Congress Cataloging-in-Publication Data
Hall, Lee.
    Olmsted's America:
An "unpractical" man and his vision of civilization / Lee Hall. — 1st ed.
      p. cm.
    "A Bulfinch Press book."
    Includes bibliographical references (p.   ) and index.
    ISBN 0-8212-1998-7
    1. Olmsted, Frederick Law, 1822–1903. 2. Landscape architects — United States — Biography.
3. Landscape architecture — United States — History. 4. Olmsted, Frederick Law, 1822–1903 —
Views on United States. 5. United States — Civilization. I. Title.
SB470.05H34   1995
712'.092 — dc20   94-34663
[B]

Designed by Peter M. Blaiwas
Typesetting in Weiss and Shelley Allegro by Dix Type Inc.

Bulfinch Press is an imprint and trademark of Little, Brown and Company (Inc.)
Published simultaneously in Canada by Little, Brown & Company (Canada) Limited

PRINTED IN THE UNITED STATES OF AMERICA

to
Robert and Janna
and
Tom and Frank

Contents

Acknowledgments

*M*any people advised, encouraged, and assisted me in writing about Frederick Law Olmsted and his vision of American civilization, beginning with the subject himself. While a college student I met Olmsted through his writing, but it was architect Paula Treder who introduced me to the magic of Central Park, and to the beginning of my obsession with the man, his parks, and his ideas. Decades later, in what would prove to be the beginning of this book, I turned again to Olmsted's descriptions of the antebellum South, secure in the belief that he was an accurate observer and fair-minded reporter. Over the years my appreciation for Olmsted has deepened with increasing familiarity with his writings, ideas, and designs.

The excellent staff of the New York Public Library and the Library of Congress provided guidance and material from the collections of rare books and manuscripts, prints and photographs, and periodicals. I am especially grateful for permission to use the Frederick Law Olmsted Papers in the Rare Books and Manuscripts Division of the Library of Congress. Ms. Joyce Connolly extended hospitality and professional assistance in photographing material at the Olmsted house (the Clarksted) in Brookline, Massachusetts. This project also benefited measurably from staff help and collections of libraries at Mount Holyoke and Amherst Colleges.

I owe special debts to Sherry Wilding White, curator of special collections at the New Hampshire Historical Society; Judith Walsh, local history librarian at the Brooklyn Public Library; George M. White, FAIA, architect of the Capitol; Tracy B. Grimm, archivist, Albany County Hall of Records; Daira D'Arienzo, archivist of Amherst College; Field Horne at the Historical Society of Saratoga Springs; Sally Thoren, Andover Historical Society; James Stuart Osbourn, senior reference librarian, New Jersey Division, Newark Public Library; Judy Haven, research associate, Onondaga Historical Association; Gail N. Colglazier, curator of collections, Connecticut Valley Historical Museum; Donald E. Loker, Niagara Falls Public Library; Pamela Scheffel, Rochester Public Library; Patricia M. Virgil, Buffalo and Erie County Historical Society; Elsa Meyers, librarian, New Jersey Historical Society; Marie Lore, South Street Seaport Museum; Joann Ryan, planner, city of

Albany; Christine M. Miles, director, Albany Institute of History and Art; Rebecca M. Rogers, United States Capitol Historical Society; Hugh Powell, Staten Island Institute of Arts and Sciences; and Susan P. Walker, archivist, United States Military Academy at West Point.

No artist could dream of a better steward of his work and reputation than Olmsted has in Bill Alexander, curator of grounds at Biltmore, Asheville, North Carolina. I remain appreciative to Bill for sharing his vast knowledge of and enthusiasm and love for Olmsted's great work in the Smoky Mountains. Janna Fitzgerald accompanied me to Biltmore, her enjoyment enhancing my own. I thank her for marrying into my family, for her years of interest in my work, and for her patience in walking miles, carrying camera equipment, and shooting many rolls of film for the Olmsted book.

Several other intrepid adventurers joined me in segments of my research. Ben Mauceri found helpful clues in my search for evidences of Olmsted on Staten Island. Phyllis Freeman added humor and zest to the Staten Island trek.

I am grateful to several dear friends for enthusiastic encouragement of the idea for this project: Abe Ajay, Phyllis Freeman, Nell Eurich Lazarus, and Ruth Weintraub. I am grateful to Steve Moseley, president of the Academy for Educational Development, for his help and understanding, and to my agent for this book, John Hochmann, for finding the perfect publisher and the perfect editor for it. Every writer should be blessed by an editor with the skills and good sense of Brian Hotchkiss, who has contributed to the book and to its author's sense of confidence and purpose. Similarly, writers only dare dream of handing manuscript and pictures to a designer as sensitive and creative as Peter Blaiwas.

Finally, I gladly thank Margaret Horsnell for hours of conversation and keen advice on this book, and for enriching my understanding of nineteenth-century America.

— **Lee Hall**
South Hadley, Massachusetts
August 1994

Prologue

The world is a civilized one, its inhabitant is not: he does not see the civilization of the world around him, but he uses it as if it were a natural force. . . . In the depths of his soul he is unaware of the artificial, almost incredible, character of civilization, and does not extend his enthusiasm for the instruments to the principles which made them possible.

— *José Ortega y Gasset*
The Revolt of the Masses

Frederick Law Olmsted (1822–1903) is today seen as a towering figure among nineteenth-century geniuses, the recognized father of landscape architecture in America, the designer whose name lives in association with parks, campuses, and planned communities in cities throughout the United States. He is venerated for his pioneering efforts in designing parks for a rapidly urbanizing America, for his role in the preservation of scenic landscape through federal parks and the conservation of natural beauty, and for his advocacy of the development of managed forests, thus spawning the "Cradle of Forestry" in the North Carolina mountains.

Now, a century after he laid down his pencil, folded his topographical maps, and passed his practice on to his sons and associates, the great works credited to Olmsted — Central Park in New York, Prospect Park in Brooklyn, and the park systems of Boston and Buffalo, for example — have the status of near-sacred lands and are enjoyed and protected by politicians, citizens, and students of design. Today, Olmsted's ideas and reputation have transcended the label "unpractical man" often applied to him during his lifetime, and he is celebrated for his work on the Columbian Exposition in 1893, for planned communities in suburbia and in the form of college campuses, and for the grounds of great private estates throughout the country.

Born into the early years of the American industrial revolution, spiritually awakened by the transcendentalists, and intellectually challenged by the promises of science and rationalism, Olmsted anticipated the social problems that would be engendered by the great changes of the nineteenth century and that to a large degree would define the twentieth century. As a very young man, curious about the progress and problems spawned by industrialization, urbanization, and the westward expansion of the country, Olmsted saw the need for social reform. He was absolutely certain about the evils of slavery, but unsure about its remedies; similarly, he wanted a role in the elevation of all people, in the spread of values, tastes, and manners that in his judgment separated "the civilized" from "the barbaric."

As he grappled with the social upheavals of the nineteenth century, trying his hand at first one enterprise and then another, he left a record of thoughtful, critical reflection of precisely what he meant by *civilization*. He observed nineteenth-century society in his own small-town New England, in the antebellum South, on the frontiers of Texas and California, in the chaos of the Civil War, in the political arenas of Washington and New York, and among the men of power and prestige with whom he sought to be associated.

Olmsted wrote voluminously, not just because he identified himself as a writer for part of his life, but also because he communicated through letters to family and friends and because he used writing as a tool for thinking. According to Charles Capen McLaughlin, editor in chief of the Frederick Law Olmsted Papers, the landscape architect's personal and professional papers comprise some sixty thousand separate items covering the span of years from 1838 to 1903 and mostly dwelling in the manuscript collection of the Library of Congress.

His books on the South, written in the 1850s, display his astute powers of observation and his analytical and rational approach to understanding society. These antebellum works, widely read and celebrated during Olmsted's life, remain important chronicles of the life and culture of the slaveholding states. In like manner, Olmsted's private letters and papers, shaped by the same powers of observation and inquisitive mind that reported on the South before the Civil War, reveal aspects of the nineteenth century as well as the personality of the writer.

Though he was what today would be termed "a late bloomer," a man who tested and abandoned a series of occupations before he dedicated himself to landscape architecture, Olmsted was appreciated in his own age, first by his family and a few close friends who early discerned in him the ingredients of genius. By the end of his career, *Garden and Forest*, a magazine that Olmsted helped to found, identified him as the "foremost artist which the New World has yet produced," but predicted that his memory "may be dimmed in the passage of years, for it is the fate of architects to be lost in their work." [1]

Although Olmsted was honored during his lifetime, the *Garden and Forest* prediction almost proved true, in part because most people have short attention spans where history is concerned, but to a larger extent due to the nature of Olmsted's work. Landscape architecture, once taken from the conceptual nursery of the designer's table, is at the mercy of people and weather. Land designed by the human hand is alive; a park has its own life and must stand up to the ravages of war, pollution, storms, and vandalism. Landscape architecture is arguably the most fragile and evanescent of art forms, for, whether looked over by a sensitive steward or assaulted by vandals, it is by its nature always in the process of changing, always becoming something other than the perfect moment envisioned by its human creator.

In reality, who, save the landscape designer himself, has a definite vision of the work? Designed landscape (no less than nature itself) hangs precariously on natural flux, with trees and grass growing and storms reshaping land and foliage, with use wearing away landmasses and altering relationships inherent to the design. To some degree, therefore, the lover of parks must always infer the designer's intention, must sense the reality of the design behind the actuality of the park at any given point in time. In this sense, the park lover collaborates with the designer and in imagination lifts the idea of the park free of the vicissitudes of neglect, mismanagement, abuse, natural cycles of life and death, and the mischief and caprice of citizens and politicians.

Olmsted's works, however admired, have changed. Few today exist precisely as they emerged from his hand and mind; and only a very few — for example, the Biltmore Estate near Asheville, North Carolina — evidence the conscientious efforts of curators or park commissioners to preserve Olmsted's original design. This contributes in part to the realization that, despite his accomplishments and recognition during his lifetime, today Olmsted might be an obscure figure in the history of the nineteenth century if he had not been brought vividly to the contemporary mind by Lewis Mumford's chapter on him in *The Brown Decades*, published in the 1930s.

By 1972, the 150th anniversary of his birth, many Americans had become aware of the importance of ecology and the preservation of nature and turned attention to the father of landscape architecture. In that year, an extensive collection of letters and documents — from Olmsted's hand as well as material written by his family and friends — was first opened to the public at the Library of Congress, having been restricted for nearly fifty years.

During the same decade, two large biographies of Olmsted were published, both based upon the newly available materials in the collection that Olmsted's son Frederick Law Olmsted Jr. placed in the Library of Congress. Laura Wood Roper, with assistance from the Olmsted family as well as access to the Olmsted Papers before the collection was available to other biographers, published *FLO: A Biography of Frederick Law Olmsted* (1973), a detailed and lengthy book about the life of the great man. Elizabeth Stevenson's *Park Maker: A Life of Frederick Law Olmsted* (1977) measures Olmsted's achievements as a nineteenth-century conservationist and characterizes him as a man seeking to reconcile the forces of nature with the powers of art. In addition, Charles Capen McLaughlin and his associates undertook the monumental task of editing and publishing a multivolume edition of the Olmsted Papers.

The two biographies extol Olmsted's admirable qualities, including his intellectual power and zeal for social reform; but neither reflects aspects of his personality and patterns of behavior that, to the reader at the end of the twentieth century, suggest that his privileged position in nineteenth-century America instilled in him stereotypical thinking that he never fully overcame regarding African Americans, Native Americans, men, women, children, families, education, the responsibility and authority of government, and the nature of "civilization." While both biographies chronicle Olmsted's fervor for work, neither probes personal characteristics that some associates found difficult, including his defiance of orders and authority, his tyranny over subordinates, and his craving for recognition.

Frederick Law Olmsted was a complicated member of the human species, and an equally complex specimen of his age. He should be neither condemned nor praised for enacting and articulating the values, prejudices, and ideals of his culture; rather, he can, and should, be viewed in that context, and his ideas and actions should be understood as those of an affluent and influential man who, in many instances, surpassed the prevailing snobbery, racism, religious and racial prejudices, and patriarchal attitudes of his age. In his manifestation of nineteenth-century ideals, he created a metaphorical landscape containing utopian pastures, transcendental outlooks, rational paths of thought and reflection, but a landscape also accommodating noxious weeds and undrained swamps.

Today, with renewed interest in community planning, in ecology, in recreation and the outdoors, and in natural resources, Olmsted is regarded by many as a retroactive guru, as a familiar and friendly personality, and as an abiding spirit in the study of environmental design and ecology, in discussions of suburbia and planned communities, and in attempts to shape urbanization to human needs. Perhaps only Abraham Lincoln has achieved a higher status among the popularized saints of the nineteenth century.

But as the twenty-first century approaches, Olmsted's ideas, though conceived and born in nineteenth-century America, continue to vitalize thinking about the role of human beings in nature, about the nature and responsibility of citizenship in a complex post-industrial society, and about the power of design to preserve natural beauty and to create oases of nature within the cityscape. In his landscape designs and in his writings, Frederick

Law Olmsted perfected a vision of America that today remains cogent, even when it is not exercised in planning.

Not only Frederick Law Olmsted's extant designs, but his numerous letters and papers, as well as his published articles and books, reveal his influence on visible America and his underlying passionate belief in the dignity of human beings, his romantic philosophy of citizenship and his efforts to shape ideal settings for people, their homes, and their institutions in a rapidly changing America. While no single work illustrates both the sources of his inspiration in nature and small towns and the evidences of his genius in landscape architecture, taken together Olmsted's works speak poignantly to the modern mind, identifying and clarifying some of the most pressing issues of environment, urbanization, and quality of human life on this planet.

Although Olmsted is credited with establishing the profession of landscape architecture in the United States, and with almost single-handedly determining what are now regarded as some of the best instances of American cityscape, these far-reaching achievements only partially reflect the man's mind, social philosophy, and aesthetics; and this achievement, splendid though it is, scarcely suggests the pertinency of Olmsted's philosophy to today's social and ecological issues.

In a life that spanned the last three-quarters of the nineteenth century, Olmsted both observed and participated in enormous social changes in the United States. He held strong views on slavery, abolitionism, transcendentalism, religion, education, travel, the role and capabilities of women, the nature of cities and urbanization, and on his own belief in an almost mystical level of citizenship ("communicativeness"). A passionate advocate of freedom for all citizens in a democracy, he supported the Union in the Civil War and, after its founding in 1854, was active in the Republican Party.

While the words *ecology* and *environmentalism* do not appear in Olmsted's writings, his work attests to his prophetic understanding of those concepts and of the interdependency of human beings, government, and nature; further, his writings reveal the inspiration that he drew from scenic nature. Indeed, inspired by transcendentalism and nature, Olmsted thought and wrote profoundly about the ethical and moral responsibilities of human beings to the planet, and about the power of nature to restore the weary and improve the moral sensitivities of all who submit to its beauty and force.

It is significant that Olmsted used the nom de plume Yeoman in signing his early letters to newspapers — articles that were collected as his books on the antebellum South. He was born in the tradition of New England yeomanry and placed high value on self-reliance, independence, and the acquisition of useful skills. At once pragmatic and romantic, he was often graceful when his ideas were rejected and large spirited when they were adopted; but when convinced he was right about policy or plans, he could be obdurate, authoritarian, and disdainful of opinions contrary to his own. Devoted to his family, he was also driven by his appetite for work. But opposing forces and paradoxical values often impelled Olmsted, making him an elitist who found democracy both practical and sentimentally appealing, and a man who identified himself as a New England yeoman but self-consciously developed (and encouraged his children to do likewise) "social graces" that would enable him (and them) to consort with "the best people." Above all else, he was a man who drew inspiration from the American landscape and cityscape, and who used the actual and possible visible features of both to embody his romantic vision of humanity and citizenship.

Through his designs Frederick Law Olmsted, nineteenth-century New England yeoman, attempted to mediate between the raw forces of nature and the aesthetic and social needs of people. Finally, like all artists, he attempted to surpass the accepted barriers between mind and matter, between human beings and nature, and between citizens and society.

Olmsted's America was several countries at once: there was the nineteenth-century world of urbanization, industrialization, westward expansion, a world of promise and hope; there was the society of the time, run by the powers of capitalism and patriarchy, that supported slavery, murdered Native Americans, and denied full citizenship to women, a world in need of high-minded reformers; there was the smaller domestic world of the New England village, the yeoman's world that nurtured Olmsted and furnished him with his basic understanding of civilization; and there was the private world of his own imagination, purpose, and ambition — the ideal world that he sought to shape.

One
Yeoman's
Beginning

It may in truth be said, that in no part of the world are the people happier . . . or more independent than the farmers of New England.

— *Encyclopaedia Britannica, 1797*

Frederick Law Olmsted was born and nurtured in the yeoman tradition of nineteenth-century New England. His mature vision of an ideal human society — whether organized around rural or city life — stemmed from his early appreciation of New England small-town customs and manners, from the physical and spiritual pleasures of domesticity, and from the scenic nature of the surrounding countryside. As the father of American landscape architecture, he would find aesthetic delight in nature's picturesque vistas, and faith bordering on the religious in the power of natural beauty to renew the human soul.

He consciously appropriated the tradition of the New England yeoman-farmer when, as a young writer, he habitually signed his earliest published works — letters to editors of New York newspapers — "Yeoman," which symbolized for him integrity, versatility of skill and mind, and purity of spirit. "Yeoman" signified to Olmsted the basic ingredient of American civilization, the ideal democratic citizen who exercised his rights and responsibilities to himself, his family, and his community.

Frederick Law Olmsted was born in Hartford, Connecticut, April 26, 1822, the first child of John Olmsted and Charlotte Law Hull. His family's history was intertwined with that of New England since 1639, when his ancestor James Olmsted came from Essex, England, to seek his fortune in the New World. Forefather James, one of the original proprietors in Hartford, settled on seventy acres of land on the road that was to become Front Street.

Throughout his childhood, Frederick Law Olmsted roamed the Connecticut River valley, first with his father and family, later alone. He wrote, "It was my fortune . . . to be taken on numerous journeys in company with people neither literary, scientific nor artistic, but more than ordinarily susceptible to beauty of scenery and who with little talking about it, and none for my instruction, plainly shaped their courses and their customs with reference [to] the enjoyment of it" (PFLO I: FLO, "Autobiographical Fragment A.")
Mount Tom, little more than forty miles north of Hartford, Connecticut, was a favorite spot from which to view the gently curving great river and its fertile valley and the spires of village churches in the small New England communities nearby.

From James's settlement onward, the Olmsted family increased in wealth and prominence in the Connecticut River valley. James's son, Nicholas, an officer in the wars against the Indians and a deputy to the General Court, acquired additional land on both sides of the Connecticut River, then as now navigable from the seacoast to Hartford. The Olmsteds, like their neighbors, spawned farmers, patriots, soldiers, and sailors in the China trade.

Frederick's mother, Charlotte, died when he was three, shortly after the birth of his younger brother, John Hull. He remembered very little about her and easily accepted as mother his father's second wife, Mary Ann Bull, a friend of Charlotte's and a deeply religious woman. Frederick, his brother, John, and their several half siblings were solicitous, respectful, and affectionate toward Mary Ann.

But John Olmsted, a well-to-do dry-goods merchant, shaped his son's values, supported his enthusiasms, and encouraged him in the several pursuits that finally combined as the foundation for his career as a landscape architect. John's large dry-goods store secured an affluent life for his family in Hartford, and, despite his lifelong regret at having achieved only a common school education, the elder Olmsted was widely regarded as a substantial citizen of the Connecticut River community. Quietly altruistic and civic-minded, John Olmsted served as a member of the fire department, as an aide-de-camp to the general of militia in his town, as a director of the Hartford Retreat for the Insane, and as a trustee of the Wadsworth Atheneum. But he shied away from public attention or acclaim, preferring the pleasures of domesticity and of traveling to marvel at picturesque scenery.

John Olmsted doted on his family and home, extolled the virtues of responsible citizenship, and determined early in the lives of his two sons that they would have the education he had not acquired. Although John included his wife and children in his numerous excursions to view scenic landscape and experience the spiritual uplift it provided, Frederick recalled that his father rarely expressed opinions about the beauty that so moved him.

Nonetheless, by the time he was twelve, young Frederick had seen most of New England and had visited West Point, Lake George, Niagara Falls, and Quebec. And he was as dedicated to the picturesque as was his father.

Olmsted's Education

Despite his father's determination to give him the best possible education in preparation for matriculation at Yale College, Frederick's schooling was erratic. After Charlotte's death, Frederick's father, believing that village ministers in Connecticut could instill piety in his son as well as prepare him to study at Yale College, turned the energetic youngster over to a series of ministers who ranged from good to cruel, and from intelligent and trust-worthy mentors to somewhat shifty and hypocritical tyrants in their dealings with their young charges.[1]

After being subjected to several schools run by rural ministers, Frederick boarded in North Guilford with the Reverend Zolva Whitmore, a Congregational minister, a kind and wise man who understood that not all learning comes from books and that the rod was unnecessary in the classroom. Olmsted later recalled his happy time with Whitmore and remembered fondly the delightful rural setting; the gently paced lessons that left time for exploring the nature of the militia and the intricacies of beekeeping; the leisure of hanging out in the country store listening to the talk of local men; and the lazy explo-ration of the nearby forests and fields. Frederick's near-idyllic life with Whitmore ended, however, when John Olmsted decided that the youngster needed a more demanding tutor.[2]

In his autobiographical notes, Olmsted recounted a particularly bitter patch of school-ing. For five years, he lived in a cold wooden building in the farmyard of minister-school-master Joab Brace in Newington, Connecticut. Brace worked the boys in his charge hard, requiring physical labor on the farm as well as hours of study in their drafty quarters. Moreover, he was quick to punish, often harshly.[3] Brace also hired teenage "teachers" from the village to instruct his charges in Scripture. Olmsted found them to be arrogant, cruel, and ignorant.[4]

By 1840, when his formal education was deemed completed, young Frederick had been subjected to twelve different programs of learning, beginning with the Dames' School in Hartford. After years of boarding with the series of clergymen, Frederick later reckoned, he had not acquired the education that he thought should have been his.

But young Frederick pursued his own education on his own terms. Naturally curious, gregarious, and adventurous, he loved the out-of-doors and, on a scale smaller than his fa-ther's far-ranging pursuit of the picturesque, Frederick explored the countryside near Hart-ford. On one occasion, he and his brother, then nine and six respectively, hiked sixteen miles through unfamiliar country to visit an uncle and aunt. The adventure took two days and included an overnight stay in a rural inn.

Throughout his years of formal schooling, Olmsted returned to his family for frequent vacations. Over the years of childhood he grew especially close to his younger brother, forming a friendship that became central to the development and maturation of each. Frederick counted John as his best friend and continually called on him to serve as both confidant and counsel. John, who would die young, selflessly served and promoted Freder-ick throughout his life.

Saratoga Springs, New York, became a favorite pleasure ground where an increasingly urban population sought the relaxation of semirural surroundings. As a child Olmsted and his family visited the town for pleasure. Later, exhausted by his work with the Sanitary Commission in the Civil War, Olmsted retreated to Saratoga Springs to recuperate.

Frederick also enjoyed the friendship and informal teaching of his uncle Jonathan Law, a friend of John Greenleaf Whittier. The patient and bookish kinsman introduced young Olmsted to his library and allotted him a fragment of garden in which to experiment with horticulture.[5]

His curiosity and natural love of learning, moreover, drew him to literature and impelled him to read voraciously during his entire life. While still a child, he surveyed the libraries of friends and relatives to find and feast on books. It was perhaps in these early foragings in the libraries of learned gentlemen that he came across prints of English park scenery and the eighteenth-century writings of Uvedale Price and William Gilpin, who praised the picturesque and instructed the British gentry on how to appreciate scenery on their travels.

In addition to books, Olmsted was deeply influenced by long family trips by coach or canal boat, by carriage or on horseback. These journeys in search of the picturesque imbued him with a lasting appreciation of nature. Before Frederick reached adolescence, his

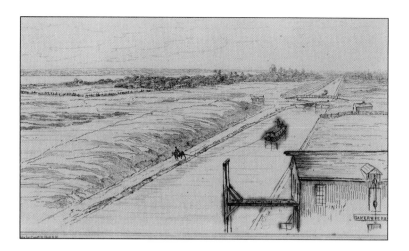

The Erie Canal was completed in 1825, linking Lake Erie with New York City via the Hudson River. The 363-mile-long-canal, with eighty-three locks, was built along a site laid out by James Geddes in 1809. It was not until 1816, however, that Congress appropriated funds for the project. The Erie Canal — and water transportation in general — was an important topic of conversation during Olmsted's childhood.

quiet and industrious father had led the family in search of scenic vistas including the White Mountains, the Maine coast, and large portions of New York State.

Although John Olmsted never spoke to Frederick about his feelings as he stood in the presence of natural beauty, it was apparent to his son that the elder Olmsted's appreciation bordered on the religious experience he sought but never found, that instead he found evidence of God's goodness in the beauty of nature. John Olmsted made it clear to his sons that he hoped they would find God in personal mystical revelations. Eventually Frederick would convince himself that

The Connecticut River south of Hartford was navigable to Long Island Sound, but the rough and swift-running reaches to the north could be dammed to capture its power for the growing industries of the valley. All over America, water power was being harnessed: the industrial revolution was under way.

he had felt his soul stirring in a desired religious conversion, but his was a short-lived conversion, and he soon realized that he found deeper emotional and spiritual meaning in nature. But John's nurturing of Frederick's sensibilities provided fertile soil for the ideas he discovered in and on the sites that they appreciated in their travels.[6]

By the time he completed his elementary and high school education, Olmsted had become romantic and idealistic. Possessing a hungry mind and the drive of an intellectual, the spirit of an idealist and romantic, and being a young affluent male in the middle of the nineteenth century, Olmsted was a social and educational elitist and ripe for the moral and intellectual challenges of his era.

But ideas alone would never fully satisfy him. Even as a young man, he sought consonance between theory and his observations of nature and human life, between scrutiny of society and participation in life as a leader for social change. From his rural New England childhood, Frederick embarked in rapid succession upon a series of apprenticeships, in turn intending to become a surveyor, a merchant, and a farmer.

The Surveyor and Merchant

Frederick contracted sumac poisoning, which threatened his eyesight and eventually kept him from entering Yale. During his convalescence, unable to read or study, Olmsted wandered the Hartford countryside to visit family members and friends. Forsaking his dream of studying at Yale, teenaged Olmsted decided to enter the field of civil engineering through an apprenticeship with Frederick Augustus Barton (1809–1881). Olmsted went to live with Barton, a surveyor and civil engineer who taught mathematics at Phillips Academy, in Andover, Massachusetts, while studying for the ministry at Andover Theological Seminary. When Barton completed his theological studies and took a church in Collinsville, Connecticut, Olmsted followed him and continued his studies with him until May 1840.

Olmsted's apprenticeship with Barton was to be the first of a long series of embarkations on careers that came to nought. While with the engineer-clergyman, Olmsted learned basic surveying, but he also found ample time to further his enjoyment of nature and life. "It followed," Olmsted recalled, "that at the time my schoolmates were entering college I was nominally the pupil of a topographical engineer but really for the most part given over to a decently restrained vagabond life, generally pursued under the guise of an angler, a fowler or a dabbler on the shallowest shores of the deep sea of the natural sciences."[7]

During this time, he later recalled, he also drew fantasy towns and cities. These active and introspective searches for pleasure, these experiences of scientific study and outdoor

America changed rapidly in the first years of Olmsted's life, with industrial expansion and growth of cities encouraged by the expanding railroads. Although he professed distaste for train travel — and for the hotels catering to rail passengers — Olmsted continually traveled throughout the country, logging miles on every available form of transportation.

life, of daydreaming on a drawing pad and of working in the out-of-doors, he later identified as the advent of interests that would culminate in his career as a landscape architect.[8]

But at the time, neither Olmsted nor his father saw any connection between Frederick's delightful escapades and his future. Indeed, John Olmsted, worried by Frederick's seeming inability to select a direction for himself, took matters into his own hands and arranged for his son to clerk in the store of James Benkard and Benjamin H. Hutton, a Beaver Street textiles firm in Manhattan. Although the lure of French silks and mercantilism did not snare Frederick, and his time with Benkard and Hutton developed in him no fondness for business, his imagination was captured by the docks and the ships he visited to check shipments of dry goods. He stayed little more than a year in New York before returning to his family and to the countryside around Hartford.[9]

At home, surrounded by his family, Olmsted socialized with his friends and visited his brother at Yale College. There, too, Olmsted enjoyed the intellectual stimulation and social whirl of other young people. After seeking the experience of religious conversion extolled by his father, he turned to a source more instinctive to him in his pursuit of spirituality, nature. And, like many other educated and privileged Americans of his century, Olmsted wanted to combine the power of scientific or rational thinking with the exaltation of spiritual and aesthetic experience.

Through friendship with Yale students, Olmsted discovered the social reform movements brewing in the United States, and he began to read the transcendentalists whose writings dealt with spirituality and nature, with civic responsibility and individual exercise of conscience. But Frederick was not ready to settle down and devote himself to good works and a career. Perhaps recalling the ships docked near Benkard and Hutton, he decided to go to sea.

Seaman

In 1842, Frederick turned twenty and his brother, John, entered Yale. The older brother must have felt that life was passing him by and must have been equally happy for his brother's fate and disappointed in his own unfocused future. At that time Olmsted seemed to make a sudden decision to set sail toward adventure as well as work. In his unsettled state, eager for knowledge of a larger world of adventure, he turned to the sea — the ultimate symbol of romantic yearning — and to the adventure that has beckoned many Americans seeking to find the meeting of mind and body.

It was not unusual for nineteenth-century young men from good families to undertake such adventures. Herman Melville served on a whaler for three years, an experience that surely fed the genius behind one of America's great literary masterpieces. While Olmsted did not know Melville, he had read Richard Henry Dana Jr.'s *Two Years Before the Mast* and was familiar with that writer's account of the cruel treatment that befell seamen, of the dangers and hardships abundant on vessels in the China trade.

On April 23, 1843, Frederick, as the lowest-ranked seaman on board, shipped out on the bark *Ronaldson*. Although some of Olmsted's forebears had been to sea, he was himself without experience to qualify as anything other than an apprentice seaman on the vessel. He began his journey with high hopes and optimism born of his own romantic nature and of his reading of *Two Years Before the Mast*. But Captain Warren Fox made life hell for Olmsted, and perhaps worse for other men on the ship.[10]

The ship, laden so heavily with what Olmsted called "Yankee notions" that it was impossible to include adequate supplies of water and food for the crew, rounded the Cape of Good Hope, crossed the Indian Ocean to Java Head, then to Hong Kong and Canton — a four-month voyage in which the captain turned tyrant and the seas turned tumultuous. Soon disabused of his romantic preconceptions about life on a sailing vessel, and thoroughly seasick a good part of the time, young Olmsted wrote regularly to his father, his brother, and his friends, revealing his growing revulsion at the ship's captain's abuse of his absolute power.

Olmsted was not fitted by experience or temperament for life as a seaman. He wrote:

> I have tried with all my heart to think well of the bark in which my lot is cast, to believe that those evils which we have felt — & which have produced so much ill feeling in others, in all my shipmates — were the result of accident, negligence & necessity. I have endeavored to think that it was from the nature and habit of the men & that in other ships I would find as much grumbling — if not from the same, from similar grievances. In this I succeeded pretty well, and as I wrote you from Anjer, there was not so contented a person on board. Since our arrival, however, I am convinced of necessity that our men not only are more discontented, but have much more cause for complaint than the crew of other vessels here, our neighbors. We are worked much longer, if not harder, & have many less privileges than are customarily allowed.

Olmsted, a slight young man, experienced misery he could not have dreamed. Seasick and afflicted by a series of maladies and fevers, unable to eat or to attend to his duties for long periods of the journey, the adventuresome young man lay on his bunk and suffered. But his physical sufferings were not as painful, he found, as the agonies inflicted on his mates by their cruel and brutal captain. Frederick was to recall the hard work, injustices, and brutalization of seafaring life for the rest of his days.[11]

Olmsted planned to visit China and witness firsthand the customs and the people, but the *Ronaldson* rested only briefly in Hong Kong, a port city beset by fever, which prevented commerce. In the next port, Canton, the ship lay at anchor, waiting for the arrival of its cargo of tea, cassia, and raw silk. Moreover, during this time when he had hoped to explore China, Olmsted was laid up by illness and constricted by his duties on board ship. He had few opportunities to go ashore and, once there, scant opportunity to venture into the closed Chinese society.

In letters to his family he did not describe the city or the Chinese countryside, but he did comment on the surprising courtesy of the Chinese toward foreigners, even in the shadow of aggravation lingering from the recent Opium War between the Chinese and British. China also provided a challenge to Olmsted's pride in country, which approached ethnocentrism. While in that mysterious country, he visited with sailors on other ships; onshore, he walked busy streets, visited workers in a variety of occupations and students in a classroom. The visible evidences of an exotic culture whetted his curiosity, while his natural tendency to faith in human goodness was supported by his observations of a foreign civilization. He later reflected:

I suppose that civilization is to be tested as much by civility as anything else, and I have recalled . . . a personal experience which made a strong impression upon me, tending to a higher estimate of the social condition of the masses of the Chinese people than, I think, generally prevails.[12]

Civilization would become a frequent topic in Olmsted's writings. He found himself nearly swept off his civilized base and into barbarity on the *Ronaldson*. Near the end of the voyage home, the crew of the bark, suffering from scurvy and overwork, threatened mutiny after a young sailor, falsely accused of swearing, was flogged. Olmsted described the reaction of his shipmates:

"How long are we to let that go on?" asked one, while another counted aloud the lashes — "Twenty-three, twenty-four" — "We are no men if we stand it longer." With this, he sprang forward, and nearly every man snatched a

Olmsted was not interested in the importing business, but the boats at the New York docks struck a responsive romantic chord in the young man. He had read *Two Years Before the Mast*, written by Harvard graduate and lawyer Richard Henry Dana Jr. The account of Dana's voyage to California as a common sailor, and of the life of sailors tyrannized by cruel captains notwithstanding, Olmsted decided to go to sea.

Olmsted's experiences on the *Ronaldson* proved uncomfortably like those detailed in the novel. Olmsted may not have been familiar with Dana's "Cruelty to Seamen," a legal paper dealing with the injustices suffered by merchant sailors. Later, however, Olmsted took up the pen to protest the treatment of men at sea and to urge legal reform.

As cities increased in size and population during the nineteenth century, newly instituted parklike cemeteries — as opposed to the rural church graveyard — served as sites to bury and memorialize the dead and as landscaped spaces for strolling and meditating. These private, or secular, cemeteries are indicative of the essential changes occurring in American society of the period: Could the forces and material goods of the industrial revolution be compatible with religious conviction?

handspike or drew his sheath-knife. I fully expected to see the officers thrown overboard, when in a moment, almost before a step was made, our oldest and best man exclaimed, "Avast! avast! Come back, you fool; put down your knife; what do you want to run your head into a halter for? Can't you wait till we get home and let the law serve them out?" This interruption led to more deliberation, and finally a single man went aft, unarmed, with a remonstrance, which fortunately was heeded.[13]

Later in his life, Olmsted recalled that he had been "strangely uneducated, — miseducated . . . chiefly taught how not to study." Soon after his return from China, however, he decided that his "secluded life, country breeding, and miseducation were not such bars to an 'intellectual life' as [he] was in the habit of supposing." While Olmsted's growing passion for the "intellectual life" had not taken form, he had had his fill of life as a seaman.

When Olmsted, thin and worn from labor and illness, stepped ashore on April 15, 1844, his father did not immediately recognize him.[14]

The sea proved no more fitting a career for Frederick than had surveying. He returned to Hartford with his father, spent the summer recuperating from his exhausting adventure and renewing friendships with old pals. Once he returned to American shores, he drew from his experiences at sea and published numerous letters in New York newspapers urging changes in maritime laws to protect seamen and passengers alike.

Olmsted's memories of his service before the mast of the *Ronaldson* and of the injustices inflicted on seamen by tyrannical captains impelled him to action. Like other nineteenth-century men of his class and character, his weapon was the pen. He believed that words, rationally and persuasively marshaled, would sway opinion, would educate, and would inspire citizens to right wrongs.

In writing his long article "A Voice from the Sea" for the *American Whig Review*, Olmsted recalled the *Ronaldson's* bullying captain and argued for the creation of schools to train sailors in seamanship, order, and discipline. Moreover, he wrote that sailors should have opportunities for wholesome recreation in their ports of call, including the use of public parks and gardens.

In a few years Olmsted would take to the pen again, but he turned first to the land and, as a farmer, added another set of experiences to those accumulating toward his ultimate passion for landscape architecture.

Lessons of the Land

When Frederick stepped off the *Ronaldson*, John Olmsted took his thin, sickly, weakened son home to Hartford to spend the summer regaining his strength. It was for Frederick an idyllic, if unpurposeful, summer. The young blade's talents lay dormant while he whittled away at romantic fantasies. Restless, unable to find a direction for his life, Olmsted enjoyed the continuing financial support and unqualified love of his father. Yet, in his random adventures and explorations, Olmsted was accruing experience and information, skills and disciplines that would eventually meld into intellectual and psychological power and would enable him to realize his dream of being a man who mattered.

Frederick's New England background included the bedrock of his attitudes about citizenship, intermingled traditions of yeomanry and puritanism, of both religion and science. Having struggled and failed to experience the religious epiphany his father coveted for him, young Olmsted's faith found root in science, in rationality, and in his own form of stoical humanism. He assumed that all men of his class enjoyed a broad education, participated in the affairs of their communities, and upheld prudent standards of conduct.

Now twenty-two, Olmsted had tried and rejected a number of possible career paths: in May he decided to be a scientific farmer and set out to find a model farmer and farm to study.

Early spring in New England is a sweet time of greening fields and opening blossoms, certain to draw poetic souls closer to the earth and seasons. Olmsted created in his imagination a muse of lyric agriculture as he went in search of an ideal farm and a scientific farmer to teach him the methods of farming in New England. After considering jobs on farms near Boston and Northampton, he found the mentor through whom he hoped to secure for himself the happy, moral, aesthetic life he imagined to be the benison of the diligent American farmer. With bright dreams and high expectations, he went to work for the summer of 1845 on Joseph Welton's farm, near Waterbury, Connecticut.[1]

That fall, taking a break from farm work, Frederick visited John at Yale.[2] Frederick's social life during this time was to prove as important as his work to his growth. John, who intended to be a medical doctor, brought Frederick into his circle of friends and their long searching discussions about society and reform. Frederick, now committed to scientific agriculture, participated in the conversations about changing society and envisioned the social good that would result from better-managed land and livestock, better-planned crops, and a farmer's life combining moral, political, and aesthetic principles in beautiful homes, educated families, and good stewardship of nature.

In many ways, Olmsted was the quintessential nineteenth-century man, an autocrat by nature and a patriarch by nurture. For him, as for most men of the nineteenth century, his home was the symbol of his position in the world, and his wife and children — however loved and honored for their individuality — the signs of his social status. When we are poised on the threshold of the twenty-first century and view the historical Olmsted as the genius progenitor of landscape architecture, it is easy to disregard the degree to which his personality and social values were shaped by his gender and his century and by his high regard for domesticity.

Like his father, Frederick placed high value on home and family; he longed to fall in love, to marry and become a husband and father. He confided to his brother:

The Maine coat of arms (1837) reflects the New England history of economic prosperity based on seafaring and agriculture. Men of the region had long extracted their livelihoods from sea and soil, often working independently and mastering numerous skills. Olmsted was firmly rooted in the yeoman tradition. Having tried his hand before the mast, he then turned his attention to scientific farming.

I sent a letter to Father yesterday in answer to one I received from him last week in which he gave me a lecture on Rash marriages, &c., saying that matrimony was a subject for me not to think of for years. I've no intention of marrying for three or four years. But I'd just as lief as not be engaged, if I came across a suitable person, before I took a farm on my own account, fearing that after that I should have no good opportunity of selection. I think I should like to cruise for about a year, then fall desperately in love & lay off and on till I could bring about an engagement.[3]

But despite longing to find a wife, playing at courtship, and casting himself as something of a would-be swain, Frederick had not managed to lose his heart to any of the young women in his group in Hartford or to find a suitable farmer's wife. He met a likely girl in New Haven, however, and embarked upon a highly formalized if lukewarm courtship. The young woman did not become his wife; she became his mentor.

Elizabeth Wooster Baldwin, the pretty daughter of Roger Sherman Baldwin, recent governor of Connecticut, may not have set fire to Frederick's heart or awakened sexual passion, but she apparently introduced him to the writings of Ruskin, Lowell, and Emerson. His lack of formal education, she assured him, did not prevent him from becoming an educated gentleman, a man of stature in society. This assurance, coming from a respected person, was just what Olmsted wanted and needed to hear. Bolstered by Elizabeth's judgment of him, he renewed his ambition to become a man of consequence and to undertake the self-education necessary to fulfill that ambition.

In addition to talking with friends at Yale, philosophizing about reform of society and self, Olmsted read widely, including Richard Whately's *Elements of Logic*, James Mill's *History of British India, The Federalist*, as well as poetry, fiction, and ecclesiastical literature.[4] Furthermore, his romantic tastes, honed by his diligent reading of the writings of Benjamin Silliman, Timothy Dwight, William Gilpin, and Uvedale Price — as well as by Elizabeth Baldwin's reading list — were continually enlivened by the friends he made while in New Haven. The conversations of that period convinced Olmsted that he had only to read, to think, and to educate himself to be and do whatever he chose. He drank the heady wine greedily.[5]

During those fall months in New Haven, Frederick seems to have attended classes, probably including lectures on scientific agriculture by Benjamin Silliman. If pretty Miss Baldwin turned one part of young Olmsted's mind toward the higher reaches of liberal learning and the ethers of transcendentalism, Professor Silliman's advocacy of scientific agriculture appealed equally to the part of Olmsted's nature that admired the practical man, the man of action, the rational man who was admired for solving problems.

Olmsted became convinced that his future, and that of agriculture as well, lay in scientific farming. As a farmer devoted to the latest scientific knowledge and methods of agriculture, he reasoned he could cultivate both parts of his ambition: he could be close to nature and simultaneously develop a model farm for others to emulate. He could be both poet and man of action; he could enjoy the spiritual rewards of transcendentalism and worldly acclaim for his bold enactment of rational principles. Farming, he believed, was an occupation that would afford him both the happy domestic life he wanted and the prestige of being a leader and reformer. "How shall I prepare myself," he asked a friend, "to exercise the greatest and best influence in the situation of life I am likely to be placed in?"[6]

In the middle of the nineteenth century most Americans were farmers, yet *scientific* farming was practiced by only a few. Olmsted the romantic and Olmsted the reformer joined as he imagined the kind of farm he would command, the life he would enjoy, and the leadership he could exercise in changing the agricultural methods of the country.[7]

In order to learn more about the latest scientific agricultural practices, Olmsted apprenticed himself to George Geddes. The son of James Geddes, the engineer on the Erie Canal, George owned and operated a model farm near Syracuse, New York,[8] and was living proof for Olmsted that the farmer's life was a good life.

Olmsted worked hard on the Geddes farm and soon gained confidence in his new skills and additional enthusiasm for his chosen career. Apparently missing family and

Farmers in the northeastern United States were considered successful if they could build and maintain comfortable houses for their families, solid barns and outbuildings, fences around grazing lots, and meadows rich in good grass, and if they owned fertile land, healthy animals, and sturdy equipment.

Olmsted, with his love of nature and deep roots in family life and ritual, began to idealize farming and to see the farmer as the quintessential free man. He dreamed of being a scientific farmer, a patriarch with time to read and ponder, and a wise and respected man who could influence others.

friends, he wrote long letters to his brother[9] about his farmer concerns: a rainstorm that washed away parts of the garden, a gate on an irrigation canal failing, fences breaking, wandering farm animals. He wrote of physical work and of his pride in handling both daily routines and emergencies.

Soon after he left the Geddes farm, Frederick persuaded his father to stake him to a little farm near Sachem's Head, near Guilford, on the coast of Connecticut. It was a small, poor farm, with little hope of prosperity; it was doomed from the start. Nonetheless, Frederick spent the year of 1847 trying to work the poor soil and to put the property in good order. When he realized that no amount of dawn-to-dusk labor would stimulate the rocky, unproductive soil toward commercial success, Frederick turned again to his father for assistance.

Olmsted listened to lectures at Yale on the newest developments in scientific agriculture and believed that a successful farm would depend in the future on proper investment, good management, and technology — the capitalist's tools — and not just physical labor.

New advances in technology included John Deere's steel plow (1833), a tool that promised to open the lands of the West. Until Deere's invention, American farmers had plowed the soil with instruments based on Thomas Jefferson's plow. A year after the appearance of Deere's innovative agricultural tool, Cyrus McCormick patented a grain reaper designed to reduce the need for labor on a farm.

NOVEMBER.

His inability to succeed as a farmer, Olmsted told his father, stemmed from the farm itself, and not farming as a career or from lack of effort on his own part. He needed a larger place, more fertile soil, and an environment that would support the life he envisioned. Again, John Olmsted helped Frederick pursue his dreams.[10]

In 1848, Frederick took possession of the Akerly farm, purchased for him by his father for the sum of twelve thousand dollars. The once-handsome farm on the south shore of Staten Island, now run-down and not fully productive, was nonetheless a fertile spread of about 130 acres. Olmsted's enthusiasm for the place grew as he perceived increasing possibilities for its use and for its visual improvement.

A neighbor on Staten Island, Dr. Cyrus Perkins, offered advice Olmsted was eager to hear and act upon. Perkins, urging Olmsted to improve his farm, theorized that it would be economical to spend money at the beginning of his venture in order to get the farm on a profit-producing basis as quickly as possible. When Frederick presented the idea to his father, however, he met initial resistance; but, as was by then usual, the elder Olmsted soon bent to his son's will. With support from his father, Olmsted spent more than thirty dollars an acre to prepare the soil for planting, an investment Olmsted calculated would be recouped within eight years. Dr. Perkins's theories, alas for Frederick, proved wrong, and Olmsted never managed to make money on his farm.[11]

But if Olmsted did not make money as a farmer, he nonetheless won prizes for his crops at the Richmond County agricultural fairs, including a silver spoon for his pears in 1852.[12] And, perhaps a better measure of the man he was becoming, Frederick made himself known socially and politically among his Staten Island neighbors.

Acting on his administrative and political instincts, Olmsted delegated much of the farm labor to hired men and invested his own time and energy in the Richmond County Agricultural Society, an organization founded to improve the tastes of local farmers in matters of architecture, landscape, and manners; to enhance their lives with better houses, better roads, and better methods of farming. As secretary of the society, Olmsted was active in advocating the higher tastes and style of living that he thought appropriate for the farmer's life and, in 1849, invited others to share his philosophy of agriculture and domesticity:

> *We ask you, then, Fellow Citizens, one and all, to associate in this Society. We entreat you to support it. We believe it will increase the profit of our labor — enhance the value of our lands — throw a garment of beauty around our homes, and above all, and before all, materially promote Moral and Intellectual Improvement — instructing us in the language of Nature, from whose preaching, while we pursue our grateful labors, we shall learn to receive her Fruits as the bounty, and her Beauty as the manifestation of her Creator.*[13]

On a more practical plane, he also led the society in developing one of the earliest cylindrical-drainage-tile works in the country and in installing English-style systems for turning soggy soil into friable fields.[14] Later, as a landscape architect, Olmsted would stress the importance of good drainage and good soil preparation, lessons he learned on his Staten Island farm.

While Olmsted's administrative and political skills were maturing, his passion for design was also finding expression. He avidly read the agricultural journals of the day, his conviction growing that farming was not simply a means to crop production, but a way of life, an enactment and realization of his romantic view of a happy and useful life. As he labored to transform his Staten Island farm from a run-down property to a gentleman's comfortable home, he impressed neighbors, including William Henry Vanderbilt, who liked what he saw and soon sought Olmsted's advice on improving his own farm at New Dorp, Staten Island. Other neighbors, too, recognized Olmsted's gift for design and management and bought trees from his nursery and sought his advice in planning their property.[15]

It is not surprising that Olmsted admired the work of Andrew Jackson Downing, the great landscape gardener in Newburgh, New York, north of New York City. He not only read Downing's magazine, the *Horticulturist*, but visited Downing at his home. Downing, like Olmsted, believed in scientific agriculture and used his magazine to promote his ideas for improving crops and living in tasteful surroundings.[16]

His scientific interests notwithstanding, and enamored of the view afforded by the Staten Island property and by his dream of an idealized rural life, Frederick may have worked harder on effecting picturesque surroundings than on taking cash crops to market. He removed the barns that blocked the view from the house and rebuilt them elsewhere on the property; he also rebuilt the nine-bedroom stucco-covered stone house; he evicted the dogs and geese from the muddy farm pond where they swam and reshaped it into a decorative pool that was host to a collection of water plants.[17]

It was a magnificent site. From the farmhouse, Olmsted could see New York City, the west end of Long Island, and the lighthouse at Sandy Hook. Whether by conscious choice or force of inchoate aesthetic yearnings, Frederick carried out a complete redesigning of the farm, many of his decisions appearing to be driven by his personal sense of beauty.

Many years later, in 1920, Olmsted's widow recalled the Staten Island farm on the main road to the shore of Prince's Bay:

Leaving the road, one entered a very pretty wood of trees of fair size, — oaks, maples, sweet and sour gum, sassafras, holly, etc. After about a quarter of a mile one came out upon the cleared land on top of a small rise. . . . There was a sort of plateau from which the land sloped gently down for about a quarter of a mile and then an almost level stretch went to the bank six feet above the beach. From all this part of the farm there was a fine view of Prince's Bay looking across to Sandy Hook, Navesink, and the New Jersey Hills stretching away to the southward.

Olmsted spent two years and large sums of his father's money to transform a nearly derelict property into a country home suitable for a cultured man. In that process he honed his talent for administration, devising systems and schedules for his workers that called forth maximum efficiency, encouraged good spirits, and rewarded excellence. He defined and scheduled chores by the hour and required his foreman to report on each day's progress at a specific time. Moreover, he often toiled alongside his hired hands in the sweat and grunt hard labor of laying drainage tiles, digging ditches, and caring for crops.

Despite hard physical work, Olmsted did not lose sight of his class membership or of his ambition to be a man of stature in society. He threw himself enthusiastically into the civic affairs of Staten Island, serving on the school board and joining other gentleman farmers in establishing the Richmond County Agricultural Society. But neither visible progress on the Staten Island farm nor stature earned in the community held Olmsted's attention. As a gentleman farmer Olmsted enjoyed a degree of prestige among his neighbors, influenced the affairs of his community, and entertained his friends. His brother, John, then a medical student in Manhattan, was a frequent guest, as was Charles Loring Brace, then studying at Union Theological Seminary. When John and Brace announced their plans to make a walking tour of England — John for his health (he had been diagnosed as suffering from tuberculosis) and Brace to study Christian social work in England — Frederick ached to join them.

He wrote to his father, described his long-standing passion to travel abroad, and argued that the trip would further his education as a scientific farmer. What he could learn from the latest English agricultural practices, he wrote, would be a solid investment in the future financial success of his farm.[18] John Olmsted generously agreed to finance his trip.

An American Farmer in a New World

At the end of April 1850, the three friends sailed aboard the *Henry Clay* for Liverpool, thus beginning their journey through England, followed by a month exploring France, Belgium, Holland, Germany, and completed during visits to Ireland and Scotland. From the beginning of his walking tour to its end in October, Frederick flooded the mails with letters detailing his experiences. Throughout the remainder of his life, he would take pleasure in travel and in recording his observations of places and people.[19]

As they walked about England, Olmsted's interests and subject of study changed significantly. He had persuaded his father that he needed to study the agricultural practices

in England and on the Continent, but his sights soon shifted. First, he perceived pure pleasure in the scenery that surrounded him daily, and, second, he discovered Birkenhead Park
and the great landscaped gardens of the gentry. After his tour of England, Olmsted's
Staten Island farm could no longer contain his vision of the ideal good life; he would seek
a larger arena in which to test his ideas.

The American farmer's change in direction began simply enough: he fell in love with
the English rural landscape. With display of neither grand vistas nor dramatically distin-
guishing features, the rolling green of England appealed deeply to the young American.
Under the spell of the countryside, Olmsted consistently overlooked the practical requirements of paying crops and submitted his senses to the visual richness of the landscape of
England.[20] Rather, in the "green, dripping, glistening, gorgeous"[21] English landscape his
mind was at work along with his eye; with acuity and sensibility, Olmsted began to identify the factors that made the English landscape so enchanting and that, in later years,
would serve as principles of design for his parks, campuses, and suburban developments.
He observed:

> The great beauty and peculiarity of the English landscape is to be found in the frequent long, graceful lines of deep
> green hedges and hedge-row timber, crossing hill, valley, and plain, in every direction; and in the occasional large
> trees, dotting the broad fields, either singly or in small groups, left to their natural open growth . . . therefore branching
> low and spreading wide, and more beautiful, much more beautiful, than we often allow our trees to make themselves.[22]

Thus, as he began to analyze the features of the picturesque English landscape, he also
studied the private parks of the great homes of the aristocracy and mentally compared and
contrasted the natural landscape and the work of the gardener. In one such garden, at
Eaton Hall, Olmsted noted his pleasure in seeing the deer park in late afternoon. John,
Charles, and Frederick sat under a tree and admired

> a gracefully irregular, gently undulating surface of close-cropped pasture land, . . . trees scattered singly and in
> groups — so far apart as to throw long unbroken shadows across broad openings of light, and leave the view in
> several directions unobstructed for a long distance. Herds of fallow-deer, fawns, cattle, sheep, and lambs quietly feeding
> near us, and moving slowly in masses at a distance.[23]

Although the gardens of the aristocracy appealed to him aesthetically, he could not divorce their cultivated beauty from the peasant labor that produced it and refused to believe that such settings could be conducive to great statesmanship in service to
humanitarian ideals.[24] And Olmsted, a New England democrat who still smarted over the
injustices done to seamen under the tyranny of ships' captains, found the English class system repugnant and could not justify the subjugation of the poor for the pleasures of the

Without relinquishing his dreamy idealization of nature and his transcendentalist values, Olmsted was convinced that the modern farm would prosper from the advances of technology. Improved transportation and agricultural machinery would mean larger crops, faster and more efficient delivery to market, and higher prices. Moreover, the gentleman farmer would not be shackled to the grunt and sweat of the fields, but manage men — mostly poor immigrants — hired to do physical labor. Such a farmer, as envisioned by Frederick Law Olmsted, would be an important man — prosperous, respected, powerful, independent, the duke of his own fiefdom.

rich. The poorer citizens of England, especially farm laborers, had little hope, he felt, for comfort and dignity earned
through honest work. As he grappled with what he found to
be the morally troubling facts that the grand and beautiful
estates could exist only through the exploitation of poorer
people, and that the beauty he enjoyed resulted from
markedly different living conditions for the aristocracy and
the poor, Olmsted's social consciousness stirred:

Is it right and best that this should be for the few, the very few of us, when
for many of the rest of us there must be but bare walls, tile floors, and every
thing besides harshly screaming, scrabble for life? [25]

In 1848 Olmsted's father bought the Akerly farm on Staten Island for his son — whose drawing this is thought to be. When Frederick took title, the property was run-down, but commanded a magnificent view of the waterways around New York and New Jersey. Olmsted undertook reclamation of the land by devising an innovative drainage system, refurbishing the house, resiting and rebuilding the barns, and instigating a series of changes to the grounds that presaged his eventual profession of landscape architecture.

Still, the young man who had pored over the books of
Uvedale Price and William Gilpin was enraptured by the
grandeur of the great gardens and grounds of the aristocracy
and deeply appreciative of Capability Brown's designs. As an
idealistic young American in England, rooted in New
England transcendentalism and the practical possibilities he
saw in scientific agriculture, Olmsted began to envision the
possibilities of shaping and tending the earth not only for its
agricultural benefits and scenic potential, but for the betterment of society.

In the newly created public park at Birkenhead, Olmsted found an example of what he believed might benefit all of humankind, regardless of class or education or wealth. The recently opened park was a pioneering public project that had transformed 125 acres of farmland across the Mersey River from Liverpool into an oasis of nature available to all citizens in a crowded, industrial city. As such, it merged the moral and aesthetic for Olmsted. He realized that Joseph Paxton, who would design the spectacular Crystal Palace (1851), had created a public park for citizens of every class. He exulted:

> *Five minutes of admiration, and a few more spent in studying the manner in which art had been employed to obtain from nature so much beauty, and I was ready to admit that in democratic America there was nothing to be thought of as comparable to this People's Garden.*[26]

The man who would one day be called the father of landscape architecture in America wrote:

> *Probably there is no object of art that Americans of cultivated taste generally more long to see in Europe, than an English Park. What artist, so noble, has often been my thought, as he who, with far-reaching conception of beauty and designing power, sketches the outlines, writes the colours, and directs the shadows of a picture so great that Nature shall be employed upon it for generations, before the work he has arranged for her shall realize his intentions.*[27]

With the model of Birkenhead clearly in mind, Olmsted first reckoned that planned parks — what would later be called landscape architecture — could be used to promote civility and to encourage communicativeness and could be characterized as the driving force behind the "genius of civilization." Aware of the power of the burgeoning industrial revolution, he speculated:

> *Whether, in this nineteenth century for the carpenter's son, the first of vulgar, whistling, snorting, rattling, roaring locomotives, new-world steamers, and submarine telegraphs; penny newspapers, free schools, and workingmen's lyceums, this still, soft atmosphere of elegant age was exactly the most favorable for the production of thorough, sound, influential manhood, and especially for the growth of the right sort of legislators and lawgivers for the people.*[28]

An
Important
Man

The Olmsted brothers returned to the United States in October 1850, leaving Charles Brace behind to continue his studies of Christian social work. Cognizant of Brace's success in supporting himself in Europe by writing travel letters and selling them to newspapers in the United States, Frederick saw the potential in his journals. Soon he turned his hand to working his letters and journals from the trip into a book. But writing a book did not fully engage him; though settled again at his Staten Island farm, Frederick was restless and discontented with his surroundings. He thought of the heightened consciousness he had shared with John and Charles on the journey, when they "were all living a great deal more — loving oftener, hating oftener — and reaching a

Olmsted held sturdy opinions about political and social matters. He made a point of being well informed and of informing others of his opinions on such matters as slavery, urban design, conservation of forests, education, and civilization.

great many more milestones." By comparison, everything around him seemed faded and silly.[1]

His interest in domesticity, however, sustained him. For still-bachelor Frederick, as for his father, the essential unit of civilization was the family, and he dreamed of being a man of consequence, a patriarch buttressed by wife and children. Social protocol required successful men of the nineteenth century to be pillars of probity and rectitude, to be modest in dress and manners but to display their power and wealth through the clothing and leisure of their wives and children, and the refinement of their homes. For Olmsted, as for other young men of his time, marriage symbolized social responsibility, worth, and maturity.

At this time Olmsted's interest in finding a wife may have been intensified also by the marriage of his friend Frederick Kingsbury, in April, and by John's decision to marry Mary Cleveland Bryant Perkins, a Staten Island neighbor, in October.[2]

But Olmsted's interest in finding a wife, and his longing for the security and social standing that accompanied marriage, had increased since his return from China. In 1844 he had worried, "I wonder if I really shall be an old bach. What a shivering idea."[3] For some years he had scanned the population of suitable young women in the Connecticut River valley, looking for the woman who could be a supportive wife to the important man he was determined to become. As flirtations and infatuations faded, Frederick worried:

> I am likely to be all along a bachelor or to marry believing that the "highest element of love" is not of earth, and so secure from disappointment if I shall not find it. . . . I do not love rashly — foolishly. I do not Love easily. My attachments are always worth more than I reckon them. . . .
>
> I doubt if I shall ever "love" till I marry (or am engaged) but I shall not marry a woman that I shall not be very likely to love very dearly when I safely can. I do not know such a one.[4]

Emily Perkins (not related to Mary Cleveland Bryant Perkins, his brother's fiancée), daughter of an influential Hartford attorney, appeared to be "such a one" in 1849, and he did his best to impress her despite her apparent lack of interest in marriage. In 1851, after visits and correspondence, she accepted Frederick's suit, but stipulated that their engagement remain their secret. Neither Frederick nor Emily gave signs of giddy delight in their anticipated union. Emily steadfastly refused to announce the engagement; Frederick, in no apparent haste to marry, told a friend that they planned to announce their engagement, but that he wanted to wait until at least November in order to take his sixty thousand cabbages to market in New York.[5]

The engagement, such as it was, ended in a haze as dense as that in which it had existed. Emily's mother asked Olmsted to meet her in New Haven, where, under circumstances not recorded, she dissolved the engagement. Olmsted's wise father noted that Frederick showed no signs of a broken heart; he wrote to a friend, "Pray tell me what it is makes Fred so happy since his *disappointment,* as it is called. He seems like a man who has thrown off a tremendous weight. Can it be that he brought it about purposely?"[6]

With his engagement over, Olmsted continued to farm, and he returned to writing his book on his English experiences.[7] The book would alter the direction of the thirty-year-old farmer's life. *Walks and Talks of an American Farmer in England,* a two-volume work published by George Palmer Putnam in 1852,[8] won critical attention and a significant readership; and it also gave Olmsted a taste of the two things he most desired to achieve, recognition and money. The doors of New York's literary society opened to Frederick Law Olmsted, measurably increasing his self-esteem and giving him cause to believe he had taken a step toward becoming a self-supporting man and an important presence in the affairs of society.

Olmsted's observations in England attuned him equally to what he perceived to be the perils of industrialization and to the inherent potential in people for good citizenship, ideas reflected throughout *Walks and Talks*. The publication of the book enabled him to see himself as a man of ideas, and he itched to find a place of influence in society and to contribute to its improvement; he wanted recognition as a leader, and he wanted power.

Walks and Talks, moreover, gives early evidence of Olmsted's singular approach to writing. He described scenery, people, slums, and great houses and gardens in minute detail; he captured and set down the speech of people he met, showing an acute ear for dialect; and he described the sights of English life, filtering and clarifying experience through reflection. His later writings — most notably those about the antebellum South [9] — would benefit from his gift for observation, reflection, and clarification.

Treating his letters and journals as if they were the field notes of a skillful anthropologist, Olmsted wrote from the viewpoint of an American in England, emphasizing the affinity between the two peoples. But he also looked through English eyes, focusing critically on slavery in the American South, an institution that, he noted, created "a hundred times more hard feeling in England towards America . . . than all [other causes]." Olmsted had been stung by the comments of Englishmen he met who, he felt, held him responsible for the hateful existence of slavery in America. Wanting to make clear his own and New England's abhorrence of slavery, Frederick wondered if a way could be found to have Southerners lecture in England and exonerate Northerners of blame for slavery. [10]

Frederick's friend Charles Loring Brace, and other young men at Yale College, were ardent abolitionists who had debated the moral issue of slavery among themselves and had often argued that the North should invade the South and free the slaves. Olmsted, more moderate in his prescription for curing the social ill, found the abolitionists distastefully pious and self-righteous. But called upon by English acquaintances to defend slavery, Olmsted recoiled from the idea of one person owning another and identified himself with abolitionist thinking.

His attention to the slavery issue was further focused by the passage of the Fugitive Slave Act in 1850, legislation that required return of escaped slaves to their owners and denied fugitives a jury trial and testimony in their own behalf. The law, a concession to the South, infuriated antislavery forces in the North.

Mid-nineteenth-century travel in America was limited and difficult. When Olmsted traveled through the pre–Civil War South, he used every known means of transportation — riverboat, rail, carriage, horseback, and foot. Other Americans were moving onto the frontier on foot or with the aid of wagons drawn by mules, horses, or oxen. Olmsted's impetus to travel was intellectual rather than economic, but he shared the frontiersman's lust for adventure. Whether affluent traveler along the eastern seaboard or homesteader pushing westward, few doubted the justice of Manifest Destiny.

Olmsted saw the law as one that made the practice of slavery an issue for every citizen in the country; it was no longer possible to be uninvolved in the festering issue. The Fugitive Slave Act so angered Olmsted that he vowed to disobey the law; he would, he insisted, not only take in a runaway slave, but he would shoot anyone who tried to reclaim that human being. Frederick pondered the slavery question in an exchange of letters with Charles Loring Brace, who, though still in Europe, tried to recruit his friend to the abolitionist movement. But Olmsted resisted his friend's proselytizing, believing that slaves required education and help before they could be freed to full citizenship.[11]

Though young Frederick Law Olmsted placed high value on justice, on citizenship, on civilization, and on the republican form of government, he also thought of himself as a scientific thinker, and for him the moral repugnance of slavery did not render it an easily solved social ill. Surely, he thought, reasonable men could arrive at a rational and civilized solution, could avoid conflict, and could see the light of reason and shared ideals.

Travels in the United States

With the success of *Walks and Talks* Frederick imagined himself being a literary man, and he increasingly left the management of his farm to others as he pursued his dreams of a literary life and of the benefits of prestige and affluence that such a way of life would provide him. At thirty years of age, Olmsted, encouraged by family and friends — especially by John Hull Olmsted — to think of himself as a man of consequence, still sought a vocation in which to fully invest his energies and ambitions. He believed his ideas about society to be sound, but he had yet to find a means for persuading other citizens to like beliefs. "I am disappointed," he complained, "in the increased power I have over others as yet." [12]

The young farmer-journalist was given the opportunity, however, to speak his mind when Charles Loring Brace initiated his travels in the South. The resulting book remains a classic on the slaveholding society of the region. After years of debate with Olmsted on the institution of slavery, Brace was convinced that Frederick would join him in the staunchest ranks of the abolitionists if he examined southern society at firsthand. Moreover, Brace was sufficiently convinced of Olmsted's powers of observation and fairness of mind to introduce him to Henry J. Raymond, editor of the year-old *New York Daily Times*. For his part, Raymond wanted to run a series of articles on the South and slavery, but did not want to reiterate the inflamed rhetoric of other northern papers. After a brief conversation with Olmsted, Raymond commissioned him to travel through the South and report evenhandedly on slavery. The editor stipulated that Olmsted write only about firsthand observations, a guideline that suited well the author of *Walks and Talks*. [13]

In December 1852, Olmsted began a four-month journey through the South, using virtually every form of travel then available, including horse, train, coach, and steamboat, returning to Staten Island on April 6, 1853. [14] Thus, prior to the Civil War Olmsted's practice of journalism took him on extensive travels through the slaveholding states to note both physical and cultural aspects of American cities and towns. His travels took him to Washington, Richmond, Petersburg, Norfolk, Raleigh, and Fayetteville. He recorded the social organization, values, and economic and political practices of people along the North Carolina coast and in Wilmington, and around Charleston and Savannah, and through the country around Macon, Columbus, Montgomery, Mobile, and New Orleans. He explored a portion of the Red River and returned to Mississippi, then visited Vicksburg and Memphis; after that he followed the Appalachians to upper Mississippi, Alabama, and Georgia, and finally returned home via Virginia.

Olmsted's writing about these and other trips during the period 1852–1854 produced passages of rhapsodic response to American scenery, evidencing his appreciation for the feeling tones he experienced in the presence of natural beauty. In a style recalling *Walks and Talks*, he once again exercised his natural tendency to analysis, reflection, and postulation of solutions to social problems. Like any good writer, Olmsted had learned to use his pen as an instrument for thinking, as a probe for finding and lifting images and thoughts from his mind; and as he thought about the South, he challenged virtually every abiding attitude about slavery. Speaking from the South, Olmsted is consistently compassionate, independent, analytical, and practical.

Olmsted's articles appeared first in the *New York Daily Times;* later they became the basis for his book *A Journey in the Seaboard Slave States.* He presented the South not as the romantic home of cavaliers and chivalric practices, but as a brutal and violent frontier; he found a society handicapped by lack of libraries and education, and people of both races unable to enjoy the freedom of speech and thought required for a democracy. Indeed, Olmsted noted, life on the western frontier was likely to be better for more people than life in the South, because, he argued, the free-labor system promised increasing civility as well as economic opportunity. Slavery, he contended, kept the South economically and socially backward.[15]

"The character of the whole agriculture of the country depends upon [slavery]," he noted. "In every department of industry I see its influence, vitally affecting the question of profit, and I must add that everywhere and constantly, the conviction is forced upon me, to a degree entirely unanticipated, that its effect is universally ruinous." [16] The more he studied slave labor, the more convinced Olmsted became that free labor, with its profit incentives, produced better work, higher yield, and greater profits. "Labor is the creator of wealth," Olmsted insisted. "There can be no honest wealth, no true prosperity without it, and in exact proportion to the economy of labor is the cost of production and the accumulation of profit." [17]

Olmsted's contemporary critics, however, point to his remarks about the sexual licentiousness and laziness of slaves as evidence of his pernicious racism. Very few people in the nineteenth century opposed the racism (as currently defined) that stained the prevailing social attitudes, the teachings of most churches, and the legal system. On balance, Olmsted was more inclined than most men of his age to believe that African Americans could and should have full freedom as citizens.

Moreover, he contended that slavery made barbarians of slaveholders. "Why," he asked, comparing the level of civilization in the South with that in the North, "is it that here has been stagnation and there constant, healthy progress?" He answered, "It is the old, fettered barbarian labor system, in relation with which [Southerners] have been brought up, against which all their enterprise must struggle, and with the chains of which all their ambition must be bound." [18]

His writings on the South, on his travels and observations, won Olmsted a degree of the fame he desired; that fame, however, issued in part from the controversial nature of his observations. His reports, under the nom de plume Yeoman, began to appear in the *Times* in 1853 and ran for a year. While Yeoman's articles — or letters — in the *Times* incited considerable discussion, heightened Olmsted's pleasure in writing, and whetted his appetite for further reports on travels, neither the abolitionists nor the slaveholders were comfortable with his observations and recommendations. The former believed him to be too tolerant of what they

Frederick and his brother, John Hull, traveled in Texas, often camping or making do with primitive accommodations. They witnessed at firsthand living conditions in several parts of Texas and among different groups of people. Surveyors mapped the territory as statehood loomed in the consciousness of Texans. Throughout the region, the Olmsted brothers felt the heat of debate about slavery. Pro-slavery forces were determined that Texas would enter the Union on the side of the South; and antislavery or Free-Soil proponents were equally determined that their beliefs would prevail.

considered intolerable and sinful oppression of human beings, and the latter found him too harsh and unyielding in his views of the corruptive nature of slavery for both slave-holder and slave.

Olmsted, savoring his independence as well as his expanding fame, had found in journalism — as he had briefly in seafaring and farming — an activity that took him simultaneously into new regions of the earth and his own mind. And, like seafaring and farming, journalism sowed seeds that would blossom in his mature landscape designs and in his ideas on society, ethics, and communicativeness.

Texas

Within months after the publication of Yeoman's essays and while still enjoying the warmth of their success, Olmsted embarked on a western trek, again under the auspices of the *New York Daily Times.* Accompanied by his brother, John Hull, Olmsted planned to travel into Texas and California and to collect material for another series of reports to the *Times.* The brothers set out in November 1853, expecting to join a larger group in San Antonio for the treacherous trip to California.

John Hull Olmsted, his health undermined by tuberculosis, accompanied Frederick on his second trip in hopes that the exercise and fresh air would improve his health. Instead, John tired easily and often found traveling difficult and painful.

On their way to Texas, the Olmsted brothers stopped in Nashville to visit John's Yale classmate Samuel P. Allison, who debated the issue of slavery with them, arguing that the South's aristocratic society, superior to northern society, justified owning and using slaves.[19] Attentive to Allison's arguments, Olmsted was unconvinced.

In Texas, traveling by horseback through rough and sparsely settled country, Olmsted was able to compare slaveholding and free societies existing in uneasy proximity. He found the slaveholding areas of Texas embodying anything but the higher aristocratic style of life extolled by Allison. He experienced inconveniences, discomforts, and poor accommodations as a traveler, and he reluctantly lived on the available diet of pork and corn bread. Slaveholding, he concluded, did nothing to further the physical and intellectual amenities Olmsted identified with civilization.

In Austin, however, he attended sessions of the Texas General Assembly, saw hope for the rise of civilization and the practice of democracy, and praised the quality of legislation he witnessed. Somewhat later during this sojourn on the frontier, Olmsted also discovered a group of people who reinforced his thinking about civilization and confirmed his belief that slaveholding prevented the quality of life he believed important for all people. He found the German settlement of New Braunfels, near San Antonio, an oasis of civilization, a community based on free labor and therefore free of the brutality bred by slavery. Olmsted quickly made friends among "the Texas Germans." He admired their community life; the importance they placed on home, education, independence, and hard work; and the level of civilization they maintained through reading, music, and good conversation. Further, these free-labor proponents inspired his political interest in land reforms and the Free-Soil movement.[20]

In August 1854, Frederick arrived home to begin his new series for the *Times*, in which he examined the events and politics behind the heated public debate over slavery and the unrest inherent in the decade preceding the Civil War. Increasingly, Frederick believed he had a role to play in the public affairs of his country. Still not a wholehearted abolitionist, and still hoping for the gradual destruction of the institution of slavery and for systematic education of slaves to enable them to participate fully in society, Frederick argued that there should be a national policy to persuade slave owners that it would be a matter of enlightened self-interest for them to train slaves for freedom, to free them, and to help them enter the economic mainstream of an increasingly industrialized society. At the same time, vehemently opposing the extension of slavery into frontier regions, he supported the Free-Soil Parties of Texas and Kansas, going so far as to supply weapons to those prepared to fight to keep slavery out of their communities.

The probability of civil war had increased with the passage of the Kansas-Nebraska Act in 1854. New territories would have what the bill's sponsor, Senator Stephen A. Douglas, called "popular sovereignty"; that is, each would be able to choose whether a territory would be admitted to the Union as a free or slave state. While the legislation contributed to the beginning of the Republican Party, it also established battle lines between those opposing slavery — like the Texas Germans — and slaveholders in the territories.

The conflict came to a head in 1855, when a vigilante army from western Missouri forced the election of a proslavery legislature in neighboring Kansas. Olmsted, outraged at this forced extension of slavery, raised money for the purchase of arms to be sent to Kansas, an illegal activity requiring both courage and cunning. He was particularly pleased to purchase a mountain howitzer and, under the noses of officials on the border, ship it to the Kansans.

Man of Letters

By 1855, Olmsted's success as a journalist convinced him that he was destined to be a man of letters and to wield influence through his pen. Anticipating publication of *Seaboard Slave States*, Olmsted wrote his father:

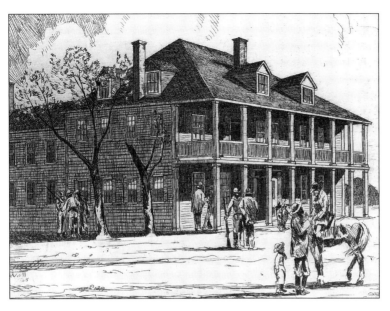

Even Houston, which was considered advanced by Texas standards, did not afford the conveniences the Olmsted brothers took for granted in northern cities. But Frederick's eye fell fondly on the Texas landscape.

Reputation or notoriety it can not fail to give me — not perhaps friendship but respect, I think. For while I strike right & left and strike hard I do so respectfully and with the grace of sincerity.[21]

Seeing the book as his means of access to the literary world, Olmsted told his father:

There is a certain kind of private advertizing of myself to be done in connection with the issue of my book which I don't want to feel so cramped in doing as I do. There is a sort of literary republic, which it is not merely pleasant & gratifying to my ambition to be recognized in, but also profitable.

In order to accomplish the "private advertizing" of himself, Olmsted needed another loan from his father. "To take & keep a position as a recognized litterateur, as a man of influence in literary matters, I need at the time of the publication of my book to be able to spend a little more than I like at this juncture . . . to be running in debt to tailors & cobblers & cooks."[22]

Olmsted wanted money and freedom to devote himself to becoming a "litterateur." Knowing that his Staten Island farm was unlikely to yield profits unless he directed all of his time and energy to it, Frederick persuaded his ailing brother to take charge of the farm. Mary, John's wife, was in the midst of a difficult pregnancy and unable to walk, and John was dying of tuberculosis. In addition, the crops were failing, the farm dogs had become sheep killers, a litter of piglets was born dead, and the house and outbuildings needed maintenance already too long deferred. But John, dutiful and loving, took over responsibilities for the farm.

Frederick, then free to apply his full attention to a career in publishing, joined the publishing firm of Dix, Edwards and Company, noted for publishing the American edition of Charles Dickens's magazine, *Household Words,* and *Putnam's Monthly Magazine.* Joshua A. Dix, a twenty-four-year-old friend of Charles Loring Brace, may have invited Olmsted to become a partner in the firm primarily to raise capital. While Dix's other partner, Arthur Edwards, invested only five hundred dollars, Olmsted was asked for five thousand dollars, which he borrowed from his father. Agreeing to a salary of fifteen hundred dollars a year, Olmsted especially looked forward to the prestige of being affiliated with *Putnam's Monthly,* a journal of ideas that he hoped to devote to uplifting spiritual messages in the style of a hybrid of *Westminster Review* and the *New York Daily Tribune.*[23]

Satisfied that he had won the bona fides of a man of letters, Olmsted considered and rejected other possible literary projects before accepting the partnership in the firm of Dix and Edwards, reckoning probably that his stake in the firm would give him editorial power. But his five thousand dollars did not buy him a place at the table where major editorial policy was determined or management decisions made. Instead, for reasons that are not clear, and perhaps not characteristic, the affable Olmsted elected to play a largely behind-the-scenes role in the magazine. He left the editorial decisions to George William Curtis, another partner; he solicited advice from Charles A. Dana and Parke Godwin, writers for, respectively, the *New York Daily Tribune* and the *New York Evening Post.*

Largely confining his activities to public relations and to dealing with authors, Olmsted did, however, work with Henry David Thoreau on his *Cape Cod* manuscript and was influential in publishing Herman Melville's "Benito Cereno."[24] He enjoyed working with *Putnam's* other notable writers, including Ralph Waldo Emerson, Henry Wadsworth Longfellow, and Harriet Beecher Stowe. He attended literary parties in Manhattan, some given by Anne Charlotte Lynch, which enabled him to meet such distinguished writers as Horace Greeley, Margaret Fuller, and Edgar Allan Poe. During his association with Dix and Edwards, Olmsted became sufficiently regarded in the literary world to make it possible for him to give a breakfast for James Russell Lowell and to attend a Press Club dinner for William Thackeray.[25]

All the while that he was enjoying the role of man-about-the-literary-world, Olmsted worked to transform his articles on the coastal South into a book. Again needing money to subsidize publication, he turned to his father for a loan of a thousand dollars. Finally, *A Journey in the Seaboard Slave States,* published in January 1856, was praised in the North, but not in the South; and it was not a financial success.

George William Curtis

Curtis, born in Providence, Rhode Island, in 1824, was a prominent American literary figure, editor, and political orator. As political editor of *Harper's Weekly,* 1863–1892, he exerted influence on popular American opinion. Pressing for an end to slavery, and for women's rights and reform of municipal and civil service, he wrote the "Easy Chair" column for *Harper's New Monthly* for years.

Influenced by Ralph Waldo Emerson and the Brook Farm experiment, Curtis spent several of his youthful years in travel in Europe and the Middle East, observing other societies. In 1850 he returned to the United States and began his long and influential work as writer and opinion shaper. He helped found the Republican Party, but broke with it in 1884 over the nomination of James G. Blaine. President Grant appointed Curtis (1871) chairman of a commission to reform civil service. He was chosen to be chancellor of the State University of New York in 1890. He died in 1892. ☙

But Olmsted's reputation — if not his bank account — was growing, and, though still financially dependent on his father, he now saw himself as a man of influence. The other partners of Dix and Edwards, recognizing Olmsted's talents for persuasion and negotiation, asked him to travel to London to develop affiliations with important publishers in England. They authorized Olmsted to offer royalty payments for the right of publishing overseas writers in the United States. Over the next few months, working in good faith, Olmsted successfully contracted several agreements, only to learn that Dix and Edwards was nearing bankruptcy and unable to honor the commitments he had made. By the time he returned to New York, the firm was irretrievably on the road to fiscal ruin.

Meanwhile, during the last year of his life, John Hull, using Frederick's notes and letters, largely wrote *A Journey through Texas; or, a Saddle-Trip on the Southwestern Frontier,*[26] published by the sinking firm of Dix and Edwards in January 1857. Later that year, the publishing house perished in the financial crisis of 1857.

Olmsted was humiliated by the failure of Dix and Edwards, mortified by his inability to repay loans to his father, without hope for another project, and no longer flying high on the promises of a writing career. Knowing too that his farm was floundering and his beloved brother dying, Olmsted retreated to the coast of Connecticut to rest and to ponder his future.

Central Park, the Beginning

The creation of the mental domain of phantasy has a complete counterpart in the establishment of "reservations" and "nature-parks" in places where the inroads of agriculture, traffic, or industry threaten to change . . . the earth rapidly into something unrecognizable. The "reservation" is to maintain the old condition of things which has been regretfully sacrificed to necessity everywhere else; there everything may grow and spread as it pleases, including what is useless and even what is harmful. The mental realm of phantasy is also such a reservation reclaimed from the encroaches of the reality-principle.

— *Freud*
General Introduction to Psychoanalysis

In August 1857, the opportunity that changed his life — and the history of the nineteenth century — came to Frederick Law Olmsted. He was thirty-five years old, unmarried, and by his own reckoning he was a failed publisher, a writer whose works had earned him a literary reputation but no income, and a student of scientific agriculture who had lost interest in his grandiose plans to become a gentleman farmer. His Staten Island farm, no longer a country gentleman's home, was under the care of a hired manager. He had found neither a sustaining purpose nor a successful career in the several ventures he had undertaken, and he was in debt to his father. In a state of depression, he took a room in an inn in Morris Cove, on the Connecticut shore of Long Island Sound, to rest and to work on his notes for *A Journey in the Back Country.*

Olmsted was a small, slight man, never physically robust and now mentally discouraged. He retreated to Connecticut hoping to work quietly on his manuscript and to sail and swim until he overcame his exhaustion and his despair. He was without means for earning his living. In each of his vocational starts, Frederick's pattern had been the same. Fired with enthusiasm and big dreams, he would throw himself unstintingly into manic-paced work until exhausted physically and dispirited; then he would return to his family and to New England's natural beauty to rest his body, repair his ragged nerves, and restore his spirit. Then in short order he would be fueled again by a new idea, a new beckoning, and he would leap at — if not into — yet another career.

After the demise of Dix and Edwards — a sour defeat that Olmsted refused to discuss for the rest of his life — he acted characteristically, withdrawing to his family for love and support and to the rocky shore of Connecticut for repose. At that time, despite his humiliation at what he perceived to be failure, Frederick's reputation as a journalist had actually grown. With the publication of Yeoman's letters, he had earned the status of a respected commentator on American life, a factor making it likely that others held him in higher regard than he granted himself.

Furthermore, in his gloomy state he may not have recognized that his writings had done still more for him than earn him a deserved literary reputation. His mode of work had served him well, his discipline repaying the effort several times over. First, of course, Olmsted had acquired information, a process of observing, analyzing, and testing data. Second, and certainly less consciously, he had acquired the intellectual burnish of the education he prized but felt had eluded him. As a conscientious journalist, Frederick had organized and clarified his thoughts on social order, civilization, and citizenship; had compared his observations and thoughts to those of writers he admired; and had combined historical knowledge with firsthand experience into an effective liberal education.

Yet despite his intellectual maturation and the public recognition accorded him as a journalist, Frederick realized that he remained financially dependent on his generous and uncomplaining father. Moreover, his prospects for financial independence ebbed with the failure of Dix and Edwards. He had no plans for the future. He had only to complete *Back Country.*

But by accident, at an inn on the coast of Connecticut, Olmsted encountered Charles Wyllis Elliott, an acquaintance who was also one of the commissioners for the Central

Park project.[1] Elliott's regard for Olmsted as a writer and political thinker, along with the favorable impression Olmsted must have made in conversation around the inn's tea table, led to the commissioner's suggestion that Olmsted apply for the job of supervisor of the Central Park project. Olmsted's qualifications may have seemed scant even to himself. While his books on England and the South suggested his familiarity with agricultural practices and the latest scientific theories, his managerial experience was limited to overseeing his hired hands at his farm on Staten Island.

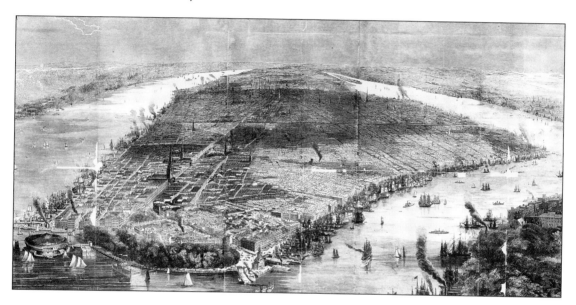

In 1857, when Olmsted was appointed superintendent of the Central Park project, Manhattan was a crowded, bustling island, a major port city, a center of commerce and industry, and the doorway to new opportunities for the increasing number of immigrants who came to the United States.

Elliott described the project for the Manhattan park and the qualities sought in the supervisor, who would handle a disorderly hodgepodge of workers, and who would train and administer a special park police squad. Olmsted was interested and probably recalled for Elliott his visits to Birkenhead, the great estate gardens of England, and the parks of Europe. The commissioner, impressed by Olmsted's enthusiasm for the New York park project, by his grasp of the problems related to managing such an enterprise, and by his familiarity with English and European parks, encouraged Frederick to apply for the job and advised him to seek support for his appointment from influential men in Manhattan.

Olmsted left the next morning for New York, where he planned to campaign systematically for the job. On his way to Manhattan, he shed the gloom that he had taken to the

Connecticut shore, and, surging with energy and eagerness, he plotted his strategy for securing the appointment. "I beg leave to recommend myself for the Office of *Superintendent of the Central Park*," Olmsted wrote.

> *For the past sixteen years my chief interest and occupation has been with those subjects, familiarity with which is most needed in this office. Economy in the application of agricultural labor has especially engaged my attention, and my observations on this subject have been extensively published and discussed in this country and reprinted in Europe. For ten years I have practically engaged in the direction and superintendence of agricultural laborers and gardeners in the vicinity of New York.[2]*

Once in New York City, he hastened to collect signatures on a petition on his behalf to present to the park commissioners.[3]

For years William Cullen Bryant, poet and newspaper editor, and Andrew Jackson Downing, the most influential landscape gardener in America, had advocated the building of a great public park in New York City. Newspaper editorials and articles made the case for a park, helping to create public support for the idea. Central Park was waiting to happen.

But Olmsted faced strong competition from well-connected men who also sought the supervisor's job. The son of a New England dry-goods merchant contended with two solid candidates, each the son of a prominent father. John Woodhouse Audubon, son of the artist and ornithologist, and Joel Nott, son of the president of Union College, also wanted the position as superintendent of the Central Park project. If they were not known in their own rights, they shone in the lights shed by their fathers. Frederick's reputation and literary connections helped him secure the signatures of Peter Cooper, August Belmont, William Cullen Bryant, *Putnam's Monthly* publisher George Palmer Putnam, Harvard botanist Asa Gray, and popular author Washington Irving,[4] men whose influence added substantial weight to the application of the merchant's son.

Another factor worked to Olmsted's favor. In a contest along party lines, Democrats and Republicans compromised, agreeing that the appointee should not be a "practical man." *Practical*, in this usage, meant a man with political debts and connections, one likely to use the powers of patronage for his own or his party's benefit. In later autobiographical recollections, Olmsted liked to identify himself as an "unpractical man," a play on the double meaning of the term. At the time of his appointment, however, Olmsted appeared to the board to be literary and therefore, by definition, "unpractical," a perception that made him acceptable.[5]

Frederick was of the right political coloration, if lacking in immediately negotiable experience for the job. When he appeared on the scene, he needed approval from the eleven

Despite the crowded shorelines at the southern tip of Manhattan, much of the island remained unfinished and often chaotic at midcentury. Streets were undeveloped and utilities unknown. The lower end of Manhattan, with cobblestoned streets and well-built structures, offered a desirable atmosphere for both living and working. But north of the commercial and residential areas, in what is now midtown Manhattan, squatters lived in shacks, kept livestock, and rendered bones for a living. The swampy land was pocked with pools of stagnant water and scrubby growth.

commissioners appointed by the New York state legislature. The appointee, carrying the title "superintendent," would report to Egbert Viele, the engineer in chief, who was a Democrat with political ties to the mayor and a known dexterity in using park jobs to further his party's power.[6] Olmsted, a titular Republican, had no political debts or ties, and therefore offended neither party.

Frederick Law Olmsted eagerly met the commissioners and displayed robust enthusiasm for the job. Some of the politicians, however, fretted that this congenial young fellow with a literary reputation might not be experienced enough. After all, his curriculum vitae contained no measurable preparation for the superintendency of the landscaping project, the largest public-works project in New York.

In September, as Olmsted sat in the office of the commissioners awaiting their verdict, he wrote John, then with Mary and their children in Europe still trying to reverse the course of his illness, "I have moved to town & done nothing else since I last wrote but canvass for the Superintendent's office: I am now awaiting the result; the Board being in session below a few doors." Olmsted passed on to his brother bits of gossip about mutual

Barnum's Museum and a variety of theaters provided recreation for those who could afford the price of admission.

friends and details about the superintendent's job, but did not mention John's health or family. "After a long session," Frederick added in a postscript, "I am elected. . . ."

Referring to his immediate superior, a former United States Army officer, the engineer then in charge of Central Park, Olmsted confided to John, "It seems to be generally expected that Viele & I shall quarrel, that he will be jealous of me, & that there will be all sorts of intrigues."[7]

Indeed Egbert Viele took offense at the appointment of Olmsted and, in a mean-spirited manner intended to undermine his authority, spitefully arranged to introduce him to the park and to the workers he would supervise. When Olmsted appeared in Viele's office, dressed in his best clothes and boots, the engineer passed his new subordinate on to a foreman who gleefully led him on a trek through a disgusting stench of mire and muck, ruining his boots and soiling his best clothes. Knowing that he was being tested in view of the men he would supervise, Olmsted hid his grimness, outrage, and anger. He attempted to impress the park workers with his good humor and heartiness.

Then, having surpassed the hazing that introduced him to the park workers, Olmsted undertook a thorough study of the park and its problems. Using the topographical plan made by Egbert Viele, he soon knew that the park consisted of 770 derelict acres of swamp, barren rocky patches, and scrub flora. In several sections squatters occupied filthy shacks and lived by slaughtering cows and pigs, boiling bones, and raising goats.[8] Moreover, the park workers, most of whom had been plucked from the pork barrel, were unskilled, undisciplined, and lazy.

When Olmsted took responsibility for the park, he inherited the continual badgering of city politicians who saw the park project as a source of jobs for constituents and thus votes for themselves. It was a grim time in New York City; joblessness following the panic of 1857 brought about demonstrations and riots. But even when faced with mobs waving "Bread or Blood" banners, Olmsted, the "unpractical man," held his ground: jobs could be kept only by those who performed their duties.[9]

Political, social, and topographical difficulties notwithstanding, Olmsted's appointment as superintendent of Central Park gave him the opportunity that, in retrospect, seems to have been perfect for him. For the first time, he would be financially independent; though he was earning only a modest fifteen hundred dollars a year, the salary symbolized a more important security and independence for the young man. The position itself carried enough prestige to satisfy Olmsted's yearnings to be seen as an influential man of affairs. Finally, his walking tour of England and his journeys in the South had awakened in Frederick a desire to be of service to the public, to affirm the values of democracy in a rapidly urbanizing and industrializing society; and the superintendency of the Central Park project afforded Frederick Law Olmsted the laboratory he needed to test his evolving theories about civilization, urbanization, and leadership.

Olmsted's first thirty-five years may have been unplanned, and his formal education may have been scant, but circumstances had prepared him well to meet the challenges of Central Park. He brought a surprisingly well-stocked set of skills to the undertaking. By the time Olmsted stepped into the park project in New York, he knew surveying and understood topography and mapping; he relished the principles of scientific farming and knew the rudiments of agriculture, including the benefits of drainage systems and painstaking soil preparation, and he had practiced good management of the workers on his Staten Island farm.

He also knew from firsthand observation the great parks and scenic landscape of England, having made it a point to learn the ingredients and dynamics of Birkenhead, and having analyzed the components of the English landscape. Through these informal studies he developed aesthetic standards for scenic beauty and a strong political belief in the importance of the public park in providing recreation and spiritual renewal in settings of natural beauty for all classes of people.

Moreover, his experiences at sea and in the South had shaped his attitudes about the decent and humane exercise of power and about leadership and good management. And, finally, as a journalist and publisher, he had honed his natural talents for communication, for clear thinking and writing.

When Olmsted was chosen to supervise the workforce of the park, he embarked on the work that would make his reputation, and the fate that would identify him as the father of landscape architecture in the United States. For the next forty years — save for time during the Civil War when Olmsted held two other jobs, as secretary of the Sanitary Commission and as head of the Mariposa Estate in California — Olmsted would make his name and fortune as a landscape architect, as the designer and builder of parks and suburbs throughout the United States.[10]

But in 1857, well before history accorded him recognition, Olmsted had private ordeals and disappointments to face. He hoped the salary for the Central Park project would make him financially free from his father and would enable him to repay the Dix and Edwards debts for which he took responsibility. The fifteen hundred dollars proved inadequate, however, and Olmsted found it necessary to ask for more money from his father, thereby incurring still more debt.

Moreover, in 1857 Frederick lost his best friend, his brother, John Hull. Fighting to survive against tuberculosis, John had sought a healing climate first in Havana, then in St. Thomas, Southampton, Paris, and Sorrento, where his father met him. They went to

Rome, then to Geneva. When his father returned to the United States, John and Mary settled in a hotel in Nice for the winter.

"Dear dear Fred," wrote John,

It appears we are not to see one another any more — I have not many
days. . . .

Well so be it since God wills it so. I never have known a better friend-
ship than ours has been & there can't be a greater happiness than to think
of that — how dear we have been & how long we have held out such
tenderness.

Then John penned his final sentence to Frederick: "Don't let Mary suffer while you are alive." [11]

Shortly after John's death on November 24, Frederick received a note from their father: "In his death I have lost not only a son but a very dear friend. You almost your only friend." [12]

Frederick Law Olmsted had also lost his youth.

FIRST STUDY OF DESIGN FOR THE CENTRAL PARK.
From a Wood-cut made in 1858.

Olmsted and Vaux never lost faith in their original concept of the Greensward design for Central Park. Winding paths and roadways, separation of strollers from horse and carriage traffic, and dense planting around open areas contributed to the rural atmosphere.

🥀 *The Greensward Plan*

But 1857 marked a beginning, too, for Olmsted. Calvert Vaux, an architect and protégé of Andrew Jackson Downing, turned to Frederick to collaborate on a submission to the competition for a new design for Central Park. At first Olmsted hesitated, worried that he might be placing himself in unseemly rivalry with his surly superior, Egbert Viele. Olmsted, mindful of doing the proper thing, asked Viele's leave to enter the competition; Viele responded with sarcastic contempt for Olmsted's ability to present a winning design. Viele's disdain freed Olmsted of any compunction to worry about injuring his arrogant superior's pride and allowed him to accept Vaux's invitation. Thus began a collaboration that influenced beyond measure the face of American cities.[13]

Calvert Vaux, a young English architect, taught Olmsted the techniques and fundamentals of design. The charming

As Olmsted wrote to the president of the Department of Public Parks in 1870, "the impracticability of making, in either section of the Park, open spaces of greensward as large as desirable, was recognized from the outset, but as much as possible was done to gain ground in this direction, and the central meadow stretches are the result in the upper Park. They supply two connected spaces, each about a quarter of a mile in extent, partially separated by trees which are already beginning to take on umbrageous forms and to cast broad shadows over the now well-established turf. These meadows constitute the only broad space of quiet rural ground on the island which has been left undisturbed by artificial objects, and much labor has been expended to render practicable the preservation of their present general character." (PFLO VI: FLO to Peter B. Sweeny, [1870].)

and intelligent Vaux, with his thorough education in architecture and seven years of experience with Downing, possessed skills and experience that complemented Olmsted's personality and ambition. Their work together on the Central Park competition was to be Olmsted's education in landscape design, as well as the standard by which parks would be designed and judged thereafter. Without Vaux's professional background, it is unlikely that Olmsted could have envisioned or realized the Central Park design. But their collaboration produced "Greensward," a concept for a rural pleasure park in a growing urban center.

The two men worked together at Vaux's home during whatever time Olmsted could wrench from his duties as superintendent, often at night or on weekends.[14] They employed draftsmen as needed, and co-opted some of the men who worked in Vaux's architectural office. In the spring of 1858, after hours of labor, discussion and analysis of the stipulations set forth by the commission, they sketched and drew; they tested concepts and reworked ideas.

Olmsted and Vaux barely met the deadline for the competition with Greensward, the last entrant submitted. It was a brilliant design. Based on the English tradition, the park provided long pastoral passages intended to offer the repose of rural landscape to the urbanite, to promote strolling or quiet meditation in picturesque dells or atop dramatic outcroppings of rock. Sheltered by the park from the jostle and danger of city streets, a citizen might take to foot or bridle path, might enjoy a leisurely carriage ride around the park — and, owing to the genius of the design, pedestrians, riders, and those conveyed by carriages would move along distinctly defined paths, freed from the possibility of collision with one another. The designers accomplished this important separation of functions by setting over- and underpasses at strategic points, the same device they used to accommodate the commissioners' requirement for cross-park traffic. They realized this separation of function without endangering park users or interfering with the overall aesthetic impact of the Greensward.[15]

The designers offered a mall to those who wanted to congregate, meet other people, and stroll to see and be seen by those who used the park. Benches were placed to provide rest and attractive vistas. Central Park, as envisioned by its designers, was to be a democratic institution, a place where people of all classes and interests could meet, share experiences, and appreciate one another.[16]

Central Park was to be the actual and symbolic beginning of Frederick Law Olmsted as a landscape architect and the infancy of the park movement in America. With the Central Park project, and then with the Greensward design, urban land — subjected to art, engineering, and management — would be transformed into rural experience, a sanctuary of spiritually uplifting aesthetic pleasure. In the summary paragraph of the text describing their Greensward plan, Olmsted and Vaux wrote:

> *It will be perceived that no long straight drive has been provided on the plan: this feature has been studiously avoided, because it would offer opportunities for trotting matches. The popular idea of the park is a beautiful open*

green space, in which quiet drives, rides, and strolls may be had. This cannot be preserved if a race-course, or a road that can readily be used as a race-course, is made one of its leading attractions.

Olmsted, Vaux, and Political Forces

Central Park was not created in a social vacuum, or under ideal protection by governing authorities. From the beginning, the project had floated on an undercurrent of political pork barreling, vote trading, and power brokerage. Olmsted and Vaux, working within the circumstances surrounding the park, not only won the competition for the design of the park, but undertook the building and management of the great urban space.

Olmsted and Vaux contributed equally to the winning Greensward design, but Olmsted, because of his work as superintendent, was named by the commissioners "architect in chief" in May of 1858. For a salary of twenty-five hundred dollars per year, he was given responsibility for employing and managing workmen and police and for seeing to the realization of the Greensward plan. Well aware of the significance of his undertaking, Olmsted described it to a friend as "the first real park made in this country — a democratic development of the highest significance." [17]

Whether by intention or happenstance, the park commissioners elevated Olmsted above Vaux, a definition of roles that chaffed the English architect for years, eventually contributing to the dissolution of the Olmsted and Vaux partnership. The commissioners also abolished Viele's job, an official action that exacerbated an already well-developed antagonism between Olmsted and Viele and set Viele on a stubborn quest to discredit Olmsted.

Olmsted, free of Viele's carping oversight, was pleased by his increase in salary and prestige. Vaux apparently successfully hid his feelings and continued to work with Olmsted toward the goals they had jointly laid out in the Greensward design. It should have been a serene and productive time for Olmsted, but the park project was threatened, Olmsted and Vaux felt, by the mischievous meddling of politicians.

After its official acceptance but well before Olmsted and Vaux could effect their Greensward plan, some of the park commissioners, for reasons of their own, began to oppose Olmsted and the design itself. August Belmont and Robert Dillon appeared determined to prevent the plan from being completed. Dillon, who had voted against the Olmsted and Vaux Greensward plan, now stepped forward and offered his own design, a formal arrangement that differed in almost every aspect with the Olmsted and Vaux plan. Dillon drew long, straight thoroughfares cutting down the middle of the park, and where Olmsted and Vaux had called for softly curving paths and seemingly natural growth of shrubs and trees, Dillon wanted a hard-edged, grid-patterned formal scheme. His design,

After winning the competition for Central Park (1858) with their Greensward design, Olmsted and Vaux undertook the development and management of the largest public-works project in the United States to that time. The public watched with interest as progress on the design produced in this urban setting such marvels of rural recreation as a skating and boating pond, paths for strolling, and decorative bridges that provided access to scenic vistas.

supported by the *Tribune* and acknowledged by both the *Times* and *Herald,* won enough public support to trouble Olmsted.[18] He feared the capriciousness and corruption of the commissioners and worried that the Greensward plan might be aborted.

Olmsted decided to fight for the plan. In order to gain press support and to kindle public enthusiasm for the Greensward design, Olmsted invited old friends, *Times* editor Henry J. Raymond and Charles A. Dana of the *Tribune,* to a picnic breakfast at the park site. Sitting on a huge outcropping of rock, looking out over the southern end of Central Park, Olmsted showed the newspapermen where Dillon's proposed thoroughfare would lie, how it would destroy all hope of establishing a rural sanctuary in the bustling city, and how it would produce a park that could be little more than a grandiose, tree-lined boulevard. Olmsted persuaded the influential editors to use their newspapers in support of the Greensward plan.[19]

This instance was to be but one of many in which Olmsted used his connections among journalists, and his skill in public relations, to further a project. But it was an omen of future political interference and personality conflicts that would threaten Central Park.

Even when work on their design was proceeding at a reasonable pace, however, Olm-

Charles Anderson Dana

Born in New Hampshire in 1819, the son of a poor merchant, Dana fell under the influence of Brook Farm. There he met Horace Greeley who hired him to work for the *Tribune*. Dana worked as the paper's city editor (1847) before becoming its managing editor in 1849. In that position he ran counter to Greeley in his vigorous support of the Civil War. When Greeley fired him in 1862, Dana was appointed by President Lincoln to serve as a special commissioner and later assistant secretary of the War Department.

After the war, and a brief period as editor of a Chicago paper, Dana became part owner and editor of the *New York Sun*, where his reputation grew for both his business acumen and his assertive writing. One of the journalists who appreciated human-interest stories, he also originated the idea for the *New American Cyclopaedia*. A year after his death, his book on the Civil War was published. ⚘

sted and Vaux were subjected to pressure to hire workers designated by the commissioners. It fell largely to Olmsted to deal with the commissioners or political henchmen who saw only the pork-barrel potential of Central Park. Patronage was so widespread that Olmsted's resistance to it was seen by most commissioners as evidence of either his foolishness or reckless disregard for the established way of doing business.

"My dear Sir," Charles Elliott hinted to Olmsted, "I have had an interview with Alderman Brady respecting the placing of a man on the Park. He feels that other members of the Board had had more of this kind of patronage than he has. . . . I think he said he had not a single foreman or assistant on the Park while other members of the Board have three and four each. . . . Will you try to see me on Monday about it? I think as the matter stands Brady deserves consideration." [20]

But against the backdrop of political intrigue and foolish meddlesomeness, Olmsted and Vaux urged the park workmen onward. Soon the public saw the Greensward design emerging, and they liked what they saw. In the future Central Park would not be protected solely by its designers, but also by legions of pleased citizens who strolled, rode, visited, skated, rowed, and looked.

Domesticity: The Building Block of Civilization

Central Park and the creation of the Greensward plan did not absorb all of Olmsted's life, however; nor was he involved exclusively in pitting his cleverness against corruption. At the same time that he joined his life to the fate of the park, he committed himself to marriage and to the realization of his dream of being husband, father, and head of a household.

Olmsted was formed largely by his recollections of a near-idyllic childhood. Although his mother had died, leaving with young Frederick only a dim memory of herself, her son had enjoyed a happy, carefree childhood. Loved and indulged, he roamed the Connecticut countryside, made friends easily, and correctly assumed that he was secure and protected by adults, whether family or stranger.

He often spoke to his brother and friends of his desire to marry, to be a husband and father, to be the holder and keeper of a household. Some years earlier, in 1851, when the woman he had planned to marry had changed her mind and precipitously ended their engagement, Olmsted, to the puzzlement of his father and close friends, displayed none of the symptoms associated with heartbreak or rejection by a loved one. Rather, he expressed enthusiasm for his brother's impending marriage to Mary Cleveland Perkins.

John, knowing that he was doomed by tuberculosis, nonetheless fathered three children and, by his own accounts, enjoyed a near paradisiacal marriage. As he felt death overtaking him in Europe, John had petitioned Frederick: "Don't let Mary suffer while you are alive." [21]

After John's death, when Mary and the children returned to the United States, Frederick assumed responsibility for them. Mary, with a modest income from a trust fund, lived first at Frederick's farm on Staten Island, but then moved to Manhattan, giving Frederick even greater access to the children and influence on the daily routines of the household. For a time, Frederick actually shared the family's living quarters, but soon quietly moved to his own apartment, perhaps a sign that the relationship between Mary and Frederick was changing from that of friends or in-laws to a courtship. Some months later, in June 1859, Frederick Law Olmsted quietly married Mary Cleveland Perkins Olmsted in the Bogardus House in Central Park, in a ceremony conducted by Mayor Daniel F. Tiemann.

Whether Frederick was impelled by romantic love or a sense of obligation to his dead brother, his marriage to Mary Perkins Olmsted — a woman who proved over the years to be firm and sometimes formidable in the exercise of her independent mind — centered his life in the domesticity he had longed for. At the age of thirty-seven, Frederick Law Olmsted became both husband and father, as he took responsibility for the rearing of his brother's children, and instantly became head of a family of five.[22]

Europe 1859

The heavy burden of Central Park, as well as the stress of taking care of his new family, soon took a toll on Olmsted. In his now-familiar pattern of overwork followed by physical and emotional fatigue, Olmsted suffered fevers and grew morose. Concerned about his physical condition and his mental gloom, the park board granted Olmsted a leave of absence from the Central Park project from September to December 1859. Although newly a husband and father, Olmsted gladly seized the opportunity to travel alone to Europe to study public parks in England and on the Continent.[23]

Olmsted's psychological condition at the time is reflected in Vaux's bon voyage note to him:

> Upon my word, Olmsted, I will not forgive you if you do not make a better show. Who will be tempted to study of nature and the polite arts if the best paid and most popularly appreciated professors cut such a lugubrious, sallow, bloodless figure as you insist on doing? I consider that the only thing to be really regretted in our last two years' operations is the absence of jollity; because you see there are so many aspects of comicality in the whole affair.[24]

Olmsted had little use for "comicality," however, unless he originated it. Ambitious and what today would be called goal-oriented, he used his European travels to good advantage. He met Jean Alphand, the civil engineer responsible for the plan of the Bois de Boulogne and Bois de Vincennes, and studied those important urban parks. He took particular note of the rich vegetation employed in both Parisian parks, as well as the trees and shrubs adorning the great boulevards of Paris. He studied the layout of the extended park-like greenbelts through the city and discussed matters of design and maintenance with Alphand.[25]

London proved similarly edifying. From Sir Richard Mayne, commander of the London police, Olmsted solicited ideas for recruiting, training, and managing a special police force for Central Park.[26] He recognized the necessity of policing public pleasure grounds, but wanted to organize a separate body for that purpose and to train its members to teach people how to use the park, how to enjoy its greenery and spaces for activities without destroying the features that defined it. Rested and hatching new ideas for park administration and design, Olmsted returned to New York.

🌺 Civil Service and Political Rumblings

Olmsted did not return to serenity after his sabbatical in Europe, however. Rather, he encountered the man who would add measurable misery to his life and to his work with Central Park — the strong-willed Andrew Haswell Green. Green, in Olmsted's absence appointed by the board to be comptroller of the park, was a nitpicker and penny-pincher who had dug himself into the daily operations of Central Park. Displaying a style of management completely at odds with that of Olmsted, Green refused to delegate authority and insisted on his right to approve personally every expenditure, every decision, and every task undertaken within the park.

Olmsted's administrative responsibilities extended from supervising as many as 3,600 workers and giving ongoing attention to the preparation of earth and drainage systems on the site of Central Park, to artificially reshaping the natural topography to produce a heightened sense of nature, planting and caring for shrubs and trees, building walkways, carriageways, and bridges, and handling vast sums of money. Considerate and fair in his dealings with workers, Olmsted was nevertheless an autocrat, a boss who made decisions

The Mall at Central Park was designed to encourage people to sit in the shade of great trees and engage in conversation with one another. Such a configuration stemmed from Olmsted's long-held commitment to the concept that a park should bring together people of all classes and interests, thus promoting democratic ideals.

Calvert Vaux

Calvert Vaux and Olmsted worked together for five years on the implementation of their design of Central Park, beginning in 1858. When two article — both by friends of Olmsted — appeared in New York papers, Vaux's festering belief that his partner appropriated credit for the park erupted. He complained to Olmsted, "The public has been led to believe from the commencement of the Central Park work to the present time that you are pre-eminently the author of the executed design."

Despite public perception then and now, Olmsted and Vaux were partners in the design and realization of Central Park. Vaux, a professional architect, had moved in 1850 from his native England to work in America with Andrew Jackson Downing, one of the early advocates of a rural park for Manhattan.

After Downing's tragic death by drowning in 1852, Vaux took over his business and promotion of a great park for New York. When the competition for a design of the park was announced, Vaux approached Olmsted and suggested that they work together on an entry.

Olmsted and Vaux won the competition with their Greensward plan. Although lacking Vaux's training, Olmsted was elevated to the post of architect in chief, and Vaux was retained as his assistant at a salary of five dollars a day until 1859, when he became consulting architect. During Olmsted's leave to serve as head of the United States Sanitary Commission in Washington, 1865–1867, Vaux shouldered responsibility for the park, performing his own and Olmsted's duties.

Throughout Olmsted's years in Washington and California, letters between the partners often dealt with the relative role and merit of design and administration in making a park. Vaux saw park design as an art and believed that he and Olmsted were creating *landscape architecture;* Olmsted maintained for years that the park was an exercise in prudent management. "I believe that this work was chiefly an example of the art of design," Vaux wrote to Olmsted, "incidental of the art of administration. You thought the administration all inclusive and the design secondary." Once convinced by

Vaux to identify himself as artist and landscape architect, however, Olmsted defended that point of view vigorously.

Even though he and Olmsted were not partners during Olmsted's sojourn in California, Vaux continued to support their work and to defend their joint achievements against a lawsuit by Egbert Viele, who charged them with having stolen his design for Central Park. Vaux fought zealously, keeping Olmsted apprised of developments.

When Brooklyn leaders invited Vaux to visit a proposed site for a park in that city, Vaux suggested a change in the perimeter and orientation of what would become Prospect Park. In 1865 Vaux received the commission to design the park. He invited Olmsted to return from California and resume their partnership.

Vaux was also responsible for having himself and Olmsted reappointed as landscape architects to the Central Park commission. When it made public Richard Morris Hunt's plans for four monumental gates to the park, Vaux mounted a campaign to maintain the integrity of the Greensward plan and, in the process, convinced the commissioners that he and Olmsted should be rehired. Moreover, under the conditions of their employment, Olmsted and Vaux had power to review all architectural embellishments and intrusions suggested for Central Park.

With the commission for Prospect Park and reappointment as landscape architects of Central Park in hand, Vaux grew impatient with Olmsted's delay in accepting his invitation to partnership. Olmsted's egotism lay behind his hesitation, Vaux thought. "Your objection to the plan is I believe at heart because it involves the idea of a common fraternal effort," Vaux wrote to Olmsted. "It is too republican an idea for you, you must have a thick line drawn all around your six-pen' worth of individuality."

When Olmsted agreed to work again with Vaux, he brought to the firm three landscape commissions from California. 🌿

and disdained second-guessing or grumbling from subordinates. But Green held the purse strings. And he loosened them to pay only for those items and projects he deemed relevant to the public park in process. In his throttlehold on the budget, Green appropriated some of the authority Olmsted and Vaux believed to be theirs, thereby truncating their ability to carry out the design of the park. Green openly considered Vaux and Olmsted impractical and uneconomical. To the designers he appeared to take sadistic pleasure in placing irritating obstructions in the way of almost everything they attempted.

By late January 1861, Olmsted, exhausted and frustrated by Green, threatened to resign unless the board restored his complete control over the park work and allowed him to spend reasonable amounts of money without prior approval by Green. The board persuaded Olmsted to remain as supervisor by acknowledging the relevance of his complaints, and by pointing out that his resignation would threaten the passage of a bill to increase the size of the park.[27]

Partnership: Olmsted and Vaux

Nothing in Olmsted's life was more fortuitous than his meeting Calvert Vaux. The association of Olmsted and Vaux, though sometimes an uneasy one, lasted for decades and produced some of the masterpieces of American park and urban design.

While Olmsted's name is firmly fixed in the public mind as the creator of Central Park and as the father of American landscape architecture, it would be impossible to overestimate Calvert Vaux's contributions to both achievements. Vaux came to the United States at the invitation of Andrew Jackson Downing, who lived in Newburgh, New York, fulfilled his responsibilities to his many clients, and published a widely read magazine, the *Horticulturist*. Downing's gardens were marked by many features that would be amplified by Olmsted and Vaux: romantic vistas, picturesque details, and a feeling of naturalness. When Downing died in a drowning accident in 1852, his protégé Vaux took over his practice. The partnership of Olmsted and Vaux was thus a direct growth from Downing's roots.

Vaux not only continued Downing's business but kept alive one of his most passionate concerns. Downing and William Cullen Bryant — poet and editor of the influential *New York Evening Post* — had long advocated the formation of a great public park in Manhattan.

From the beginning of their association, Olmsted and Vaux gently quarreled about the nature of their work, Olmsted insisting that it was largely a matter of engineering and administration, Vaux maintaining that they were artists working to shape the land according to aesthetic principles. Olmsted, steeped as he was with the rudiments of scientific agriculture, shied away from talk of art, however, thinking it too grandiose a term for the practical business that occupied the partners.

Civil War,
Civil Servant

*I*n 1861 Olmsted saw the approach of the Civil War. His well-known abhorrence of slavery had not abated during the years he had given to the Greensward plan and Central Park. As the likelihood of war increased, so did Olmsted's loyalty to the Union.[1] He had hoped and argued earlier for the powers of sweet reason to persuade southern slaveholders to free slaves voluntarily and to take responsibility for their education and preparation for participation in society; but now he accepted the inevitability of war. Now, he reasoned, only one economic and social system could prevail in the United States; and only war could determine whether it would be based on free labor or slavery. Believing war inevitable, Olmsted's patriotism for the North swelled; he wrote to Brace, "My mind is made up for a fight. The sooner we get used to the idea, the better, I think." [2]

At the same time Olmsted accepted the inevitability of war, the thirty-nine-year-old park administrator, smarting under the growing power of comptroller Andrew H. Green, demanded of the board of commissioners that he be given full authority to manage the park, including power over hiring and firing employees. That failing, he asserted, he would not be able to function as general superintendent. The board's response was not

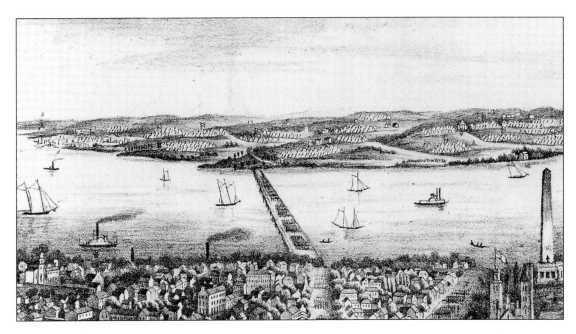

Washington, teeming with bureaucrats and military men, proved to have as many administrative pitfalls as Central Park. Olmsted deplored the lack of discipline, the poor sanitation, and the haphazard treatment of the wounded that plagued the Union's volunteer army.

what Olmsted expected. In June 1861, Olmsted's powers were further limited to merely overseeing the final aspects of the Greensward design.[3]

The fraught atmosphere of his Central Park work probably served to heighten Olmsted's interest in escaping to another job. By joining the war effort he could remove himself from Green's reign and could also further his vision of a just and civilized society. When the Confederates fired on Fort Sumter on April 12, 1861, Olmsted, like many citizens persuaded to the Union cause, searched for a way to participate in the looming war. He weighed his experience and skills against the needs of his country. He was no longer a young man; his leg had been badly damaged in a carriage accident the previous year, leaving him too lame to serve in the military. Nonetheless, his craving for a significant role in the Union cause was so strong that he considered joining the navy, where, he believed, his lameness would not be as detrimental as it would be in the army. When he at last accepted the impossibility of engaging in battle on either land or on sea, he decided to contribute his administrative talents to the war effort in another manner.

Aware that runaway slaves were being designated "contraband" by the Union army, with the approval of Secretary of War Simon Cameron, Olmsted saw an opportunity for himself. Slaves, he had long held, could not be thrown into freedom without preparation; they needed education, he insisted, to enable them to work and live in a free society. Olmsted decided to seek appointment as superintendent of contrabands, a position that would permit him to realize his educational and social reforms and to assist slaves in their new freedom. He approached Henry Whitney Bellows, a Unitarian minister in New York who had praised Central Park and Olmsted's management of it in an article published in the *Atlantic Monthly*, and asked him to lobby on his behalf.[4]

Bellows, as Olmsted had hoped, strongly supported him as a public servant and administrator, but he had a different job in mind for Olmsted. Influential in the organization and authorization of the United States Sanitary Commission, Bellows believed Olmsted to be a near-perfect candidate to serve as its executive officer. Olmsted responded eagerly when he was offered the job.[5]

The Sanitary Commission

Accounts vary regarding the birth of the United States Sanitary Commission, but there is general agreement that its inception was laced with political strife.[6] A group of wealthy New York men led by Bellows had responded to pleas from a large number of women who wanted to volunteer to aid the war effort.

President Lincoln was less than enthusiastic about the prospects of introducing an organization of independent civilians into the war effort, but by June 13, 1861, he bowed to pressure from powerful citizens and signed an executive order establishing a "Commission for Inquiry and Advice in Respect of the Sanitary Interests of the United States Forces."[7] Modeled on the British Red Cross, the Sanitary Commission had no official authority but was a philanthropic organization of volunteers whose executively defined purposes consisted of collecting and disseminating supplies to care for the wounded on battlefields, in camps, and in hospitals; informing and advising the Army Medical Bureau on the latest and best practices of hygiene and sanitation; and promoting the health of the Union troops in camp and in battle. In short, the Sanitary Commission, as defined, had no real authority and was destined for turf warfare.

On June 20, a week after Lincoln created the Sanitary Commission, Henry Whitney Bellows invited Olmsted to serve as its chief executive officer, with the title "general secretary." Olmsted was eager to accept the leadership of the largest voluntary organization in the history of the country. In late summer he took leave from his responsibilities at Central Park and moved to Washington to organize and direct the commission's affairs.[8] He thus optimistically began what he later described as his most important single public service.[9]

Olmsted may not have known the stresses that preceded Lincoln's reluctant executive order creating the Sanitary Commission, but the causes of his later frustration were seeded in that rich turmoil. With considerable effort, Bellows had obtained approval for the idea of the Sanitary Commission from career army officer and acting surgeon general Robert C. Wood. That approval was rescinded a month later by the elderly Clement A. Finley, shortly after his appointment, in June, as surgeon general.

Finley had been persuaded to accept the commission if its role was restricted to serving the volunteer army. With Secretary of War Cameron's approval, then, Lincoln had called the Sanitary Commission "a fifth wheel" and signed the executive order inaugurating it.

When Olmsted took charge of the Sanitary Commission, he reported to a board of commissioners consisting of its founders — Henry Whitney Bellows, Elisha Harris, and William H. Van Buren, as well as Alexander Dallas Bache, director of the U.S. Coast Survey; Samuel Gridley Howe, a reformer from Boston; Cornelius Rae Agnew, a physician; George Templeton Strong, a lawyer; Oliver Wolcott Gibbs, a chemist; and John S. Newberry, a physician and scientist. Three army officers also sat on the board: George W. Cullum, Robert C. Wood, and Alexander Shiras. These were well-educated, wealthy men from privileged backgrounds; several held professional or postgraduate degrees and were recognized leaders in medicine, law, and religion; none was a businessman; but only three — Bellows, Howe, and Olmsted — had been active in reform movements. They were united in belief in the Union cause, in their belief in rational solutions to problems, and in their determination to meet the Sanitary Commission's goals in an efficient and effective manner.[10]

Olmsted, the only member of the commission lacking a college degree, brought his skills in administration and communication, as well as his interest in science, to his assignment. During his years on the Central Park project, he had shown himself to be a creative and practical administrator, able to deal with myriad details and disparate problems. The other commissioners were aware of his record in establishing and training a special park police force — drilling them in military discipline and teaching them to educate the public concerning park use — as well as in instituting timekeeping systems for the workers, developing a system for breaking tasks into smaller units and assigning each to a specific crew, and teaching his men to understand delegated authority and responsibility. While setting model administrative practices in place, Olmsted had supervised the work of as many as four thousand men on a project that was spending millions of dollars. He was, by all measurements, an outstanding manager and in later years believed that his major contribution to the development of Central Park had been the "[a]dministration & management of the public introduction to and use of the Park." [11]

His new job was as complicated as that at Central Park and put him under more pressure than Green and New York politics had ever done. The role of the Sanitary Commission's leader was in part defined by the entrenched hierarchical power struggles of the professional army officers, in part by the political churnings of Washington, and finally by the disparate viewpoints and purposes of the individuals who composed the lay governing board of the Sanitary Commission. During his tenure, Olmsted would rail against the Washington bureaucracy, which shielded indecision, and as in the Central Park project, he would find himself at odds with the governing board of the organization he headed. He would work himself to the point of emotional and physical exhaustion, would enmesh himself in details of logistics and administrative structure, would command the loyalty and respect of subordinates, and would alienate those to whom he reported. He would perform heroic feats of administration and resourcefulness and would see his role somewhat grandiosely in the light of his reformist values and deep convictions about the nature of civilization. His letters from the period indicate that, all difficulties and frustrations notwithstanding, he believed that he had an important role to play in support of the Union cause, and that he had a mission of near-sacred trust to take the actions he deemed appropriate. Indeed, under Olmsted in two years the Sanitary Commission collected and distributed medical supplies, clothing, and bedding worth more than half a million dollars and contributed significantly to the well-being and survival of countless Union soldiers. [12]

But as head of the commission, Olmsted, as when he was superintendent of Central Park, resented his superiors, often ignoring their policies and directives and unilaterally spending extravagantly to achieve his own ends. He had the soul of a zealot. He exhibited a near-religious intensity in his beliefs — whether scientific farming, the Free-Soil movement, Central Park, or the Union — causing him to overwork to the point of nervous exhaustion. Moreover, he tended to place his faith at the center of a grander scheme of civilization, and to see himself as contributing to the reform and betterment of American life. Not surprisingly, he believed that the Sanitary Commission could not only supply the latest scientific information to army doctors, but could be a force in educating officers and men in their duties. Finally, as a patriot, he believed he was serving his country by committing himself to the Sanitary Commission.

When Olmsted enthusiastically accepted the post, he anticipated making a major contribution to the war effort. At that time politicians and army officers drinking in the hotel bars of Washington reflected the abiding opinion of the day that the war would be over shortly. Olmsted was prepared for a longer struggle. He believed the Union was unprepared for the war it faced, estimated that the conflict would last two or three years, and that it would cost the government as much as six hundred million dollars.[13] But he nonetheless expected to whip the Sanitary Commission into shape in six weeks and return to Central Park.

During the summer, however, he recognized fully the seriousness of the war and the importance of the commission. When Olmsted took office, he found the Sanitary Commission without adequate funds to sustain a staff and thus turned to other members of the organization to carry on its day-to-day work. After little more than two weeks in Washington, Olmsted began recruiting and training a corps of inspectors to work with military doctors in distributing donated supplies and to study and advise on the sanitary conditions of the military camps. Olmsted chose physicians educated in the eastern medical schools, men like the commissioners, men of influence and social standing.[14]

In addition to the inspectors, Olmsted hired men recommended by friends or commissioners to do office and other nonmedical work. Two had worked for him on Central Park: Alfred J. Bloor, an architect, became his secretary and assistant, and Joseph Curtis, an engineer, worked for his former boss until he joined the army. As the commission grew, he added other employees, including two others from Central Park, John Y. Cuyler and Howard Martin. A year after its inception, the commission had employed office workers, teamsters, cooks, security guards, and domestic servants.[15]

Olmsted planned to employ men with specialized skills to perform specific duties, again delegating responsibility and authority so that he would not be burdened by the routines of day-to-day operations. He wrote to his wife in September, "I have completed a *large* organization which leaves me only matters of the first importance to personally attend to."[16]

At first, Olmsted supervised all of the inspectors, but after September 1861 he divided them into regional groups, each headed by an associated secretary who reported to Olmsted. He continued to tinker with organizational structure and, according to the chief inspector for the Sanitary Commission with the Army of the Potomac, "After the battle of Gettysburg, Mr. Olmsted prepared the outline of the Field Relief Corps of the Army of

As the war progressed, Olmsted detected a noticeable improvement in the discipline and appearance of the Union army, and came to believe that victory was possible. He urged President Lincoln, whom he had disliked and labeled a boor at first meeting, to appeal personally to civilians in order to fire up the population for better mobilization of resources.

the Potomac, which served afterwards as a species of model for similar Relief Corps in the other armies." [17]

The Sanitary Commission's branches — such as its New York City parent organization, the Woman's Central Relief Association — sought, received, and sent to the commission the supplies needed. In this way Olmsted folded the work of the grass-roots volunteer corps into the intricate organization he built. Paid employees handled correspondence with the volunteer groups, logging, indexing, and filing all letters received and their answers. Olmsted stipulated similarly precise procedures for the filing of financial reports. [18]

Olmsted's greatest contribution to the Sanitary Commission was to its organization of structure and procedures. [19] His administrative genius permeated his creation of the organizational structure for the Sanitary Commission, and his fondness for power similarly saturated his separation of functions he identified as administrative and executive. He saw the administrator's role as supervisory, and the executive's as hands-on attention to the task.

He wrote: "The further (i.e. the more distinctly) removed an administrator is from pure execution the better. I am the Commission's executive, but with reference to my executives, I am pure administrator, and it is just as absurd & as fatal for me to take my executives' business, or if you please, other executives' of the Commission's business out of their hands as it is for the Exec. Com. to take my business out of my hands." [20]

He offered advice on administration to his stepmother, Mary Bull Olmsted, then president of the Hartford Soldiers' Aid Society:

> *Your first business is to read the newspapers, the whole aim & object of your organization being with regard to matters of which you can only get early and sufficient information from them. You can deputize any responsibility better than that as a general rule. If, in an emergency, it is otherwise & you are obliged to give personal attention to matters of detail, your first duty is to remedy the imperfection of your organization which makes this necessary — meantime employing father, Mary, Bertha, or someone as clerk to read the newspaper & furnish you, verbally or in writing, with an abstract of all matters bearing upon soldiers, directly or remotely.*

As was the case with Central Park, lines of authority in the Sanitary Commission were not as clearly defined as Olmsted would have had them. Both he and Associate Secretary John S. Newberry were members of the commission's board, and both were its employees. On the board they had equal status; in the operation of the Sanitary Commission, Olmsted was Newberry's superior. In actuality, however, this was an intolerable distinction without difference for Olmsted, resulting in disputes within the board as well as between Olmsted and Newberry.

Shortly after his appointment to the Sanitary Commission, Olmsted, assisted by Elisha Harris, reported on an inspection of the camps of volunteer soldiers. Olmsted noted that the army's diet should be improved with the addition of fresh fruits and vegetables, but blasted the soldiers as "really much dirtier than it can be believed they have been accustomed to be in their civil life," observing that they lived in crowded dirty tents and used filthy latrines. Blaming these unhygienic practices on army officers who failed to instruct volunteers in proper military life, Olmsted insisted that they made the army susceptible to epidemics of contagious disease. Inspectors from the Sanitary Commission, he suggested, would "without special effort or intention, really be the best possible missionaries of sanitary science to the army." He requested that the War Office give the Sanitary Commission the authority to enforce standards of hygiene in the army camps. His request was ignored.[21]

Olmsted's interest in sanitary reform rested on his conviction that habits of personal cleanliness and grooming were necessary to civilized living. He added to the Sanitary Commission's official role his personal mission to educate soldiers to the virtues of healthful living. Olmsted saw, too, a correlation between personal hygiene and discipline, the essential ingredient in a good army and one he believed was lacking in the Union officers and troops alike. But Olmsted's personal convictions had not been adopted as the policies of the Sanitary Commission. Moreover, his attempts to force his ideas on the army brought only anger from the commanders who believed him to be intrusive and abrasive.

But Olmsted had cause to be concerned about discipline. In midsummer of 1861, in the battle of Bull Run, the Union troops fought well until the afternoon when, their flanks broken by Confederate forces, they retreated in disorder, many of them returning to Washington. The following day, Olmsted observed the dirty, demoralized soldiers on the streets of Washington and, more to his displeasure, their officers drinking in the hotel bars of the city.

"Beloved!" he wrote to his wife. "We are in a frightful condition here, ten times as bad as anyone dare say publicly. . . . The demoralization of a large part of our troops is something more awful than I ever met with." In Olmsted's opinion the situation in 1861 was so dire that "Unless McClellan . . . becomes a military dictator & rules over our imbecile government, we should & must have a resolution before we can do anything with the South." As for himself, he confided, "I am overwhelmed. I have suffered intense humiliation. Our Commission can do something and I from my position in it can do something to set public opinion in the right direction & to overcome . . . the prevailing inefficiency and misery. You would not have me do less than I can." [22]

Disheartened soldiers, dirty and undisciplined, were, in Olmsted's view, uncivilized, unpatriotic, and unlikely to win the war. Olmsted regarded discipline as a soldier's acceptance of authority, which, on the other side of the coin, entitled him to fair and respectful treatment from his military leader. In Olmsted's thinking military leadership, and the army's resulting effectiveness, required an overall discipline and organization to provide healthful diet, adequate clothing and shelter, and standards of hygiene, along with instruction in using arms, drilling, fighting, and obeying orders.

Olmsted wrote a blistering report on the causes of what he considered the disgraceful defeat of the Union army at Bull Run. His *Report on the Demoralization of the Volunteers* focused on the poorly clothed, fed, shod, and protected volunteers, a motley and disorderly mob with neither the skills nor the disciplines required for soldiering. Fired with principle and theory, as well as with practical sense and patriotism, Olmsted's report on the Sanitary Commission's study of reasons for this blamed military officers — and, unstintingly, the government itself — for lax discipline.

Olmsted was not alone among Republicans in fearing that Lincoln's administration was unequal to the demands of the war. Along with his friend Charles Loring Brace, Olmsted believed after Bull Run that a temporary military dictatorship would be better to win the war and to free the slaves. Ironically, Olmsted's strong support of civil liberties and representative government had led him to this extreme position. Convinced that the South was willing to sacrifice anything to win the war, and already on record as vehemently opposing southern suppression of free speech, press, and personal liberty, Olmsted's despair following Bull Run led him to his willingness to forgo temporarily the freedoms he valued in order to defeat the evils inherent in the southern system of government.[23]

Olmsted organized the Sanitary Commission to receive medical supplies and other donations from the private sector and to deploy them to Union army hospitals and battle stations. He engaged in political efforts to change the operation of the army's Medical Department and to funnel medical supplies and food through that official agency.

The first version of Olmsted's report, finished in September, has not survived but, according to George Templeton Strong, was judged so potentially damaging to the Union's ability to attract volunteers that the board of the Sanitary Commission suppressed it. Olmsted laid blame on Lincoln, viewing the government incompetent to mobilize the country for war and the army unprepared for battle. Olmsted's second version, less harsh in its criticism, was not released to the public, but printed privately for circulation only among the members of the Sanitary Commission.

The report indicted the Army Medical Bureau for ineptness, for inability to provide adequate care for soldiers. With limited funds and supplies from public donations, the Sanitary Commission, according to the report, could not compensate for the Medical Bureau's failures. Olmsted called for "a general reform, enlargement and vitalization of the Medical Bureau," and for the appointment of a new surgeon general, one who would be "big hearted and energetic." [24]

The report was hardly diplomatic, since the Sanitary Commission was subordinate to the Medical Bureau. But Olmsted and other commissioners appealed to Secretary of War Cameron and to General McClellan to retire Surgeon General Finley. When Cameron forwarded the confidential correspondence from the Sanitary Commission to Finley, he threw fuel on hot ashes, virtually guaranteeing continuing discord between the two groups. [25] Shortly afterward, Lincoln rebuked the Sanitary Commission for its efforts to remove Finley from office. But the commission had a candidate in mind — William Alexander Hammond, a physician who had resigned his commission in the army, then reenlisted at the beginning of the war, thus losing his previous rank.

Olmsted's frustration increased when McClellan interfered in his plan to solicit blankets for soldiers from the public. Convinced that "it is so necessary to the safety of the country that the war should be popularized that I can hardly be loyal to the Commission and the government, while it is required of us to let our soldiers freeze & our armies be conquered for the sake of maintaining a lie," Olmsted believed that the administration would sooner let soldiers suffer and die than risk public perception that the war was not under control. He held Lincoln responsible for not making a greater effort to win the support of the Northerners. [26]

Olmsted also believed that the supplies collected and distributed, the work done by the Sanitary Commission, obscured the failures of the Medical Bureau. By November the commissioners began anonymously to plant articles in newspapers detailing the shortcomings of army doctors. [27] After a virulent attack on Finley, however, the strategy resulted in ricocheting accusations. Henry J. Raymond, editor of the *New York Times*, now strongly supported the surgeon general. Although he had earlier commissioned Olmsted's articles on the South, that friendship dimmed in the light of his "Platonic friendship" with Elizabeth Powell, a young nurse who took some of the sting from his unhappy marriage. She wrote under the pseudonym Truth, praising Finley and accusing Olmsted of being power hungry and meddlesome and suggesting that his personality and imperious ways — and not the entrenched powers of the Army Medical Bureau — endangered the success of the Sanitary Commission. Heaping it on Olmsted, Truth praised Finley as a wise, nearly god-like man of great virtue and identified Olmsted as a "man of consummate abilities," who sought personal power "and the handling of millions" through his office with the Sanitary Commission.[28]

Olmsted appealed to Raymond, brandishing his *Report to the Secretary of War,* which — unlike his earlier ill-fated diatribe against the administration — was widely read and much praised. Perhaps Olmsted's sweet reason or the document he authored brought about Raymond's change of mind. It seems more likely, however, that Mrs. Raymond's display of anger with her husband for his dalliance with Miss Powell forced the *Times* editor to back off.[29] At any rate, Raymond shifted the newspaper's policy and began to support the work of the Sanitary Commission and the appointment of Hammond.

Meanwhile, the Sanitary Commission's ongoing efforts to reform the Medical Bureau finally focused on getting legislation to reorganize the Medical Bureau. Senate Bill 97, written by William A. Hammond and introduced by Henry Wilson, created the office of inspector general and provided for eight inspectors who reported to the surgeon general and took responsibility for the sanitary conditions of army camps, hygienic standards for hospitals, and dissemination of materials and information. It also required mandatory re-tirement of officers over sixty-five and promotion of officers based on merit rather than seniority.[30]

Olmsted, acting for the board of the Sanitary Commission, campaigned for the bill, arranging to have it delivered to the War Department when Cameron was absent so that it was received by a supporter, Assistant Secretary of War Thomas Scott. In addition, Olm-sted and Hammond called on their friends with political influence and lobbied congress-men.

In January 1862 Edwin M. Stanton was appointed secretary of war. Olmsted and his friends organized visits to him by influential citizens from eastern cities, all urging passage of the bill and reform of the Medical Bureau.[31] Conducting his campaign for the passage of the bill, and anxiously watching its various permutations in the legislative process into February, Olmsted grew frustrated and, along with the other commissioners, began to wonder if the Sanitary Commission had achieved or would be able to achieve its goals.

By the end of February, having persuaded other commissioners not to resign even when he himself despaired, Olmsted perceived a sign of victory. Stanton's needed support for the bill came not on the merits outlined by the commissioners, but because Surgeon General Finley badly treated one of Stanton's friends. With the secretary of war's support, and with legislative tinkering to allow the president to appoint the surgeon general, the

House of Representatives passed the medical reform bill in April 1862. Olmsted saw this as a major accomplishment for the Sanitary Commission, one in which principle triumphed over politics. It was a "great benefaction" he wrote to his friend Bellows. "I refer to the reform and enlargement and to the popular support of the reform and enlargement of the Medical Department of the army and to the wonderful suppression which in the midst of this period of intense popular excitement, we have witnessed, of Quackery, Pedantry and the conservatism of ignorance."[32]

But Olmsted and the other commissioners could not rest until Hammond was appointed surgeon general. Political forces again delayed matters, and Hammond was not confirmed by the Senate until April 25. With Hammond in place, the Sanitary Commission intensified its efforts on behalf of its candidates for the inspectorships.[33]

Convinced that the Sanitary Commission was meddling in political affairs, however, Stanton and the Army Medical Bureau continued to ignore Olmsted and his colleagues until McClellan's spring campaign on the Virginia peninsula in 1862. Throughout that operation the Sanitary Commission efficiently provisioned the army with supplies and medical aid, and Olmsted led his staff in around-the-clock labors to save lives and relieve suffering.

At that time, too, Hammond was at last appointed surgeon general. Under him — and in view of the commission's good work during the Virginia Peninsular Campaign — Olmsted's advice became the army's standard operating procedure. In a spirit of cooperation between the army and the volunteers and within a year after Hammond's appointment, Olmsted estimated that the Medical Bureau supplied nine-tenths of the medical care needed by troops on battlefields and in hospitals.[34]

Olmsted was plagued by fatigue and despair as early as December 1861. At that time, working to file a report with the secretary of war on the activities and observations of the Sanitary Commission, he studied findings from questionnaires on the physical condition of the troops, described the achievements of the commission, and recommended changes, all implicitly heaping criticism on the Medical Bureau for its poor care of soldiers. But in order to prepare the report before Christmas, Olmsted worked himself and his staff to the point of exhaustion. He jestingly commented that one staff member, actuary E. B. Elliott, was so fatigued that he fell asleep if left alone.[35]

In addition to the regular work of the Sanitary Commission, Olmsted continually expanded his efforts, often stepping on powerful toes well planted on protected political turf. He began to lobby the War Department and Congress on matters related to hospital construction and the welfare of soldiers, a venture that required hours of waiting, talking, more waiting, and persuading.[36]

Olmsted and Hospital Ships

While Olmsted administered the Sanitary Commission mostly from his office in Washington, he spent time in the field, notably two and a half months with the Army of the Potomac in the Peninsular Campaign, during which he directed the activities of hospital ships under his office. Characteristically industrious and resourceful, Olmsted borrowed boats and rapidly transformed them to serve as hospital ships; he then led the Sanitary Commission volunteers in the enormous task of transporting the wounded to hospitals in the North, thereby saving countless lives.[37]

In the spring of 1862, when the Sanitary Commission took responsibility for outfitting hospital ships to transport the wounded from the battlefields of McClellan's Peninsular Campaign, Olmsted plunged heart and soul into the work.[38] But even this undertaking was not free of the corroding political atmosphere and pervasive administrative chaos that plagued the Union effort.

When Stanton conceded to Sanitary Commissioner William H. Van Buren that only inadequate plans existed for the evacuation of the wounded in the imminent campaign, the sanitarian offered to staff and provide material for a hospital ship if Quartermaster General Meigs — reluctant at best — could be persuaded to assign a vessel to the project.

Olmsted and Frederick Knapp, his friend and associate on the commission, took charge of a rickety steamboat, the *Daniel Webster No. 1*, on April 25; recruited and briefed staff and volunteers; and set sail from Ship's Point on Cheeseman's Creek on April 27.

On the voyage Olmsted led the women and men under his supervision in completely refurbishing and outfitting the ship, whitewashing walls, building bunks and kitchens, storing supplies, and establishing procedures to be used in the care of the sick and wounded. Throughout the coming eleven weeks Olmsted and his band would be physically and mentally tested in their combat against filth, gore, suffering, death, and also by their frustration with poor hygiene and discipline in the army.

Within a month the Sanitary Commission took command of another and better steamboat, the *Ocean Queen*, which, despite needing equipment and stores, added significantly to the ability of the sanitarians to transport the wounded. But the *Ocean Queen* was scarcely in operation before Quartermaster General Meigs recalled it and diverted it to use in transporting troops. Several days later, the *Elm City*, another ship used by the Sanitary Commission, was recalled from hospital service, stripped of its bunks, and, token of yet another change of mind among those commanding the war, returned to the Sanitary Commission. These and a chain of similar instances plagued both the Sanitary Commission and the Medical Bureau. In addition to getting and keeping ships for use by the Sanitary Commission, Olmsted had to wrestle with the frequently changing crews employed by the government. Fearing contagion, resisting discipline and work, the men who ran the ships were never far from insubordination or even desertion.

By begging, cajoling, and reasoning, Olmsted and the Sanitary Commission managed to assemble a well-equipped and efficient fleet of hospital ships, including the *Webster*, the small shore boat *Elizabeth*, and the large *S.R. Spaulding*. They also used river steamers such as the *Knickerbocker*, *Elm City*, *Daniel Webster 2*, and *State of Maine*, and the two handsome sailing vessels *Euterpe* and *St. Mark*, which were used as receiving hospitals. In addition, the *Wilson Small* served as headquarters for the Sanitary Commission.

Olmsted's administrative brilliance sharpened the effectiveness of the operation, while he also attended to minute details and solved problems that were small in relationship to the larger picture. His staff consisted of volunteers as well as employed physicians, male and female nurses, medical students, pharmacists, cooks, quartermasters, stewards, and servants. There was continual turnover, especially among the volunteers, and severe problems of overwork, exhaustion, and illness. Even so, Olmsted commanded a steady and dedicated staff through most of McClellan's Peninsular Campaign.

Olmsted valued and respected the people who shared his work, recognizing their often-heroic efforts. Knapp, a gentle and quiet man, shot and dressed a cow to provide the essential ingredient of beef tea for the wounded. Physicians James M. Grymes and Robert Ware, both of whom died in the war, worked day and night to relieve suffering and to save lives. But the volunteers who most amazed him were the gentlewomen, often of intellectual bent and high social standing, who sang hymns and did fine stitchery on the ship decks when they had a few hours of rest, but who comforted the sick and wounded, cleaned festering wounds and human filth, quietly vomited when the stench of decay and death choked them, and scrounged for materials and innovated methods in order to provide nourishing food for the soldiers. These women included Katherine P. Wormeley, Georgeanna Woolsey, and Christine Kean Griffin. Olmsted said of them, "They beat the doctors all to pieces. I should have sunk the ships in despair before this if it had not been for their handiness and good nature." [39]

The Sanitary Commission's relentless attention to hygiene did not convince the army of the need for a clean water supply. Typhoid plagued camps in swampy areas when human waste and water supplies were not sufficiently separated. At the beginning of the Peninsular Campaign, as soldiers waited in camps to be sent into battle, the commission confronted sickness and disease, rather than wounds. Moreover, the sanitarians grappled with the inability of the army doctors to provide adequate care. Olmsted found poorly managed hospitals, inefficient and sometimes inhumane care of the sick, and military physicians without the system or supplies necessary for caring for soldiers.

Often, Olmsted noted, sick soldiers needed only rest and nourishing food in order to be prepared to return to their units. These men, he felt, should be nursed in clean, orderly hospitals on the peninsula, an efficient policy that would care for the genuinely ill and discourage malingerers.

After the battle of Fair Oaks on May 31, 1862, when the Confederates attacked McClellan's army at the Chickahominy River, Olmsted's worst fears were realized. Working out of White House, the Custis family plantation then owned by William Henry Fitzhugh Lee, Olmsted realized that the wounded were pouring in, but that the army physician in charge — Henry Hollingsworth Smith, surgeon general of the state of Pennsylvania — was disregarding the Sanitary Commission's plans for an orderly and effective use of the hospital ships. Instead, ships were filled with soldiers whose conditions had not been assessed and wounds had not been cleaned. Olmsted, often disregarding conflicting orders from the army physicians, loaded as many soldiers onto the boats as he could and removed them to better medical facilities.

Disheartened by the government's chaotic response to the battle of Fair Oaks, Olmsted felt that the Sanitary Commission existed in an untenable never-never land squeezed between government inefficiency and army medical incompetence. He believed himself to occupy an ill-defined status and to possess inadequate authority for accomplishing the work before him.

In June, as McClellan waited to march on Richmond, Olmsted anticipated heavy casualties and urged the Medical Bureau to prepare by bringing in more doctors and support staff, by providing better shelter and adequate supplies. Before McClellan made a decision to move, however, Lee's troops attacked, setting off the Seven Days' Battle.

Olmsted, already disposed favorably toward McClellan, worked closely with his officers during the shift of their headquarters from the Pamunkey to the James River. Just as he learned to temper the Union officers' estimates of Rebel strength, Olmsted realized that the soldiers fought bravely and fiercely. He called them heroes and believed that their courage and strength could win the war for the North. Worried nonetheless about the outcome of the war, Olmsted began to petition every source he could identify for more men and supplies for McClellan's army. He went to Washington to confer with Quartermaster General Meigs and other high officials in the administration. They failed to promise what Olmsted wanted, so he turned to President Lincoln, urging him to appeal personally for volunteers. If volunteers did not come forward, Olmsted argued, it was time for the Union to initiate conscription.

At the same time, aware that blame for the war's unfavorable progress was being laid on McClellan, Olmsted embarked on a campaign to praise the general. He urged the edi-

The refitting and use of hospital ships was one of Olmsted's triumphs of will, administrative skills, and leadership. Working in great haste with reluctant crews and volunteer medical people, he used a small fleet to deliver medical supplies to army encampments along the Virginia rivers and to remove the wounded to hospitals where they could receive better treatment than that provided in the medical stations near the battlefields.

tor of the *New York Daily Tribune,* Sydney Gay, to attribute responsibility for the Peninsular Campaign to Stanton.

In July, Bellows, noting Olmsted's poor physical condition, admonished him to give up the Peninsular Campaign. Exhausted, gaunt, and badly sunburned, Olmsted left for New York on July 16. He believed the Sanitary Commission had saved lives on the Virginia peninsula, but he also believed that the job done by the sanitarians was one that properly belonged to the army. In compensating for the inadequacies of the Medical Bureau and the army, he wondered, was the Sanitary Commission performing a public service? And as he had for months, he fretted over the lack of authority granted to the Sanitary Commission and about his own lack of power to command the actions he believed vital to the war effort.

Olmsted found himself as frustrated by his mission with the Sanitary Commission as he had with that of Central Park.

Slavery, Freedom, and Civilization

Olmsted, working at his manic pace in February 1862, without rest or adequate sleep, managed the dispersement of relief agents and supplies to hospitals and battlefields and supervised the efforts of 7,009 aid societies in northern communities. But he was restless, often frustrated, and increasingly at odds with the commissioners. As reform of the Medical Bureau inched forward, threatening to stall at countless twists and turns in the political landscape, Olmsted considered two other positions of public service: superintendent of streets for New York City or administrator of a program to aid contraband slaves in their transition to freedom.[40] Both required political appointment, and both appealed to Olmsted's interests.

The Streets of New York

Mayor George Opdyke of New York invited Olmsted — still on leave from Central Park — to serve as the city's street commissioner. This position carried the power to influence the growth and character of the city and to supervise street construction and maintenance, street lighting, and the docks.

While spacing and placement of the crosstown streets had been determined in 1811, that for the avenues — the uptown–downtown thoroughfares — had not been settled. The commissioner might create avenues of parklike splendor, with spacious medians and handsome plantings. For Olmsted, this would be an opportunity to manifest his theories about urban planning, including his conviction that the grid pattern produced unhealthful and unattractive living conditions for city dwellers.

Olmsted vacillated between the New York City job and his other possibility at that time, superintending freed slaves at Port Royal in the South Carolina Sea Islands. In a letter to Treasury Secretary Salmon P. Chase he promised that, as a gentleman, he would not campaign for the New York post but that he would make no decision regarding Port Royal until the New York aldermen had accepted or rejected him as street commissioner.[41] Knowing that he had enemies among the aldermen, Olmsted, by this course of action, risked losing the superintendency of the Sea Islands project.

The street commissioner, like the superintendent of Central Park, managed numerous jobs that the aldermen considered coinage in the realm of patronage. Olmsted had already exhibited his unwillingness to join the accepted political practices of the day, and although he wanted to be street commissioner, he made no effort to convince the aldermen that he was willing to assist them in dispersing patronage. On the contrary, as he recalled later, he reaffirmed their notion of him as an "unpractical man."

When politicians called on him to ascertain his willingness to be "practical" in hiring and firing, Olmsted made it clear that he intended to employ men fit for the work at hand. Olmsted recalled, "When one of the mayor's friends in the city-hall understood that I seriously meant to be my own master, or defeated, he exclaimed, "Why, the man must be a fool!'" [42] Convinced that the aldermen would not approve his appointment, Olmsted turned his attention toward the superintendency at Port Royal.

Port Royal

In the early months of 1861, Olmsted's concern for the welfare of freed blacks, rooted in his travels and articles on the antebellum South, had prompted him to suggest to both Cameron and McClellan roles the army might play in hastening the collapse of slavery in the South.[43] In November an army-navy offensive resulted in the capture of one of the South Carolina Sea Islands — Port Royal, a region of rich plantations. White owners abandoned their land and slaves, leaving the army in charge of both, a happenstance that promised more harm than help to the slaves. The army not only seized the corn and animals that the blacks might have used, but also spread disease and, in some cases, physically abused the slaves, who were considered, at least unofficially by the army, to be contraband.

Treasury Secretary Chase, strongly opposed to slavery, saw Port Royal as an opportunity. Citing the Union laws relating to abandoned property, he sent Treasury agents to Port Royal, among them Edward L. Pierce, who shared Chase's ideals and set out to make the Sea Islands a model community for assisting freed slaves. With help from antislavery groups in the eastern cities, he brought teachers to Port Royal in the spring of 1862.[44]

But Olmsted, still in New York and still hoping to be appointed to the superintendency of the Sea Islands project, protested what he considered to be stop-gap measures.
On January 27, 1862, Olmsted, accompanied by Bellows and another sanitarian, Professor
Alexander Dallas Bache, had visited Chase to push for a comprehensive government policy and program to accomplish goals he had long advocated. Olmsted was not a disinter-
ested party. He wanted to influence government policy regarding the Sea Islands project,
and he wanted to manage it.

In the meeting with Chase, he argued that slaves should be guided into full freedom,
educated to the responsibilities and rewards of free labor, and helped toward full economic
and social independence. Moreover, he argued, the Port Royal project could be used to
demonstrate that slavery itself was based on economic fallacies, thereby serving to instruct
the South in the superiority of free labor.

Preoccupied with other problems, Chase all but ignored Olmsted's counsel. Unsatis-
fied by Chase's reception, Olmsted turned to Connecticut senator Lafayette S. Foster, a
Republican who was already agitating for legislation to cover government handling of
Port Royal. Foster encouraged Olmsted to draft legislation on the subject. Within days,
Olmsted presented the senator with a proposed government policy for Port Royal, and
Foster introduced the bill on February 14.[45]

Foster's bill, as prepared by Olmsted, not only promoted Olmsted's policies for guiding slaves into freedom, but established a bureaucracy and administrative post tailored to
Olmsted's measurements. Olmsted, recognizing that blacks had been damaged by slavery,
believed that a gradual process of moral and mental healing would enable them to participate in a democracy and to reap the rewards of a free-labor system. In his book *A Journey in
the Seaboard Slave States*, Olmsted had earlier called for a step-by-step system of emancipation whereby slaves would buy their freedom with wages earned from labor, at the same
time learning the values of planning, thrift, and work. He strongly believed that the damage done to the minds and morals of the slaves could be repaired, but he expected the
process to be gradual rather than immediate. Foster's eagerness to sponsor a bill on Port
Royal gave Olmsted an opportunity to turn his dreams to reality.

Moreover, the proposed bill established the government's obligations for the protection of the blacks at Port Royal, reasoning that the slaves needed to be taught to support
themselves and to respect the law. Olmsted anticipated a role for private benevolent organizations to cooperate with the government by supplying education and religious instruction to the Port Royal blacks. The plan called for a three-member board of commissioners
to lease land from the government and oversee cultivation of it and called for wages-for-
work as a program of incentives and to allow blacks to buy their freedom.[46]

Desiring an immediate passage of the legislation, Olmsted tried to prepare a bill with as little controversy as possible. He characterized his efforts in a letter to James R. Spalding:

The Bill is drawn with especial care to void all issues of a radical character. Neither slave-holder nor abolitionist would be compromised in voting for it — and, as it will not stand in the way of more thorough measure, one way or the other, when the policy of the country with regard to slavery is determined, it may be hoped to unite all who do not wish to establish at Port Royal, another evidence of the folly of ever hoping to see negroes usefully employed in any other condition than that of abject slavery.[47]

But Olmsted decided to work on another level as well to ensure passage of the bill. As he had done in other instances when he wanted to influence opinion, Olmsted orches-trated publicity in the *New York World* — a journal that had already identified him as the perfect supervisor of slaves under government control. At the same time, Olmsted drew up and circulated a petition to Congress asking for appropriate management of the Port Royal blacks. Olmsted's father circulated the petition in Hartford and got seventy-five sig-natures; Edward Everett Hale circulated it in Boston; and Charles Trask in New York. With support from "well known capitalists and bankers," the petition made its way to Congress. And Olmsted let it be known that, if asked, he would accept appointment to the superin-tendency of the Port Royal project.[48]

On March 13, while the bill was before the Senate, Chase officially offered the job to Olmsted, but by the time the two men met in early April, Olmsted was convinced that he and Chase viewed the Port Royal position from strongly differing points. Turning away from Chase, Olmsted then requested from Secretary of War Stanton the authority he con-sidered necessary to supervise the government's project in the Sea Islands. Little is known of these meetings. But Olmsted was not appointed to the post; rather a brigadier general stationed in South Carolina was assigned to Port Royal.[49]

Olmsted rejoiced when Lincoln signed the Emancipation Proclamation in 1863. He believed that slavery had harmed the white as well as the black population, and that its ex-istence in America made both democracy and a full realization of civilization impossible. In Olmsted's mind, frontier society was marked by barbarism, by absorption — whether truly necessary or not — with the use of force to survive, to obtain food and shelter, leav-ing little time or energy for attention to the spiritually and intellectually uplifting tools and products of culture. To Olmsted, civilization was rooted in domesticity — in an at-tractive and well-organized home, a family unit controlled by a powerful but benevolent patriarch; in a style of life that included social and cultural amenities such as books, con-versation, music; and in adherence to the values and disciplines inherent in citizenship.

Slavery, as Olmsted viewed it, not only demeaned blacks, but tempted their masters to protect the evil system by limiting freedom of expression, religion, and press. Moreover, he believed slavery promoted a wasteful form of agriculture, and a frontier mentality.[50]

Later, in the spring of 1864, Olmsted would be under consideration to head the Freedmen's Bureau, then being established. He rejected overtures, however, claiming poor health, but adding mysteriously, "This consideration is at the present moment so strong as to leave me under no necessity of enquiring what my duty would otherwise be. What my inclinations are I need not tell you." [51] In 1865, urged by friends to consider again the superintendence of the Freedmen's Bureau, Olmsted wrote:

> I do not much incline to it, because I do not believe the government would allow me to do what I should think best to be done. It would be, I fear, not only a vexatious, aggravating and thankless duty but a puerile pretence & fizzle.[52]

Olmsted offered no further plans for guiding slaves to freedom.

Contemporary readers find Olmsted's comments about blacks confusing. While his papers leave no doubt that he favored the protection and education of freed slaves, that he wanted them to be guided into citizenship, and that he believed they would prosper in a free-labor system, those same writings sometimes also reflect the mind-set of nineteenth-century Americans regarding blacks. Although modern readers may recoil at the nineteenth-century racist shadows in Olmsted's writings, two specific evidences leave no doubt as to his democratic and humanistic beliefs and his dedication to including African Americans in mainstream American civilization.

In the 1850s, critical of the North's treatment of blacks, he argued that "the negro is endowed with the natural capacities to make a good use of the blessing of freedom" and that "the negro [should] have a fair chance to prove his own case, to prove himself a man, entitled to the inalienable rights of a man." [53]

Olmsted had not attended the 1847 Rochester Convention, one of the "Hundred Conventions" planned by the American Anti-Slavery Society, and one at which Frederick Douglass spoke,[54] but he nonetheless cited it as evidence of the natural equality of the races:

> It may be doubted if there has ever met a Convention of white men in our country in which more common sense, more talent, more power of eloquence, a higher civilization, more manliness, or more of the virtues and graces of the Christian and the gentleman, were evidenced than in that Convention of the despised Northern negroes.[55]

The Union League Club: Citizenship and Civilization

Wolcott Gibbs met Olmsted in New York on Election Day, 1862, and grimly acknowledged that the Democrats had won. Distressed by this and other evidences of sentiment against the Union that bordered, in his opinion, on disloyalty, Gibbs wanted to form a private club of influential citizens to propagate faith in the northern cause and fealty to the Republican Party. Now converted to admiration of Lincoln and distressed by the anti-Lincoln sentiment he heard often and vehemently expressed, Olmsted responded enthusiastically to Gibbs's idea. On November 5, the day after the election, he wrote at length to Gibbs outlining the goals and organization of such a club.[56]

Olmsted was ripe for Gibbs's idea. He had been struggling against the factionalization of the Sanitary Commission, seeing the problem as a manifestation of lack of discipline, of self-interestedness, and of insufficient loyalty to the Union cause on the part of the various insubordinate branches. During the autumn of 1862, in a series of letters to his old friend Charles Loring Brace, Olmsted articulated his views concerning the Republican Party, the Union cause, and the evils of slavery. Lurking behind these letters — and responsive to Gibbs's idea for a club of private citizens — was Olmsted's strong commitment to citizenship and civilization as he perceived them.

Along with the Radical Republicans of the day, Brace held McClellan responsible for the slow progress of the war and specifically believed that the general's indecisiveness had made a debacle of the Peninsular Campaign. Olmsted disagreed and argued that McClellan could lead the Union army to victory if he had support from Secretary of War Stanton. For Olmsted, the United States government — not McClellan — was the root of the problem. At first he had found Lincoln not only boorish, but inefficient and possibly incompetent. In the ensuing months, however, his assessment of the president had changed for the better; but Olmsted now believed that Lincoln's generals and cabinet officers exercised authority without the president's approval and that they worked more for themselves than for the common good of the Union. Even so, in Olmsted's opinion, the Democratic Party was worse, having failed to criticize slavery and, in the fall of 1862, having actually proposed negotiating peace with the South.[57]

Olmsted proposed to Gibbs that a small number of important men should initiate the club, specifically men like Gibbs, Cornelius Rae Agnew, Robert Minturn, James Brown, George Templeton Strong, and John Jay. In addition, Olmsted proposed adding a layer of members distinguished in arts and letters, including such "clever men" as Frederick Knapp, George Waring, and George W. Curtis, who would work hard for the club. Finally, Olmsted urged they include a group of "those innocent rich young men . . . who don't understand what their place can be in American society, gentlemen, in the European sense, in a society which has no place for 'men of leisure.' The older and abler established men ought to fraternize with them to welcome and hold every true man of them in fraternity — so soon they may govern us if they will." He called for modest dues and modest quarters.[58]

Olmsted advocated a profile of membership reflecting his idea of an "American aristocracy" composed of men of stature and achievement, unlike the European titled aristocrats. Olmsted's ideas about class — no less than those he expressed about race — may seem to the modern reader to be ambivalent. While he professed belief in meritocracy, a degree of snobbishness tempered his recognition of achievement and leadership and, later, would color much of the advice he pressed upon his children.

Men from privileged backgrounds, members of established families, Olmsted believed, might naturally be drawn to the club and might suit its purposes. Other men — despite their prominence and apparent possession of the qualities listed as desirable for membership — should be rejected. Among those he cited as unworthy were two Central Park commissioners who had disagreed with him: nouveau riche August Belmont, who had signed Olmsted's petition in 1847 for the superintendency of the Central Park project, but later opposed the Greensward plan and attempted to substitute one of his own, and banker Henry G. Stebbins, who, as chairman of the commission's Committee on Statuary, Fountains and Architectural Structures, offended Olmsted by requesting design proposals from Richard Morris Hunt, an artist whose aesthetics he deplored. In stating his opposition to these men, however, Olmsted joined George Templeton Strong on a public high road, belittling attempts by Belmont and others to establish a hereditary aristocracy (based largely on wealth and display) in America.

While admitting that the Union League Club would have a social function, Olmsted and Gibbs rehearsed rhetoric appropriate to an organization that would promote citizenship and, especially, the aims and values of the Republican Party.[59] Olmsted was convinced that Gibbs's club could bolster the Republican administration's war effort and patriotism and suggested in January 1863, "Your league ought to be extended over the whole country before Congress adjourns."[60]

By the time the club opened, it had strayed far from the dreams of Gibbs and Olmsted. Mere loyalty to the Union was sufficient for membership, and not the high level of achievement and patriotism Olmsted had urged. Moreover, the membership dues were set at twenty-five dollars a year, not at the modest ten dollars Olmsted thought appropriate. Finally, the club professed neither the social nor the political goals that had inspired Olmsted and Gibbs. Although loyal to the Lincoln administration, it did nothing to recruit and educate those men Olmsted and Gibbs believed to be the country's natural aristocracy.[61]

More Bureaucracy

After he returned from the Peninsular Campaign in July 1862, Olmsted met with the New York members of the Sanitary Commission — Agnew, Gibbs, Strong, and Van Buren

— who composed the executive committee. He soon sensed that during his absence from the Washington office, his position had been undermined. The staff members he had assigned to supervise the office and the work of the Sanitary Commission had been less than diligent, creating an administrative vacuum the executive committee had been quick to fill. By the time Olmsted returned, the executive committee had not only taken over day-to-day operations and decision making for the Sanitary Commission, but criticized Olmsted for his absence and for his want of knowledge regarding the operation of the commission. The committee members particularly displayed their displeasure concerning Olmsted's lack of control over the western branch, a segment of the operation he had delegated to John S. Newberry. Newberry had disregarded several requests from Olmsted for regular reports from the western branch. And, moreover, Newberry appears to have actively sabotaged Olmsted's position with the executive committee.[62]

By August 1862 Olmsted showed the stress he was under. He was jaundiced, itched incessantly from a skin disorder, and was close to nervous collapse. He retreated to Saratoga Springs to recuperate, but was soon ordered back by the executive committee to oversee the Sanitary Commission's care of the wounded from the second battle of Bull Run.[63]

When he arrived in the Washington office of the Sanitary Commission on September 17, Olmsted faced more criticism of his handling of affairs during the summer. He prepared a report for the executive committee, defending the commission's role in the Peninsular Campaign and his own administration.[64] Although he temporarily reduced the executive committee's criticism, Olmsted's absence from the office, arguably, had permitted a number of problems to take root. He now faced a factionalizing organization, with various state and local groups insisting that the funds and materials they solicited be dispensed only to soldiers from their regions. This was a hateful notion to Olmsted, one akin to secessionism and states' rights. Moreover, other philanthropic organizations took advantage of the competitive atmosphere that developed around the regionalist sentiments within the Sanitary Commission and began to solicit funds from sources previously loyal to Olmsted's group. Worse still, the western branch of the Sanitary Commission began to solicit in New England. By the fall of 1862 factionalization so alarmed Olmsted that he and his staff referred to the tendency as "old boss devil."[65] But on a more serious note, Olmsted could no longer argue that he controlled his staff or the benevolent association under his supervision.

Olmsted responded to the situation by writing and publishing a pamphlet, *What They Have to Do Who Stay at Home*, intended to aid in fund-raising and to show the virtues of centralized efforts to aid the soldiers, specifically the Sanitary Commission. As the author later recalled in his effort to appeal "for an improved organization of those who stay at home, to the end of obtaining a more secure supply, to the distributing depots of the Commission, urged by a presentation of the essential rightness, justice, and beauty of its federal or fraternal purpose, in distinction from any merely local or sectional purpose of benevolence," [66] he preached discipline and loyalty to the local groups. But the pamphlet did little to improve conditions.

When Unitarian minister Starr King raised two hundred thousand dollars from Californians, he stipulated to his former mentor, Bellows, that the Sanitary Commission must share the funds with the St. Louis commission. Even meeting that condition, the Sanitary Commission found that the California windfall considerably eased their financial situation. But the money also exacerbated competition between the Washington office and its western branch offices.

Newberry, his failure to report to the central office notwithstanding, had created a strong western branch, with vigorous organizations in Cleveland, Chicago, Louisville, and Cincinnati, all of which showed increasing independence. By the beginning of 1862 the Cincinnati and Chicago groups flaunted their self-sufficiency. Olmsted held Newberry responsible.[67]

In a blatant move for autonomy, the Cincinnati office demanded that it receive a portion of the California contribution; that failing, it threatened, it would disassociate itself from the United States Sanitary Commission and join forces with the St. Louis commission. In November the Cincinnatians charged that the U.S. commission consisted of a group of eastern men with no authority, and with no interest in or understanding of the West.

Olmsted's anger with Cincinnati mounted through November and December 1862. Calling the Cincinnatians swindlers and confidence men attempting to extort money from the United States Sanitary Commission to serve their own interests, Olmsted wrote a 138-page rebuttal to their claims. He detailed the purposes, organization, and procedures of the Sanitary Commission and reiterated the necessity for central control. While he cited facts — including the president's creation of the Sanitary Commission and its base in federal government — he also insisted that the commission could not delegate powers to local groups and that his office had full authority over disbursement of funds and materials collected. Olmsted also reviewed the history of the commission's operations and pointed out that employees had been assigned to regional offices in an effort to ensure full participation by all sections of the country.[68]

In writing the report, Olmsted seems to have realized that the western branches had never participated or cooperated as he had envisioned. Members of the Sanitary Commission were torn. Although they officially upheld Olmsted, they also wanted to make peace with the westerners. Their impossible ambition, however, served to increase their criticism of Olmsted, who, they believed, had caused much of the rift.

Recognizing the insidious threat of the factionalization, as well as the potentially harmful effects of the executive committee's continual hum of disapproval of his administration, Olmsted planned a tour of the West.

By the end of 1862 Olmsted's position with the Sanitary Commission was threatened, and both he and the commission would be pummeled by external political forces and internal dissention until his resignation in the summer of 1863. The members of the executive committee, unable to agree among themselves as to the power they were willing to delegate to Olmsted, confronted him steadily with carping, criticism, and second-guessing. George Templeton Strong served as treasurer of the commission and worried continually about Olmsted's extravagance and his expenditure of money without precise authorization from the executive committee. As the Sanitary Commission collected and handled increasing amounts of money, Strong's anxiety increased proportionately. Strong wanted strict business procedures in place to guide Olmsted's operation of the Sanitary Commission; Olmsted, in this post as in the superintendency of Central Park, wanted the authority to respond to problems and spend money as he deemed best. As he had expected the park's commissioners to give him leave to exercise his best judgment, Olmsted also expected the Executive Committee to trust him and to give him nearly absolute authority over the operations of the enterprise. Strong and Olmsted were at opposite ends of a dilemma, and without means for compromise.

By the end of the Peninsular Campaign, Olmsted smarted under criticism by the executive committee and responded by writing a report detailing the philosophy of his management as well as his history of action and accomplishment. In what can be read as a rejection of Strong's proposed system of accountability, Olmsted wrote to Bellows, "You can't have red-tape when your object is to get clear of red-tape. You can't have the ordinary securities here against waste and extravagance and petty peculation. You can't have your cake and eat it." [69]

By October 1862, Olmsted's tone with the executive committee recalled the emotional trauma of his Central Park experience and reflected his growing frustration and anxiety. He had been harassed over accounts and petty expenditures at Central Park; he did not relish a repeat of that drama at the hands of the executive committee of the Sanitary Commission. The situation at Central Park had become unbearable; work for the Sanitary Commission seemed to be locked onto a similar course. [70]

Tensions mounted between Olmsted and the executive committee during the remaining months of 1862, and especially after the executive committee reduced Olmsted's power to grant raises without its prior approval. It had been his custom — usually after consultation with Bellows — to award salary increases to valuable workers who considered leaving the Sanitary Commission for better-paying jobs. The committee denied Olmsted's request for reconsideration of the rejection of this policy. Indeed, the executive committee tightened the screws on Olmsted: in December the commitee members instituted a policy requiring him to seek their approval for any expenditure over one thousand dollars. Although they amended their prerequisite and granted him authority to act in cases of emergency, Olmsted was not placated. He was a reformer at heart and an executive by position: he wanted to take action as he saw fit. Strong, however, led the executive committee in requiring standard business practices that, in the members' minds, need not interfere with Olmsted's good works.[71]

Newberry's operations, too, galled Olmsted. He consistently failed to respond to Olmsted's requests for information and regular reports on western operations. By the fall of 1862, Newberry let it be known that he felt Olmsted was dictatorial. Olmsted angrily replied that he acted on behalf of the executive committee in requesting regular reports, that he had in actuality been diligent in allocating money to Newberry's operations, and that he had honored his subordinate's position. In January 1863 the committee again held Olmsted responsible for Newberry's operations, but nonetheless praised Newberry for his performance. Moreover, despite Olmsted's protests, the executive committee ordered him to travel to the West and inspect the operations of the Sanitary Commission there.[72]

Olmsted was near the breaking point. He described his state to Bellows, "My brain simply vomits all the business that I bring to it. I can lay hold of nothing right end foremost. I have my way of carrying on business, and it plainly is not your way."[73] This condition grew out of circumstances he had earlier described to his wife: "[F]rom this plain rise constantly mountains of the steepest sort, and no sooner do I feel that I have got things prepared to overcome one than another arises over topping it beyond."[74]

By January 1863 Olmsted suffered from the conditions created by the war, by the executive committee, and, according to George Templeton Strong, by himself. Although Olmsted had rented a house in Washington for his family, he only rarely left his office. Rather, as Strong observed, he practiced the "most insanitary habits of life," often working until four in the morning, then sleeping in his clothes on a cot in his office, and breakfasting on coffee and pickles.

A Trip to the West

In the spring of 1863, Olmsted undertook his last service to the Sanitary Commission, traveling west to Cincinnati, Chicago, and St. Louis; then down the Mississippi to confer with General Grant before the Vicksburg battle. The trip, envisioned as bringing the west-ern branch of the Sanitary Commission under control of the United States Sanitary Com-mission, was not entirely successful. Olmsted secured from General Grant a steamer for exclusive use by the U.S. Sanitary Commission for transporting supplies, and confirmed Grant's prohibition of state sanitary commissions competing with the national organiza-tion in the area under his command. But Olmsted failed in his efforts to bring the officers of the branch commissions under national control. Moreover, the executive committee had little interest in Olmsted's campaign to consolidate the volunteer groups and provided him with only nominal support.[75]

When the commissioners ordered Olmsted to inspect the western branches, he and Frederick Knapp began a six-week journey ostensibly to consolidate efforts of the central office and the western branches, as well as to assess the effectiveness of Newberry's opera-tion. In actuality Olmsted's western tour did little to further the work of the Sanitary Commission, to consolidate the regional offices, or to strengthen his own position within the organization.

Olmsted and Knapp found inefficiencies and small failings in some of the activities of the branches. They stopped a relatively small black-market enterprise with stolen Sanitary Commission goods.[76] But they stressed the helpful and collegial purposes of their mission. Olmsted was willing, he said, "to cultivate a friendly feeling amongst all concerned by a little white lying," and hoped to bring the western branches into closer alliance with the central office. Unbeknownst to Olmsted, however, Bellows undermined any hope of a better relationship between Olmsted and Newberry.

Olmsted thought the journey west an exercise in futility, but undertook it in response to direct orders from his superiors. Since his journeys in the South, the trip was his first to supply him with new observations and intellectual excitement about American life, about domesticity and manners, and about what he believed to be the uniqueness of American civilization.[77]

As Olmsted traveled into the Middle West, he scribbled comments and observations into his notebooks.[78] Trains were late and dirty. Hotels in Cincinnati, Nashville, and Mem-phis offered neither comfort nor decent food, and service was worse. He also dis-covered applaudable features of American life. He found the independent farmer self-sufficient and proud, without "the smallest particle of servility." He liked what he saw in midwestern cities — middle-class stability, comfortable homes, well-constructed public buildings, and attention to aesthetics as well as the practical needs of urban life. In one burst of enthusiasm, he declared Euclid Street in Cleveland to be grander than Fifth Av-enue in New York, calling it "a thousand-fold more . . . distinctively American."[79]

Olmsted was unable to centralize the volunteer efforts and bring the various philanthropic organizations under the management of the Sanitary Commission. Within his own organization, a western faction headquartered in Missouri insisted on collecting supplies for "their" soldiers and neglected to follow directives from, or communicate with, the Washington office.

The popular hero General John Frémont led the Missouri forces (seen here in Frémont's camp near Jefferson City). Frémont freed the slaves in that state in unilateral action that brought slave owners near rebellion, infuriated Lincoln, and cost him his position. Olmsted's dislike of Frémont flowered later as a result of the buccaneer officer's involvement with gold mines in California.

His appetite once again whetted for his studies of civilization, he noted that concern for business in Chicago and St. Louis took precedence over education and public parks and libraries; that teachers were paid poorly in comparison with railroad superintendents and steamboat pilots who played a more direct and observable role in the commercial well-being of the cities.

His criticism notwithstanding, Olmsted believed he had found real evidence of civilization in the Midwest. After a visit with Sarah Elliott Perkins, a model of midwestern womanhood, Olmsted praised American women for their "cheerful, quiet, deep, patient, religious patriotism." He declared that the region held promise of an ideal he had long cherished, an education of all classes to the "mental & moral capital of gentlemen." [80]

As he traveled from the midwestern states into the South, however, Olmsted found the region only slightly different from the time of his earlier travels there. Nor did he find any reason to look with more tolerance on the institution of slavery and its results.

Writing about travels in the South in the 1850s, Olmsted had mentioned concern for two factors mitigating against a general uplifting of society: the sparsity of settlement, with great distances between homesteads often limiting social contact outside the family; and a paucity of manners and habits — reading, public education, libraries, music, lectures — to nurture the best in the human spirit.

Although the journey to the midwestern and southern states again called Olmsted's attention to his abiding interest in the variables affecting civility, his return to Washington necessitated his placing his full concentration on the workings of the Sanitary Commission.

Personal and Public Turmoil

Despite Olmsted's achievements, he and the commissioners were on a collision course. George Templeton Strong described Olmsted as one of the most gifted men he had ever met, praised his administrative skill as well as his personal integrity. But Strong also noted Olmsted's reluctance to follow directions from the board. To Strong it seemed that Olmsted wanted complete authority over the working of the Sanitary Commission, that he was "a lay-Hildebrand," and that he mired himself in detailed paperwork and impractical schemes, which prevented him from attending properly to the policies adopted by his employers. Strong visited Olmsted in Washington, observed him working without sleep for four or five days at a time, not changing his clothes or giving heed to advice or directives from the commissioners. Two months later, convinced that the headstrong general secretary of the Sanitary Commission was unlikely to change his manner of working, Strong reluctantly concluded that Olmsted should be fired.[81]

Members of the Sanitary Commission blamed Olmsted for the difficulties encountered by the commission. Secretary of War Stanton, having already limited Sanitary Commission use of government printing facilities and having openly fought with Surgeon General Hammond, now stripped the United States Sanitary Commission of considerable authority when he assigned to the western Sanitary Commission the care of all Union armies in the West. Moreover, the commissioners were alarmed by the competition from other philanthropic groups bent on aiding the Union soldiers, specifically the United States Christian Commission, founded by the Young Men's Christian Association.

After the Christian Commission's founding in the autumn of 1861, Olmsted had tried to cooperate with its members, mostly volunteers and unpaid clergymen who, in Olmsted's judgment, symbolized equally the zeal and unprofessionalism of the organization. But Olmsted objected to more than the management systems of the rival group. He objected to their view that the Sanitary Commission, because it included Unitarians like Bellows and because it was secular in outlook, was a godless and un-Christian force among Union soldiers. Olmsted insisted that soldiers deserved care from their government, and that their religious persuasion had no proper role in their service to their country or their country's responsibility to them.

In late 1862, the Sanitary Commission members, attempting to counter the U.S. Christian Commission's sentimental publications and emotional appeals for support, wanted to publish a monthly bulletin reflecting their good works. Olmsted opposed the publication on principle, to no avail.

Olmsted found himself at odds with his employers on other principles and practices as well. He was criticized for giving a second chance to a man found drunk on the job, for insufficient supervision of employees alleged to have character defects, and for his management of the affairs of the Sanitary Commission. Olmsted, stung by the wall of criticism he encountered on his return from the West, informed the executive committee that, henceforth, responsibility for management would be theirs, that he needed time to think, and that he refused to resume general superintendence of the Sanitary Commission.[82]

The friction between Olmsted and the commissioners was due in part to the inherent distinctions between professional managers and volunteer directors, resulting in tension and conflict over who has responsibility and authority over which procedures and policies. Central Park had given Olmsted rich experience in the vicissitudes of administration. But the parallels between his relationships with the directors of Central Park and the Sanitary Commission call into question Olmsted's personality and his mode of operation.

One of Olmsted's contemporaries portrayed him as a complex, gifted, and self-destructive man. George Templeton Strong, the New York lawyer and diarist who served on the Sanitary Commission with Olmsted, expressed amazement at Olmsted's intelligence, but saw him as also volatile and arrogant. When the two men began to work together in June 1861, Strong noted in his diary, "We have elected Olmsted . . . secretary and general agent to reside in Washington, and a member of the Commission. I like him much." [83] Three months later Strong observed Olmsted's depressive tendencies in "letters [that] indicate that excitement and hard work acting on a sensitive, nervous temperament are making his views morbid. He sees only present imbecility and future inevitable disaster. Seems to think the army a mere mob; War Department, paralyzed by corruption; Navy Department, ditto." [84]

When Strong and other commissioners accompanied Olmsted on his visit to Virginia battlefields in the spring of 1862, Olmsted ostentatiously rode ahead on horseback, leaving the others to travel by coach. By the time Strong and his party arrived at the battlefield, the diarist observed with a wry mixture of annoyance and dismay that Olmsted, brandishing the souvenirs he had collected, looked like "Robinson Crusoe . . . bristling with bowie knives and shooting irons picked up on the ground." [85] Throughout the next few months Strong noted in his diary the receipt of Olmsted's lengthy despondent and complaining letters, but mentioned that Olmsted, on his return to Washington from the Virginia Peninsular Campaign, seemed "less doleful in prophesyings than I expected. When Olmsted is blue, the logic of his despondency is crushing and terrible." [86]

But by November 1862, Strong wrote that he wished "F.L. Olmsted were Secretary of War! I believe that [his] sense, energy, and organizing faculty, earnestness, and honesty would give new life to the Administration were he in it." [87] But Strong soon recognized that Olmsted's increasingly shrill insistence on power and autonomy threatened to disrupt the workings of the Sanitary Commission, and at the beginning of 1863 he wrote, "Olmsted is in an unhappy, sick, sore mental state. Seems trying to pick a quarrel with the Executive Committee. Perhaps his most insanitary habits of life make him morally morbid. . . . It will be a terrible blow to the Commission if we have to throw Olmsted over. We could hardly replace him." [88] The situation worsened in Strong's view, as he observed:

> Olmsted is unconsciously working to make himself the Commission. Perhaps he is competent to do all the work of the Commission without advice or assistance. If so, I for one am inclined to withdraw and let him have all the credit of doing it. [89]

Finally, Strong's concern for the effectiveness of the Sanitary Commission overwhelmed his admiration for Olmsted, as he wrote, "I fear Olmsted is mismanaging our Sanitary Commission affairs. He is an extraordinary fellow, decidedly the most remarkable specimen of human nature with whom I have ever been brought into close relations. Talent and energy most rare; absolute purity and disinterestedness." But Strong also looked on the other side of Olmsted's nature of "[p]rominent defects, a monomania for system and organization on paper (elaborate, laboriously thought out, and generally impracticable), and appetite for power." [90]

On leaving the Sanitary Commission, Olmsted did not disappear from Strong's diary. Fascinated by the administrator's brilliance and passionate nature, Strong noted during the organization of the Union League Club that "the effort to follow Olmsted's clear, compact, well-considered statement of plans and probabilities made me desperate and fidgety." [91] Later Strong summarized Olmsted's personality as "wary, shrewd, and never sanguine." [92]

When Olmsted later moved to California to manage a gold-mining enterprise, Strong was not surprised to learn from a mutual friend that "Olmsted is living in a great state and dignity as chief of Mariposa." [93]

In addition to the upheaval Olmsted met — or created — in his role as public servant, he faced two other equally painful situations. In February 1863 Vaux had informed Olmsted of his intention to resign from the position of consulting architect of Central Park, an appointment held jointly by Vaux and Olmsted since April 1862. For more than a year, Olmsted had given little attention to the park and had left Vaux to deal with the intensifying conflicts with the Central Park board. Olmsted sadly accepted Vaux's verdict on the impossibility of the situation. He had, he admitted, always hoped to return to the park.[94]

For Olmsted, however, the unkindest cut came in the form of a reproach from his father in a letter that has not survived. From Frederick's answer, however, it can be inferred that John Olmsted reviewed his son's history: At forty-one Frederick had amassed a history of enthusiastic embarkations on projects and careers, followed by shift or loss of interest or by conflicts with superiors and ending in overwork, fatigue, exhaustion, and near physical and nervous collapse. Over the years John Olmsted had supported his mercurial son financially and psychologically. Now, however, John Olmsted apparently felt compelled to remind his son that he had a family to support, and to reproach him for not making sufficient political effort in the spring of 1861 to remain superintendent of Central Park. Frederick replied angrily, insisting that he had been unjustly faulted and unfairly expected to be successful in all that he did. The rift between father and son lasted several months and occurred at a time when it was particularly painful to Frederick.

Quandary . . .

Olmsted did not need reminding of his precarious financial position or of the family he supported or of his need to find lucrative work immediately. In 1863, as possibilities of continuing at the Sanitary Commission thinned, Olmsted began to discuss another publishing project with Edwin L. Godkin, an Anglo-Irish journalist then living in New York City. Their past conversations had often ranged into theories and dreams about the kind of weekly newspaper America needed. He now assured Godkin of his interest and of his willingness to join such a venture if he could be assured of its financial underpinnings.

Olmsted and Godkin prepared a prospectus in June 1863, laying out the philosophical and practical particulars of their proposed publication. It would, they said, be a significant force in American intellectual life, serving as a platform for discussion of political events and social issues. Olmsted, perhaps still sore from his bruising as a partner in Dix and Edwards, insisted somewhat uncharacteristically on solid financial backing for the publication.

But caution did not dim Olmsted's enthusiasm. He saw the weekly publication as an opportunity to preach his ideals of reform and patriotism, to participate in public educa-

Edwin Lawrence Godkin

Born in Ireland in 1831, Godkin had reported on the Crimean War for the *London Daily News* prior to immigrating to the United States, where he founded the *Nation* in 1865. Under his editorship it quickly became an influential publication. He sold it in 1881 to Henry Willard, owner of the *New York Evening Post*, and two years later became editor in chief of the *Post*.

Godkin's moralistically charged writing won him respect among Americans during the Civil War and made him a respected and influential journalist during Reconstruction. A moderate, Godkin opposed excessive punishment of the South, pressed for free trade, currency reform, and the overhaul of the civil-service system. He is also known for several books critical of U.S. society. 🦋

tion and a general uplifting of tastes for the betterment of civilization in America. He was not one to tinker with small ambitions. Indeed, he had long viewed himself as a man of letters. As early as 1853 he had written about the need for a publication supporting "a higher Democracy and a higher religion than the popular" and had attempted to bring out such a journal by means of Dix and Edwards. He suggested names for the weekly publication: *Householder, Yeoman's Weekly, Work of the Week,* the *Loyalist,* the *National,* and the *Holdfast* — all reflecting his point of view about American life.[95]

For a while it seemed as if Olmsted's dream might come true. Influential men responded favorably to the prospectus, several even pledging financial support. But in the end the support was not forthcoming, and Olmsted had no cushion, dream or real, against the growing difficulties with the executive committee of the Sanitary Commission.

Already exhausted from overwork and the pummeling from the executive committee, he discovered in June 1863 that a collection of letters by sanitarians describing their experiences during the Peninsular Campaign, to be published as *Hospital Transports,* required his editorial hand. Overworked and overwrought, Olmsted was ill prepared for the blow he then received from Newberry. The associate general secretary, Olmsted's titular subordinate who had long failed to file requested reports on the activities of the western branch, now published a bulletin full, in Olmsted's opinion, of self-serving "puffery." Feeling undercut by Newberry, unsupported by the executive committee, Olmsted sensed that his position was untenable. He was, as he had been in Central Park, responsible for operations over which he had no authority; he blamed the commissioners.[96] On July 25, 1863, Olmsted resigned his position at the Sanitary Commission.[97]

In his two years with the Sanitary Commission, and in spite of bitter conflicts with his supervisors, Olmsted later believed he had performed his best service for his country.

Nature, Barbarity, and Civilization

When Frederick Law Olmsted left the helm of the Sanitary Commission, it appeared to some that he abruptly changed character. In changing directions in his career, he ended his personal work for the Union cause and turned his back on his reformist and philanthropic proclivities. Olmsted unapologetically insisted that he was going to California to seek his fortune; but, he added, he intended to plant civilized ways on the frontier. However, his years in California, 1863–1865, did not follow his plans; he neither amassed a fortune nor stitched civilized ways into the frontier crazy quilt.

His California experience nonetheless influenced Olmsted's attitudes about civilization, his commitment to the preservation of natural scenery, and his ultimate identification as a landscape architect. During those years on the West Coast, despite his involvement in a troublesome gold-mining enterprise, he added to the intellectual and practical stores that contributed to his confirmation as a nineteenth-century American genius. His personal fortune increased little, and only as a result of some astute investments. But while in California he reflected on and refined his sense of civilization, coming to characterize its highest aspects with his concept of communicativeness; he grasped the importance of federal protection and preservation of natural beauty and determined to work for that cause; and he sharpened his focus on the profession of landscape architect, working independently from Vaux for the first time and adjusting his designs to meet the requirements of the arid California landscape.

Mariposa

Frederick Law Olmsted was forty-one years old. He had managed the largest public-works project to that time, Central Park, and the largest private philanthropic endeavor in the history of the country, the United States Sanitary Commission. During the approximately two years he spent with each of these jobs, he had shown himself to be a brilliant, if erratic, administrator, with work habits and obsessions that drove him to extreme fatigue; he left each job after prolonged squabbling with the directors to whom he reported. When the board of directors of the Mariposa Company chose him to manage the investment they expected to make them multimillionaires, Olmsted briefly worried that they might want his good name to bolster the company's reputation.

The Mariposa Company had its beginning in the shady dealings of adventurer, celebrated explorer, and politician John C. Frémont, who bought the floating land grant in 1847 from the Mexican government. Son-in-law of western-expansion promoter Senator Thomas Hart Benton, Frémont's strengths lay more in mapping wilderness than in managing a mining business. When he needed cash to bolster business, he borrowed against the Mariposa Estate, but retained enough interest to attempt to sell shares to overseas investors. Soon the Mariposa Company was bound in a network of debts, conflicting claims for ownership, and complicated stock deals.

Trenor Park, a lawyer from Vermont, bought into the Mariposa Estate but insisted that he be permitted to manage it in his own manner and without interference from Frémont. Park, after a quick and high profit, extracted nearly a hundred thousand dollars' worth of gold in one week from one mine, a feat witnessed by James Hoy, a would-be New York investor. Hoy reported the high yields from the Princeton mine and the studies that promised riches to come. At best the board accepted optimistic records born of data flawed by insufficient examination over too short a time, but in time it appeared to some that the outlook was purposely adjusted to kindle the greed of potential investors.

John C. Frémont

The Pathfinder, John Charles Frémont, was born in 1813 in Savannah, Georgia, and grew up in near poverty. After military training in South Carolina and early mapping expeditions, he eloped in 1841 with fifteen-year-old Jessie Benton, daughter of powerful Senator Thomas Hart Benton. Through the senator's influence, Frémont was chosen in 1842 to lead a surveying team along the Oregon Trail, up the Platte River to South Pass.

During his second expedition, 1843–1844, Frémont circled through virtually unknown areas of the West, mapping the Colorado Rockies north to the South Pass, northwest to the Columbia, south along the Cascades and Sierra Nevada into California, then southward and eastward across the desert to Salt Lake. He then returned to St. Louis by crossing the Colorado Rockies.

His wife helped him write and publish his journals, by which he became famous as an adventurer, mapmaker, and heroic military leader. Returning to California in 1845, Frémont led the American settlers in the Bear Flag Revolt against Mexican rule. Later Frémont became embroiled in the dispute over command of the American territory by supporting Commodore Robert Stockton over officially appointed General Stephen Kearny. Court-martialed in 1847 for insubordination, he resigned from the army, but found private backing to continue his explorations of the West.

He entered political life as senator from California (1850–1851) and was defeated in 1856 in his bid for the presidency of the United States. Appointed commander of the Union Army's Western Department during the Civil War — again with the assistance of his powerful father-in-law — Frémont was removed from office when he unilaterally ordered the emancipation of slaves in Missouri. Then placed in command of the Mountain Division of the Union forces (1862), he performed so badly that he was subordinated to General John Pope. After resigning from that post, Frémont threw himself into numerous schemes to get rich — including a transcontinental railroad and the Mariposa Estate — but all of them failed. Three months before his death Congress granted him a pension in appreciation for his explorations. ✤

Largely on the basis of Hoy's observations, two other New York investors entered the gold-mining business. Distinguished banker Morris Ketchum and New York mayor George Opdyke joined Hoy, Frémont, and Park on the board; Olmsted called them "careful capitalists." Three of the investors — Ketchum, Hoy, and Opdyke, the New Yorkers on the board — assured Olmsted that the Mariposa Estate was prosperous, doubtless believing the faulty information they had been supplied. But the other two members of the board, Park and Frémont, had laid the foundation for the financial disaster that awaited the "careful capitalists" and Olmsted.[1]

But Olmsted did not realize that he faced the aggregate of the Mariposa Estate's history of unsavory business and legal dealings, unmet financial obligations, and unrealistic expectations. On September 14, 1863, Olmsted sailed from New York harbor on the *Champion*, a dirty and unsafe vessel with uncomfortable accommodations. His French valet, Charles, accompanied him, as did Howard A. Martin, a bookkeeper, J. H. Pieper, an engineer who had worked for Olmsted on Central Park; and Pieper's family. Ten days later the *Champion* landed at Aspinwall, a tropical village on the edge of the Isthmus of Panama. At nine o'clock that same morning, Olmsted boarded a train for a journey across Panama, through swamp and jungle, alongside dazzling foliage about which he wrote rhapsodically to his wife.

Banana trees stood among several varieties of palms — fan, sago, date, and cacao — bamboo swayed in the wind, mahogany trees stood majestically straight, and everywhere flowers bloomed amid the flourishing greenery. "I think," Olmsted wrote Mary, "it produces a very strong moral impression through an enlarged sense of the bounteousness of Nature." [2]

On the west side of the isthmus, Olmsted and his party boarded the Pacific Mail Steamship Company's *Constitution*, a large and clean ship, for the trip to San Francisco. Passing through Golden Gate and coming to rest in the lovely harbor, Olmsted quickly went ashore and found the town laid out in a rigid gridiron pattern, with plank sidewalks flanking the streets.

The discovery of gold in California lured fortune seekers from afar, with an estimated eighty thousand people converging on the promising West Coast fields during 1848. Some crossed the heartland of the country; others went by ship to Panama, crossed the isthmus on horse- or donkey-back, then completed the journey by ship.

Within hours after Olmsted landed in San Francisco, a horse kicked him on his already lame leg, causing no serious damage but considerable pain to the limb previously broken in a carriage accident in New York. While nursing his injury and waiting for the small boat that would take him to Stockton, the nearest town to the Mariposa Estate, Olmsted received a San Francisco lawyer, Frederick Billings, who warned Olmsted that the New York investors were dangerously optimistic about the future of Mariposa. In fact, he said, production had fallen since Hoy's investigation of yield, and the estate was in debt.

Billings stressed the importance of strong capitalization for the mining venture, telling Olmsted: "Your success will depend entirely on whether the company will sustain you in sufficiently radical and expensive operations. The estate is of no value unless they do, and if they do it is of enormous value."[3] But the situation was worse than Billings intimated. Indeed, the Mariposa mines had been sunk at the wrong end of the lode, and in time Olmsted would understand that no amount of investment, administrative skill, or technological razzle-dazzle could extract profitable amounts of gold from them.

After an overnight boat trip from San Francisco to Stockton, Olmsted, Billings, and Charles set out for Bear Valley and the OSO Hotel.[4] The trip through a desolate, sere landscape was dusty and tiresome. Fresh from the lush growth of Panama, Olmsted found the arid California desert landscape depressing. The hotel that was to be his temporary home — a badly built and furnished frame structure, with only cleanliness to its credit — did little to cheer him.

The brown desolation of the landscape assaulted his sensibilities again the next morning as he began to explore the place he expected to live for the next five years. Situated in the western foothills of the Sierra Nevada, near Yosemite Valley, the Mariposa Estate contained seventy square miles. A smattering of small make-do villages or mining camps dotted the area, with Mariposa, the largest, serving as county seat; Bear Valley was the headquarters of the company. The population of about seven thousand was a mixture of Americans, Chinese, Mexicans, Europeans, and Digger Indians, mostly men.

For the missionary of civilization, the challenges may have surpassed the opportunities at Mariposa. The cemetery behind the buildings on the main street communicated to Olmsted the barbarity of the frontier mining village. According to the makeshift tombstones, most of the men in the untended graves had died on the wrong end of a gun, a knife, or a rope. He wrote, "It is just a miners' village — no women, and everything as it must be where men don't live but merely camp."[5]

During the next few days, with Billings as an almost constant companion, Olmsted traveled over the entire area, explored mines, met the men, and educated himself to the workings of the estate. He then wrote to James Hoy and cataloged the problems he saw before him. He reported that he found the situation daunting, with worn and outdated machinery, the timbering and ventilation of the mines in unsafe condition, trespassers cavalierly mining while managers lost license fees by ignoring them, and the financial situation in disarray. "These facts," he wrote, "all new and entirely unexpected to me, coming to my knowledge mostly in one day, added to a landscape which for aridity, sterility, dust and desolation, neglect and slovenliness, I never saw anything approaching before, gave rise at first to a feeling of very great disappointment." [6]

Moreover, he found the miners rude and disrespectful, hostile to any show of authority on the part of management and without any sense of loyalty to the company. He wrote, "A store has been robbed; two men have been killed with knives; another severely wounded in a fight; another has been stoned; and a plot of murder and highway robbery is reported to have been detected — all in the three days I have been on the estate." [7]

If Olmsted had dreamed of bringing civilization to a frontier, he probably had not imagined the disparities to be overcome between his idea of a frontier and the qualities he identified with civilization. But in accordance with prevailing frontier priorities, before he could attend to the high-toned niceties of civilization, he attacked the practical business of the estate.

In surveying operations at Mariposa, Olmsted became convinced that a steady source of water was the greatest immediate need and proposed that a canal be built to divert the Merced River through the estate. But before he could design and begin construction on a canal system, Olmsted was mired in his attempt to unknot the financial disarray of the Mariposa Company.

By this time the ownership of the estate was in litigation, a result of long-standing legal wrangles over deeds, debts, and assets. First, having purchased the property from the Mexican government, Frémont had his right to possession upheld in the American courts. Using deeds and questionable data on mine production, he borrowed from banks and individuals against the mines. When he failed to repay the loans, his debtors made claims on the mines. Second, as both investor and manager, Trenor Park had proved himself adept at exploitation, studiedly heedless of sound management practices, and blatantly far more interested in stripping profit from the property for himself than in ensuring long-term goals and productivity for other investors.

After the shady management of both Frémont and Park, and without the full understanding or support of the New York investors, Olmsted faced the likelihood of ever-diminishing production, failing equipment, poor workers, and the fruits of disreputable business practices. He soon discovered, however, that the New York investors, forced to pay off debts against the property, were compelled to face the financial reality of the Mariposa Estate. They simply had no money for improvements or operation of the venture and had to admit that the mines were losing money. Against this background of imminent disaster, even so vital a project as the canal system was put aside temporarily.

But Olmsted remained hopeful that he could apply rational solutions to problems and extract gold from Mariposa. As was his practice when fired by optimism, Olmsted set himself a rigorous schedule of work, rising late in the morning and breakfasting about noon, then tending paperwork before riding around the property for six or seven hours. After collecting information and impressions about the operations of the mines, and seeking ways to deal with the ominous signs of approaching bankruptcy, Olmsted dined at his

When Olmsted arrived in San Francisco, he found another city whose placement of houses and streets was determined by a grid pattern, a rigid scheme that denied the natural topography — and beauty — of the location.

hotel with associates. Around eleven o'clock each evening he readied himself for another session of paperwork.[8]

In a frenzy of overwork and zeal, Olmsted replaced Park's superintendents, instituted reforms, and established new procedures for operations. He met little resistance and soon boasted to his father, "I have got pretty good command of the machinery and shall soon knock something out of it or burst the boilers."[9]

About two weeks later, in the middle of November, he again turned his attention to the necessity of building a canal system to bring water onto the estate. He presented his case for the investment to the New York board members. The proposed canal, which would cost about a million dollars, was both possible and practical, he insisted, and absolutely vital to the successful operation of the property. A reliable source of water would not only allow the mines to operate without regard to seasonal droughts, but would encourage settlers and support profitable crops and livestock.[10]

Olmsted realized that social changes — steps toward the civilization he treasured — might be even more difficult to effect than the crucial overhaul of the business of Mariposa Estate. Olmsted's youthful quest for spiritual or mystical experience had been replaced by a combination of aesthetic appreciation and intellectual reliance on scientific or rational thought. Now, appalled by the frontier society he observed, he sought to find rational means for changing it and, simultaneously, to collect information on American civilization for his book.[11]

He analyzed the frontier mentality and style of life and tried to describe the opposing factors that, in his judgment, composed civilized life. Insisting that democracy could promote and sustain a high degree of civilization, he believed that Americans had already begun to overcome the significant obstacle of deriving, as they were, he said, "largely from [British and European] dangerous classes, mainly from [their] poorest classes and the more useless of the poor — little from the gentle and educated and highly civilized classes, and scarcely at all from what are called its upper and ruling classes, that is to say, the recognized leaders of civilization." Thus, he said, America had issued not from European civilization, but from its "uncivilization," largely from prisoners, adventurers, and the socially undesirable who were unable to function in the old society. He asked, "How far beneath gentlemen are Americans?" and then dismissed the question, replacing it with the more pertinent, "How far above peasants are they?"[12]

Echoes of the sermons of Hartford minister Horace Bushnell, an influence on Olmsted in his youth, appear in the notes Olmsted kept toward writing his book on civilization. He marveled that the rogues and rascals and misfits who had come to the shores of the New World had not degenerated further, marveled even more that they had produced leaders from among themselves and had founded a political principle to promote independence and citizenship. It was not democracy, Olmsted argued, that mitigated against civilization; it was the frontier condition. As the hardships of the frontier diminished, he believed, stable families and community institutions would nurture in citizens a sense of justice and duty. On balance, he concluded, democracy offered a far more fertile ground for civilization than did the aristocratic governments of the Old World.

Considering that Mariposa County had been available to white settlers for less than two decades when Olmsted knew it, he accepted the inevitability of the unsettled, tran-

Olmsted took charge of the Mariposa Estate, a gold-mining enterprise begun by Frémont. At the time Olmsted accepted the chief executive's position at Mariposa, he was sympathetic to Frémont's political stand against slavery and appreciated "the fascinating power he is reputed to have over many who are intimate with him. Here at Mariposa I stand in his shoes and am paying his debts. I live in a community which he founded." Pointing out that he also worked with men who had been employed by Frémont, and that he had inherited the results of Frémont's business dealings within the mines and with the outside world, Olmsted concluded, "[Of] his character there is only one opinion; that is, that he is a selfish, treacherous, unmitigated scoundrel. He is credited with but one manly virtue, courage or audacity; with but one talent, persuasiveness. . . . [In California] he is universally despised, detested, execrated." (PFLO V: FLO to Frederick Knapp, Apr. 6, 1864.)

sient, often-violent nature of the population. He wrote, "There have been a great many robberies here lately, and half a dozen men have been hung and two or three shot." Men carried arms and used them; they fought and killed one another; and white men took for granted their right to rob, mistreat, and kill blacks, Indians, and Chinese. The frontiersmen around Olmsted did not consider the aboriginal Digger Indians, who lived on grass, acorns, and insects, fully human. White men, Olmsted noted, shot the gentle Digger Indi-

Horace Bushnell

Born in Connecticut in 1802, Bushnell served from 1833 to 1859 as pastor of the North Church, an American Congregational parish in Hartford, Connecticut. Emphasizing the metaphorical nature of language, he propounded doctrinal relativism and the importance of personal spiritual experience. Without making any distinction between divinity and humanity or the supernatural and natural, Bushnell preached about God as a force of reconciling love rather than an arbiter of punishment.

Through his books — including *A Discourse on Christian Nurture*, *God in Christ*, and *Nature and the Supernatural* — he became known as the father of religious liberalism in America. ❦

ans for sport and looked on their deaths not as murder but as the trophy killing of wild animals. Olmsted, horrified by the treatment of the Digger Indians, noted their apparent practice of their religion, their willingness to work, and their kindness toward one another. They were, he insisted, fully human.

He was distressed, too, by the mistreatment of the Chinese, who were hated by the white men not only for their different appearance but also for their willingness to work for "coolie" wages. Without fear of reprisal or any apparent sting of conscience, the white miners persecuted the Chinese laborers, robbed them, and burned their houses and camps. Olmsted noted that, though heathen, the Chinese workers were temperate and hardworking, more dependable than the tough-guy white miners. "There seems to be less essential vice in opium smoking than in our national excitements. If they have ever learned anything of white men except new forms of vice and wickedness," he wrote, "I can't think by what means it has been. I never heard of the slightest effort or purpose on the part of any white man, woman or child to do them good."

He concluded that Mariposa County, an example of the frontier society, was a loose confederation of gangs, of groups banded together in an "us-against-them" contest that promoted the antithesis of civilization — violence and competition rather than cooperation. He wrote,

> The foundation of civilized society is not a community . . . which is bound by arbitrary lines, or by lines which may be stretched or contracted by individuals according to their personal opinions or prejudices. These corruptions with regard to the Indian, the Negro and the Chinese cannot exist without making other corruptions, and the man who has learned to think that Negroes, Indians, Mexicans, Chinese, half-breeds may properly enough be treated as . . . outlaws or on different principles of right and duty from other men, does not require the inducement of a very strong

demand from his passions, his prejudices, his lusts, his covetousness or his pride . . . to make him forget the law and

civilized customs in dealing with any other man. . . . If there is such a thing as eloquence for modern minds, it should

not require much of it to make any intelligent man realize that want of respect for a brute, want of respect for a "nig-

ger" and want of respect for the dearest rights of those nearest and dearest to him all rest on one common criminal defect

of judgment and will, and that he cannot protect the virtue of his wife, prevent his children from being brutally over-

ridden or enforce the smallest benefit from his own industry with any degree of manly energy unless he makes "common

cause" with all who are inconsiderately abused.

Looking out of his window one day, Olmsted was inspired to describe a scale for placing men on the ladder of civilization. First he described the "savage," a painted Indian
wearing undressed furs and a blanket, carrying arrows and a bow, and standing immobile
for hours. "He is," concluded Olmsted, "a dull, silent, stupid savage."

Only slightly higher stood a "tall and large-framed white man of English stock, born
(in Kentucky) in a state of society which he speaks of as 'the highest reach of civilization.'
He leans against a tavern door, a cigar in his mouth, a Colt revolver visible in one pocket,
a Swiss watch in another. He enjoys warm baths, good food, Cognac and soda water, and
discoursing on 'the mockery of justice, the debasement of the ermine, the ignorance of
law, the degrading demagoguery, the abominable infidelity, By God! ' of a court decision
on 'the rights of colored people in public conveyances.' " Using words and ideas cultivated
in thousands of years of hard work by other brains, Olmsted noted that this specimen
might hum a hymn based on Handel or read a French novel translated in England and
published in Boston; and he might play billiards or cards for amusement, might spend
hours gambling and drinking. He was known to have fathered several children of different
colors, and not to have supported them; to have married a widow for her money and mis-
treated her.

Little separated these two barbarians; neither embraced civilized virtues, and neither
could be counted on to act in accordance with high principles. But Olmsted's open window permitted the sounds made by a German shoemaker and a Chinese worker chopping
wood, both low on the social ladder in Mariposa County, yet both civilized:

These two men again I at once range together very far above the Indian and the Fruit of Civilization — not perhaps

more than half way to the higher notches yet not a majority of my neighbors stand higher than these two steady,

plodding, short-sighted, frugal workers. But it is not industry, nor well-balanced supply and demand, nor sobriety

and inoffensiveness only that I lay to the scale. There is some general quality . . . which I look for most and find feeble

in the stolid German and the weazened Chinaman. . . .

I come to the conclusion that the highest point on my scale can only be met by the man who possesses a combi-

nation of the qualities which fit him to serve others and to be served by others in the most intimate, complete and extended degree imaginable. Shall we call it communicativeness? Then I find not merely less of a community but less possibility of a community, or communicativeness, here among my neighbors of all kinds than in any other equal body of men I ever saw. And the white men, the Englishmen, the Germans, and other civilized men do not possess it often in as high a degree as the Mexicans, Chinese, and Negroes — nor do the good men always possess as much of it as the rogues, the wild fellows.

Olmsted's curiosity about his neighbors in Mariposa County took the form of the detached, rational observation associated with scientific anthropology. He did not consider himself a member of the community, but a somewhat superior outsider with the competency and moral right to view those around him as specimens. He was pleased, however, by the lack of self-consciousness and pretension he saw among the Mariposans; he openly admired their self-reliance and independence even while he found their education and manners flawed; and he was amused to be called Fred. Given their energy and good nature, Olmsted believed that in time he would see communicativeness among the frontier folk. In the meantime, however, he lamented the lack of common cause and shared duties of citizenship, deplored the observable fact that he saw little evidence of "men who have any deep abiding faith in living by intelligent industry directed to the essential benefit of their fellow citizens."

People on the frontier, Olmsted observed, had not put down roots in communities or in professions and trades; they had not invested themselves in a visible purpose or role in the community. He cited the German baker who, though excellent in his chosen craft, spread himself thin in his shop by selling tobacco, beer, and gold; working as an express agent and business officer for mining companies; and serving as justice of the peace. Similarly, the local surgeon, French by birth and educated at the University of Paris, also managed a mine, ran the apothecary shop, practiced law, and was a candidate for political office. This tendency to serve too many masters resulted in social irresponsibility, in rootlessness almost as pernicious as that seen in the drifters, the adventurers, the wanderers who worked for short periods in one place before moving on to another location, another job. Olmsted wrote:

Since I have been here, the District Attorney's office has been twice vacated by resignation and is now filled by the third incumbent. The two leading lawyers in the county have left it; four other lawyers have changed their residence. Three citizens previously engaged in other occupations have entered upon the practice of law. The principal capitalist, the largest merchant, and three other leading merchants have left the county; at least a dozen storekeepers have sold out and as many more come in. The men of my acquaintance who were running mills of various kinds (saw, grain, and stamp) when I came here have left them. In one case a mill has changed hands three times, in several others twice. I know of not one which has not changed hands. The justice of the peace, the seven successive school committeemen, three out of four of the physicians, the five butchers, the five innkeepers, eight out of twelve tradesmen and their assistants, the blacksmith, the two iron founders, the two barbers, the daguerreotypist, the bathing house keeper, the seven livery stable keepers, the three principal farmers, the three school teachers and about seventy out of one hundred miners and laboring men who have lived nearest me or who have been most readily accessible and observable to me have moved from one house, office or shop to another, or have left the county within two years. I count in this village forty-seven separate places of residence and of business which have been occupied by eighty-seven persons, not including housewives and children. Of these eighty-seven, eighty-five have changed their residence or place of business within two years. This has not been on account of a destructive fire or any extraordinary occurrence; population on the whole has not decreased, and so far as I can ascertain the changes have not been markedly greater than at previous periods of the early history of the district.

All the while that Olmsted was pondering the causes and evidences of civilization, speculating on ways to engineer the society in which he found himself, struggling vainly to make Mariposa Estate a success, he was also appreciating the natural beauty of the region. Awed by the Mariposa Big Tree Grove, he wrote to Mary, "They don't strike you as monsters at all, but simply as the grandest tall trees you ever saw, . . . you recognize them as soon as your eye falls on them far away, not merely from the unusual size of the trunk but its remarkable color, a cinnamon color, very elegant. You feel that they are distinguished strangers, have come down to us from another world." Rain had coaxed green from the mountainsides, he reported, making the landscape altogether more hospitable to his New England eye than it had seemed at first. The scenery, he promised Mary, who was then preparing herself and her children to join Frederick in Bear Valley, is "at some points great-terrible. One or two annual trips into it are the highest gratifications peculiar to the country that you have to look forward to." [13]

Strike

In an effort to cut costs in the operation of the mines, Olmsted proposed to cut wages of the miners. He reckoned the cut in earnings to be fair because he also proposed, at the same time, to reduce the miners' living expenses — largely controlled by company stores and company-run services — and to improve their living conditions. The miners saw neither the necessity nor the fairness in Olmsted's policy change and responded with an ill-organized but potentially violent strike.

But Olmsted would not be bullied, nor would he have his authority to manage undermined by obstreperous miners. He took the precaution of arming himself and prepared to hold fast, telling his friend Henry Bellows, "I have a general strike to meet now, every mine stopped and some little rioting, but as I am satisfied my demands are just it does not give me any trouble and I am personally rather enjoying the lull." [14]

Although labor unions were organizing around San Francisco at the time, the Mariposa miners were not inclined to join anything and, as Olmsted had observed, were so locked into a pattern of rootlessness that they scarcely kept the strike alive for three weeks. Indeed, most chose to collect their wages, shrug off the dust of Mariposa, and move on to what they expected to be greener pastures. Olmsted, delighted to see men he considered shiftless and disloyal go, hired cheaper replacements and soon had the mines running again, but with a significantly reduced overhead.

Exhausted from the management of the mine and from long hours spent in preparing a massive report on the affairs of Mariposa for the investors, Olmsted did indeed use the time of the strike to recuperate from a growing number of symptoms resulting from overwork and stress. The vertigo and indigestion he had suffered during his time at the Sanitary Commission returned, to his annoyance; but now hammering heart palpitations alarmed him.

When business later took him to San Francisco, he consulted a doctor who informed him that he had an enlarged heart and that he might have to return east and content himself with a life of inactivity and semi-invalidism. He chose to remain in California, however, and continue his pursuit of fortune.

Elusive Fortune

Despite the insularity of Mariposa, Olmsted remained interested in the affairs of the world and continued to involve himself in matters that concerned him, maintaining a vigorous correspondence with former colleagues on the Sanitary Commission. But he did not lose sight of his purpose in being in California. He was on the western frontier to make his fortune; he looked for opportunities.

Despite his growing knowledge of mining in general and the Mariposa Estate in particular, Olmsted, with help from Ketchum, bought and traded stock in the Mariposa Company. Convinced of California's importance to the United States, he investigated other business opportunities, borrowed two thousand dollars from his father, and invested twenty-five hundred dollars in a telegraph company, the Pacific Steam Navigation Company, and the San Francisco city water corporation. He wrote, "I think San Francisco is bound to be one of the greatest cities of the world, from the position and advantages it has already gained."

News from Vaux and Central Park

When Olmsted took leave of Central Park to serve in the Sanitary Commission, he left Vaux to complete the Greensward design and to cope with the politics and politicians of New York City. Vaux and Olmsted remained in close contact even when Olmsted was on the other side of the continent.

From his frontier outpost, Olmsted took an especially keen interest in Egbert Viele's lawsuit against the city, in which the disgruntled engineer sought back salary as superintendent of the park plus a payment of five thousand dollars owed him, he claimed, for *his* plan of Central Park. In 1856 Viele, a West Point graduate whose political contacts had succeeded in placing him in charge of the Central Park project, had submitted to the city a topographical map of the land set aside for the great urban park, having made the map at his own expense. He expected the map to serve as the guide to the ultimate design of the park and expected that he would continue in a supervisory position. When the trial came to court, Viele claimed that Olmsted and Vaux (as well as several others who entered the competition for the design of Central Park) had plagiarized his work. Although the topography of the area, as well as the stipulations set forth by the park commissioners, guaranteed that certain similarities would pervade all of the designs, the jury nonetheless awarded Viele slightly more than nine thousand dollars, but did not suggest that Olmsted and Vaux had stolen the engineer's work.

Nonetheless, the *New York Herald* reported the decision, construing it to mean that Olmsted and Vaux had indeed copied Viele's plan. Vaux was furious at the newspaper coverage of the lawsuit. As his anger at the newspaper flamed, so did his heretofore mostly submerged feelings of resentment toward Olmsted. Vaux believed his partner had taken more than his fair share of the credit for the Central Park project. When he sent to Olmsted news of the *Herald*'s coverage of the story, he added a hearty expression of his own grievances toward his absent partner.

Olmsted, agitated and passionate, assured Vaux that Central Park remained his major interest, saying, "I have taken more interest in it, given more thought to it, had greater satisfaction in it, than in all else together." He explained that he had kept the title "architect in chief" because of his executive role and cited as an example of his special responsibilities his role in educating the public to use the park. He felt, moreover, that all aspects of his work on the park had been successful and insisted that he was owed special recognition for promoting the public's interest in the park, a force that had proved vital in the political milieu of the project. Without that public support, Olmsted argued, the commissioners might well have abandoned the park before completion "if it had not been for the fact that the heart of the people was with us and was kept with us." [15]

Olmsted identified himself as the manager who used his contacts among the press to marshal public support and felt that achievement merited his having been designated architect in chief, insisting to Vaux:

There was no hope on earth that I would not have sacrificed to my desire to hold that position. . . . A great deal of disappointed love and unsatisfied romance and down-trodden pride fastened itself to that passion but there was in it at bottom a special instinctive passion of my nature also. . . . It existed essentially years before it attached itself to the Central Park as was shown by the fact that while others gravitated to pictures, architecture, Alps, libraries, high life and low life, when travelling I had gravitated to parks . . . and this with no purpose whatever except the gratification which came from sources which the Superintendence of the Park would have made easy and cheap to me. . . . What I wanted in London and in Paris and in Brussels and everywhere I went in Europe, what I wanted in New York in 1857, I want now and this from no regard to Art or fame or money. . . . You know what the most obvious and constant obstacle to the realization of this desire — habit — passion — folly or whatever you choose to call it — was. I mean Green and what he embodied. You know that matters had got so arranged . . . that relinquishment of the title of architect-in-chief would have been equivalent to a relinquishment of a great and obvious vantage ground for contending with that chief obstacle. [16]

Olmsted recollected for Vaux his bitterness over Green's treatment of him, recalling the harassment and humiliation he had suffered at the commissioner's hands. Still, he insisted, "I don't know that I regret my course because the object was worthy . . . whatever it may cost me." [17]

Perhaps his mild nature, or friendship alone, impelled Vaux to accept Olmsted's description of their division of duties on the park project and to end the argument. But a shadow lingered over the friendship and the association between Olmsted and Vaux. In the future, Vaux's resentment would erupt again.

Domesticity on the Frontier

After answering Vaux's letter, Olmsted put the quarrel aside and prepared to receive his family in Bear Valley. The Olmsted children, their governess Miss Errington, her pupil Ruth Tompkins, Mary Olmsted, and her cousin Henry Perkins (who was to be Frederick's secretary) were to arrive in San Francisco on the *St. Louis* on March 11. While Olmsted awaited the ship's arrival, he was consulted on the design for the new Oakland cemetery, Mountain View, which was to be his first landscape architecture commission in the West.

After their arrival in San Francisco, the Olmsted household traveled to Mariposa, where they filled the large upper floor of a stone-and-stucco building across the street from the OSO Hotel. There, amid newly purchased walnut furniture, Olmsted settled his family and retinue into a comfortable routine. Charles, the French valet, cooked; a German woman cleaned and took care of the children. "I don't allow myself to be worried about [the expense]," Olmsted wrote, "we are all I think gaining health for it." [18] Mary Olmsted, some years later, recalled the family's happy life in Bear Valley:

There is a great dearth of incidents in our life here so that I can only tell you that we live comfortably and that strange as it may seem, time does not hang heavily on our hands. We are near two hundred miles from San Francisco, to the East is a long narrow Valley that runs from North to South and is picturesque enough in its outlines. Next to the entire absence of grass and any substitute for it except flowers (such as escholochyia, white heliotrope, drummond phlox, crane bill nemophila etc) the open way in

Olmsted's family joined him in California. When the heat of the valley grew uncomfortable, they went into the foothills of the mountains and camped near Galen Clark's cabin. Clark, whom Olmsted called the Doorkeeper of the Yosemite Valley, was a New Englander and one of the earlier explorers of Yosemite. He had been one of the discoverers of the stand of *Sequoia gigantea* and had named it the Mariposa Big Tree Grove. Like other visitors to the region, Olmsted stopped at Clark's camp on the South Fork of the Merced (Wawona) River.

which the oaks, our only tree, stand, separately, the shade of one scarcely reach to the shade of the next, — most strikes one. There are many hills covered entirely and only by chaisal, a shrub that looks like a combination of a tall heather and a fine white blossomed spirea.

To the East we have noble views of the higher Sierras and the Yosemite valley — and as there isn't a fence in the country, except round door yards in the villages, we canter about at our own sweet will and never need take quite the same path twice.

We are just beginning upon the dreary dry season and don't hope for a shower again in six months. You can imagine the dusty state of the country except in the small gardens kept constantly watered by wind mill pumps (at wells) there will soon be no shade of green visible. The live oaks being natu-rally rather olive colored and soon losing even that shade from dust and the other leaves disappearing altogether.

Olmsted wrote a friend that he had visited the Mariposa Big Tree Grove several times. "It is several hundred feet higher than our camp — which is not much if any short of 6000 feet above the sea. It is one of the most impressive sights I ever saw — coming over one like St. Peter's." (PFLO V: FLO to Edwin Lawrence Godkin, July 24, 1864.)

We live over the company's store in quite pleasant and roomy quarters in a little half Mexican looking village and have a pleasant little flower border in front of our windows, a kind of hanging garden.

We have an admirable English governess for the children and Henry Perkins for Mr. Olmsted's secretary. Outside we see no one in a social way, and you cannot conceive of the loneliness of our situation. It is entirely a pioneer life. However the only unpleasant feature is that one sees so many abandoned villages and unused houses. As gold gives out in one spot people move to another and leave all behind till fire sweeps off all but the chimney stacks, which remain standing in a ghostly monumental fashion. Another *unpleasant peculiarity is the number of murdered men's graves marked only by rough wooden crosses. There are very few farms our not being the agricultural portion to the State, so there is little to relieve the desolate impression. Here the whole population is dependent on the mines of which there are five and all produce is brought from a distance. Fortunately provisions are plenty and good and we can manage to keep a good table. We have had strawberries and green peas these two months and now apricots, pears, and apples, beef is 20 cents per pound — but servants wages $30 per month and so on to 40, 50 & 60.*

We have a liberal supply of horses and two donkeys so we all ride out every day and so far have kept ennui at bay.

Books we have in plenty, pictures and newspapers and keep well up in the national interests, but how long our resources will hold out I can't say. I read Robinson Crusoe a great deal for solace and we all take sides with Christian in his contempt etc. for Vanity Fair.[19]

Yosemite

As summer came and the temperature rose and hung fast near a hundred degrees, Olmsted moved his family; Miss Errington; the German housekeeper, Meta; California state geological surveyor William Ashburner and his wife; and a black cook and guide, Bell, to Clark's Station, a campsite on the South Fork of the Merced, some forty miles away. There, relishing the cooler air, the Olmsted party pitched camp near the small framed cottage of Galen Clark, an early explorer of the region dubbed by Olmsted the Doorkeeper of the Mariposa Big Tree Grove. Clark, who lived alone in the great forest, welcomed others who came to witness the magnificence of Yosemite.

During the next three weeks, Olmsted and his entourage camped among flowering white azaleas growing out of great granite boulders and within sight of a vast pine forest and a fresh stream. They rode their horses, visited the Mariposa Big Trees, collected wildflowers and rocks, and enjoyed the smells and sights and cool air of California.

One day, the Olmsted party watched as a group of Digger Indians set up camp near them on the South Fork. Awakened the next morning by their loud high-pitched howling, Olmsted learned from Bell, who had lived among the Diggers and knew their language, that it was their custom to gather annually to fish. Olmsted, as he had often done in his travels in the South and elsewhere, recorded Bell's information in the man's lingo, "Dy must be good Injuns and stick by dere tribe and be mighty kerful dey don't do nothin that'll be any good to anybody dat don't belong to dar tribe, and den dey get plenty fish allers, and when dey die a great wite bird wid his wings as long as from dat yr mounting to dat un'll come and take up to a big meadow war de clover heads don't never dry up and dars lots of grasshoppers all the year roun."[20]

After a brief period of relaxation in the mountains, Olmsted left his family at their cool campsite to return to the heat of the Mariposa mines to examine operations. Surprisingly, he gleaned new optimism for the future of the business, but it was an unrealistic euphoria, based more on Olmsted's projection of his hopes and dreams than on the hard reality of the production of the Mariposa mines. The situation of the Mariposa Estate was soon further weakened when the banks of California, responding to Civil War–induced fluctuations in the economy, no longer accepted greenbacks. Olmsted faced the severe problem then of paying the mines' debts with gold.

But inspirited by his hopeful outlook, Olmsted put aside any business worries that might have harried him, returned to his family, and led them on horseback into Yosemite. They visited Inspiration Point and looked out over the Great Valley; they stood in awe before chalky mile-high cliffs, and they marveled at the cascades. Olmsted found the magnificence, the grandeur, and the heroic beauty almost overwhelming. He wrote:

> There are stupendous cliffs, there are deeper and more awful chasms, there may be as beautiful streams, as lovely meadows, there are larger trees. It is in no scene or scenes the charm consists, but in the miles of scenery where cliffs of awful height and rocks of vast magnitude and of varied and exquisite coloring are banked and fringed and draped and shadowed by the tender foliage of noble and lovely trees and bushes, reflected from the most placid pools, and associated with the most tranquil meadows, the most playful streams, and every variety of soft and peaceful pastoral beauty. The union of deepest sublimity with the deepest beauty of nature, not in one feature or another, not in one part or one scene or another, not in any landscape that can be framed by itself, but all around and wherever the visitor goes, constitutes the Yosemite, the great glory of nature.[21]

In this and similar reports, Olmsted exhibits an important quality of mind for a landscape architect. He perceives and conceptualizes experiences in both time and space, remembering one or more previous experiences while absorbing another, mentally collecting and combining aspects — fragments — of natural beauty into a total captivating experience. This interplay among vision, memory, and creation identifies an effective intelligence and an elegant mind, qualities that did not abandon Olmsted when, in tranquillity, he recollected high emotion:

> The Merced . . . is here a stream meandering through a meadow, like . . . the Avon at Stratford — a trout stream with rushes and ferns, willows and poplars. The walls of the chasm are a quarter of a mile distant, each side, nearly a mile in height — half a mile of perpendicular or overhanging rock in some places. Of course it is awfully grand, but it is not frightful or fearful. It is sublimely beautiful, much more beautiful than I had supposed. The valley is as sweet and peaceful as the meadows of Avon, and the sides are in many parts lovely with foliage and color. There is little water in the cascades at this season but that is but a trifling circumstance. We have what is infinitely more valuable, a full moon and a soft hazy smoky atmosphere with rolling, towering, white fleecy clouds.[22]

Olmsted culminated the vacation by traveling for a week into the High Sierra, accompanied by John, a guide, and by William H. Brewer, a member of the Geological Survey

Olmsted described Yosemite Falls, where: "[b]anks of heartsease and beds of cowslips and daisies are frequent, and thickets of alder, dogwood and willow often fringe the shores. At several points streams of water flow into the chasm, descending at one leap from five hundred to fourteen hundred feet. One small stream falls, in three closely consecutive pitches, a distance of two thousand six hundred feet, which is more than fifteen times the height of the falls of Niagara. In the spray of these falls superb rainbows are seen." (PFLO V: FLO, *Preliminary Report upon the Yosemite and Big Tree Grove*, Aug. 1865.)

team. Climbing high into the mountains, where nighttime temperatures dropped to uncomfortable lows, Olmsted turned his eyes from great mountain vistas to tiny alpine flowers. As they climbed still higher and reached the peak of a mountain, Olmsted claimed the
privilege accorded to those who first reach the pinnacle of a mountain; he named it Mount
Gibbs, in honor of his associate on the Sanitary Commission, Oliver Wolcott Gibbs.

At the end of the week in the High Sierra, Olmsted said that the scenery was "the
grandest I ever saw." [23] With that grandeur very much in mind, he began to think about the
future of Yosemite.

Correspondence with Vaux had brought Central Park vividly to Olmsted's mind, and
his landscape projects in California further focused his attention on the problems of creating pastoral scenery in urban settings. Moreover, he not only enjoyed natural beauty, he
measured a park's success in terms of its intensification of appreciation of nature.

Olmsted was not alone in his romantic perception of nature, but joined a formidable
brotherhood of other Americans, including writers like Washington Irving, James Feni-
more Cooper, William Cullen Bryant, and Henry David Thoreau, and painters Albert Bier-
stadt and Frederick Church. As early as 1833, painter George Catlin, exploring some of
the Lewis and Clark territory, had advocated that portions of the West be preserved "in
their pristine beauty and wildness" as national parks.[24] And even earlier, in 1815, Thomas
Jefferson had refused to sell land around the Natural Bridge in Virginia, writing: "I view it
in some degree as a public trust and would on no consideration permit the bridge to be in-
jured, defaced, or masked from the public view." [25]

By the summer of 1864, when Olmsted took his family camping in the Sierra Nevada,
explored the Mariposa Big Tree Grove and the Yosemite Valley for the first time, and pro-
claimed the area to be "the greatest glory of nature," [26] the area had already been designated for protection. Just a few months earlier, almost unnoticed during the chaos of the
Civil War, President Lincoln had signed legislation removing from public lands the
Yosemite Valley and the Mariposa Big Tree Grove, putting both under state of California
stewardship "for public use, resort, and recreation . . . inalienable for all time." [27]

The legislation put forth by California senator John Conness secured the area under
state control, not federal, but nonetheless laid the foundation for the United States national park system.[28] Until that time there had been no widespread movement to preserve
such areas, although Yosemite was already a tourist attraction.

Prior to his exploration of the area and his pronouncement on its visual and spiritual
glories, Olmsted had been appointed by California governor Frederick F. Low to serve as
the area's commissioner; subsequently he was chosen by the commissioners to chair the
group and to prepare a report on Yosemite and the Mariposa Big Tree Grove. Other mem-

bers of the board were Israel Ward Raymond; Josiah Dwight Whitney, director of the California State Geological Survey; and fellow survey member William Ashburner, who had joined Olmsted and his family on their camping trip into Yosemite.

During his last months on the West Coast Olmsted wrote this report for the California legislature. Advancing five hundred dollars of his own money, in the absence of an anticipated allocation from the state, Olmsted had already worked with a team to make a topographical map of the area and to determine the best locations for roads. In preparing the report, Olmsted built a case for land use for the public good.

At a campfire meeting in the late summer of August 1865, Olmsted read his report to fellow commissioners and a group of visiting dignitaries from the East and early advocates of federal protection of scenic beauty, including Samuel Bowles, editor of the *Springfield (Massachusetts) Republican*; the Speaker of the United States House of Representatives, Schuyler Colfax; Albert D. Richardson of the *New York Tribune*; William Bross, lieutenant governor of Illinois; and Charles Allen, attorney general of Massachusetts.[29]

Olmsted laid out what he believed to be the self-evident reasons for establishing state and national parks, stressing their purposes, social values, and proper uses by the public. Citizens of all classes, he said, had a right to enjoy natural beauty, and government should protect that right.

Olmsted believed that western expansion would bring about private ownership of property that would result in a situation similar to that seen in Europe, where aristocrats owned the most attractive parcels of nature. Without government protection, Olmsted believed that "all places favorable in scenery to the recreation of the mind and body [would] be closed against the great body of the people." He also felt that that great body of people needed supervision and instruction in the appropriate use of public parks.[30]

Olmsted insisted that great scenic beauty should be preserved in its pristine state — it should suffer no adornment or improvement. He wanted strict limits on artificial construction and insisted that rigid regulations should be established to prevent the destruction of natural beauty for profit — lumbering, hunting, farming, mining. Roads should be carefully plotted to effect as little damage as possible to the natural state of the land and to serve as firebreaks, a further protection for the great trees.[31]

A few months after delivering his paper to the commissioners and their important guests, Olmsted left California to return to New York. The report itself was withheld from the legislature by Josiah Whitney and William Ashburner, who wanted no competition for state funds for their project.[32]

Olmsted learned of the treachery of Whitney and Ashburner, chose not to engage in a public dispute with them, but to accept the unjust defeat they had engineered for his report. Governor Low officially accepted his resignation from the Yosemite Commission in 1867.[33] The California state legislature, acting without benefit of Olmsted's report, appropriated twelve thousand dollars (rather than the thirty-seven thousand dollars requested in the report) for the Yosemite Commission's work. Unable to agree on administrative policy for the park, however, the legislature did not prevent private exploitation of the resources and did not maintain the region.

Olmsted never forgot the lessons he had learned from Yosemite or the philosophy he had constructed to preserve it. In *Governmental Preservation of Natural Scenery*, a pamphlet distributed in 1890, Olmsted protested lumbering in the area and the "narrow, short-sighted and market-place view of the duty of the State in the premises."[34]

An Ending, a Beginning . . .

Between September 1864, when Olmsted and his family returned from their vacation in the Yosemite, until the fall of 1865, when he abandoned his dream of making a fortune at Mariposa, Olmsted worked in three directions at once. For a while he tried to wrest profit from Mariposa, then tried to meet its debts, and finally tried merely to remove himself from the sinking company with as much money as he could salvage for himself. But during this time of growing anguish over the mining business, Olmsted worked for the preservation of Yosemite and activated his career as a landscape architect.

Olmsted realized by the end of November 1865 that the mines were yielding increasingly less and, despite several earlier and promising studies by mine experts, that the trend was irreversible. Before the New York stock market could reflect the certain loss in value, Olmsted asked Ketchum to sell his stocks.

As the prospects grew still dimmer for the mining company, Olmsted signed four thousand dollars in bullion over to himself, an amount almost equal to the salary he was owed. In San Francisco, he conferred with bankers and realized that, as he wrote journalist Edwin Godkin, "They anticipate and intend the worst. Think it a great Wall Street swindle." He assured his friend, however, that his management was not in question.[35] Similarly, he hastened to inform his father that the company's creditors accorded him "every possible favor and mark of confidence."[36]

Still clinging to the possibility of finding a lucrative business venture in California, Olmsted made a few exploratory trips on behalf of potential investors interested in sources of oil. But as his business dealings with Mariposa headed toward a disaster even greater than his earlier venture into the business side of publishing, Olmsted devoted his serious attention to designing the Oakland cemetery. When the board of the cemetery accepted his plan, Olmsted hired an engineer to begin the project.[37] Other landscape projects beck-

Samuel Bowles

Born in 1826, Samuel Bowles became editor of the *Springfield (Massachusetts) Republican*, a paper founded by his father in 1824. Under Bowles's leadership the paper was widely circulated. Bowles used his power as a journalist to further a variety of social and political reforms. In 1855 he attacked political favoritism and established an editorial policy for fair treatment of both sides of issues.

A devout Republican, Bowles nonetheless joined the mugwumps in an unsuccessful effort against Grant's reelection in 1872. ☙

oned as well. The trustees of the College of California — later to be the University of California at Berkeley — hired Olmsted to lay out a new campus for the institution. Soon he had two private commissions as well: estates for Ogden Mills and George P. Howard, both near San Francisco.

During the spring of 1865, Olmsted was cheered by Lee's surrender and the end of the Civil War, then cast into grief and a sense of doom at the news of Lincoln's assassination. He wrote, "This awful calamity of the country . . . almost disables me from thinking of anything else." [38]

In the summer Olmstead learned that the Mariposa Company would not honor its commitment to him and that his responsibility to the company was ended. On July 26, 1865, good fortune opened the next chapter in his life: Olmsted and Vaux were reappointed landscape architects to Central Park, this time with a salary of five thousand dollars a year for Olmsted. At the age of forty-two, Frederick Law Olmsted was about to embark on the most productive years of his life.

But he had no way of knowing that. To Olmsted, his future appeared anything but bright.

A
Civilized Man
Professes Landscape
Architecture

*L*ife on the California frontier had stimulated Olmsted's nearly obsessive reflection on the ingredients and requirements of civilization and whetted his
appetite for the role he might play in advancing the patterns of belief and behavior
he held dear as the highest levels of human culture. His reflections on *communicativeness* and
domesticity, now the terms he consistently used to describe the social contributions and
obligations, now connoted as well the private pleasures and responsibilities of the ideal
citizen. Olmsted, despite reformist beliefs and liberal leanings, nonetheless accorded full
citizenship only to men like himself — white, upper class, affluent, privileged — but, in
keeping with his age, insisted that much in the way of social responsibility was required
from those so blessed.

Mariposa had removed Olmsted from the bureaucracy surrounding Washington and New York that had frustrated him to the point of near physical collapse in his work on both Central Park and the Sanitary Commission. On the frontier, he had power; he lived well and was recognized as a man of authority and consequence. Although he did not finish his proposed book on American civilization while at Mariposa (or ever), his concepts expanded and deepened. Olmsted matured as a man and as a thinker.

No wonder he did not easily relegate Mariposa to his past. Life with his family on the frontier had been particularly sweet for Olmsted. They had enjoyed a degree of comfort that they had not previously known, had savored the natural beauty of the landscape, and, after a period of adjusting to the freedom and easygoing manners of the society, had appreciated their colorful neighbors. Moreover, as manager of the Mariposa Estate, Olmsted had the power and prestige of the ruler of a small princedom.

Now, thinking about what he would do after Mariposa, he not only faced the necessity of supporting a large and lively family, but he also hoped to find an appropriate platform from which to profess his ideas and to persuade others to adopt his values and schemes for ensuring the success of the American republic. Characteristically Olmsted had hold of an idea — in this instance, communicativeness — and, convinced of its irrefutable validity, looked for ways to apply it to society.

For nearly twenty years, as he identified himself with a variety of disciplines and concocted programs for solving social problems and elevating humankind, Olmsted had never had what he considered an adequate opportunity to put his ideas to the test. Thwarted by politicians and bureaucrats who held the purse strings for Central Park and the Sanitary Commission, he had long felt himself underappreciated and limited as to influence and power. Since his faith in his own ability to solve society's problems remained undiminished, he hungered for the power that would enable him to effect solutions. While Olmsted's absolute certainty of the rightness of his ideas had caused others — especially his superiors at the Sanitary Commission — to regard him sometimes as self-serving, somewhat bumptious, and stubborn, Olmsted saw himself as a leader.

His craving for recognition and authority, for the freedom to act upon decisions and influence society, had been whetted by the Mariposa experience. As he left California, his vision of America's future enhanced by the examples of self-reliance and energy he had witnessed on the frontier, he needed a means for promoting his concept of civilization to a wider population.

Now a middle-aged man of forty-three, still with no discernible profession or career, he systematically pondered the options he had for reaching the authority he desired and for reforming society to fit his dream. He could remain in the private sector and cultivate the several financial investments he had made while in California; riches, he believed, carried power and influence. He could complete several landscape design commissions that had come to him in the West; he could remain in the West and seek other landscape projects, a course of action that guaranteed neither riches nor success, but contributed visibly to social improvement. Or he could return east, renew his partnership with Vaux, and simultaneously keep his hand in journalism.

During his time in California, Olmsted attracted attention from influential men who called on him to undertake several important landscape design jobs. On the basis of his reputation for work on Central Park, he was asked to advise on the development of two estates south of San Francisco, and he was invited by trustees of the College of California (Berkeley) to design a community consisting of a campus and residential park across the bay from San Francisco. Moreover, partly as a result of his own letters-to-the-editor campaign for a public park in San Francisco and partly because of support from the editors of the *San Francisco Bulletin*, Olmsted was also invited to advise the city's municipal board on the location and plans for a large rural pleasure ground in the City by the Bay.

At the same time, however, as the Civil War came to a close, correspondence with two friends in the East reminded Olmsted of opportunities there. His friend the Anglo-Irish journalist and editor, Godkin, had secured the financial backing for the journal he and Olmsted had dreamed of starting several years earlier. In June 1865, Godkin wrote that he wanted Olmsted's help with the weekly publication of the *Nation*. At the same time, Calvert Vaux, despite expressions of resentment toward Olmsted, wanted his partner to join him again in working on a newly secured commission for a great public park for Brooklyn.

Olmsted returned to New York, intending to pursue two ventures at once: he would rejoin Vaux to continue landscape design projects, and he would merge his social interests into publication of the *Nation*. In both undertakings, Olmsted combined his search for personal recognition and fulfillment with his desire to influence society and to further civilization as he defined it.

Civilization and Education

All the Olmsted and Vaux plans for colleges and universities mirror Olmsted's personal experiences and convictions about education; few of the programs and designs would prove acceptable to educators or to the trustees who sought Olmsted's advice, and, indeed, few institutions actually applied his designs to their sites. Yet Olmsted's ideas and plans for colleges and universities stand as vivid evidence of his reverence for institutions of formal education and of his dreams of the possibility for an almost utopian America.

Olmsted's interest in designing college campuses was influenced by his regret that he had not received a college education, his romantic impressions of college campuses he had visited, and the importance he assigned to learning. A college, he believed, was a special kind of community of men preparing for leadership as citizens in a democracy. These same men, he believed, needed instruction in basic military discipline.

As a young man he visited West Point with his father. Later, in a series of letters and visits, he advised the commanding officer of the United States Military Academy about campus design. His advice was not adopted, however.

Olmsted's education was compounded of serendipitous experiences with nature, chance encounters with adults, book-learning meted out by rod-wielding tyrants, and his habit of critical reading and thinking. Perhaps his often-expressed concern for the inferiority or incompleteness of his education impelled him to glorify learning and venerate its institutions. He believed that a true democracy could prosper only on the foundation of formal education, even though he (and most other men and women of his time) saw higher education as the right of privileged white males preparing for law, medicine, teaching, or positions of power in business and society.

The curriculum for these advantaged citizens should include more than academic subjects. A young American man, Olmsted argued, should be schooled in outdoor recreation — including physical fitness — should be made to be at home in the forest or on the sea, should know the rudiments of surveying and of scientific agriculture.[1] In an essay, probably written in 1868, Olmsted's advocacy of outdoor activities appears to rest on two points: first, and most obviously, outdoor activity is good for the growing child; second — and reflective of Olmsted's tendency to couple causes to single solutions he advocated — the presence of the children of wealthy parents would elevate public education. He observed that wealthy parents seemed unwilling to send their children to public schools, fearing the influences of the lower classes. But wealthy parents might be persuaded to send their children to public schools, he asserted, if those schools sponsored safe, attractive, and healthful forms of outdoor play. The presence in public schools of children from wealthier homes, he argued, would in turn bring about the stabilization of the role of public education in perpetuating the American republic.[2]

Convinced of the rightness of his viewpoint on education, Olmsted consistently stitched his philosophy into all of his reports on college- and university-campus planning. In doing so he often strayed far from the mere physical boundaries of the grounds and facilities of the particular institution and from the guidelines set forth by trustees. He typically disregarded most existing buildings as well as roads and paths and returned to what he considered the proper beginning for a design project — topography and purpose.

Beginning with a clean slate, Olmsted usually first articulated the principles that should guide the trustees in developing policy for the institution under consideration, the mission that should be established and honored in the physical layout and buildings and in the curriculum, and the daily routines and lifestyles of students that should be enforced as a means for instilling in them the virtues of civilization. Higher education, Olmsted insisted, had a grander mission than preparing men for success in law, medicine, teaching, engineering, or agriculture: education should transform boys into civilized men and should provide them with a gentleman's passport into society.[3]

Yet Olmsted held no brief for purely theoretical learning. To the contrary, he insisted that an educated man needed to be practical. Writing to Frederick Knapp — his old colleague from the Sanitary Commission, who now operated a school for boys — about the education he desired for his stepson John, Olmsted said, "[N]o student should be graduated with honor who could not construct and use a camp oven and camp kitchen, or who was not prepared to undertake himself and to instruct others in all the duties of a regimental commissary officer." Training of this sort, Olmsted reckoned, would have given the Union better volunteers for the Civil War; and, moreover, formal education in a democracy should ensure a ready reserve of military leaders to protect the Republic.[4]

Education should not drive wedges between men, Olmsted insisted, but should draw them together in common purpose. Since his youthful visits to the campus of Yale, Olmsted had worried about the tendency of "head workers" — the traditional liberal arts students — to take a snobbish view of their superiority over "hand workers," the young men intent on careers in engineering, agriculture, and other applied sciences. Writing to Charles Eliot Norton, Olmsted argued his point:

> *Can we associate a superior education for men who will be engaged in pursuits other than "professional" or scholarly with an university? . . . Can the university be democratized? To draw such a line between an education of head-workers and hand-workers . . . will go far to establish in the minds of each class a very undemocratic habit.*[5]

Throughout his life, when Olmsted wrote about the purposes and benefits of education, he spoke as he had about slavery, about the need for reform of maritime law, and about civilization: he spoke in Yeoman's passionate voice. In his view, an educated man was one prepared to think rationally, to uphold democratic ideals in the planning and running of society, and to invest hard work in the good causes of a community's shared purposes. And when Olmsted and Vaux designed a campus community, Yeoman's say did not go unheeded.

Berkeley

Olmsted's plan for the College of California at Berkeley, like his plan for pleasure grounds for San Francisco, place him in the historical ranks of city and urban planners. Given the task of creating a community from the ground up, of laying out a coherent town consisting of residential areas as well as a college campus, Olmsted wanted to provide "scholars, at least during the period of life in which character is most easily molded, [with surroundings of] refined domestic life, these being unquestionably the ripest and best fruits of civilization."[6]

While still in California, Olmsted was invited to design a campus for a new college being planned. He and Vaux collaborated on a master plan for the Oakland campus. In preparing a report for the trustees of the College of California, Olmsted wrote: "With regard to dwelling for the students, my enquiries lead me to believe that the experience of eastern colleges is equally unfavorable with regard to the old plan of large barracks and commons, and to the plan of trusting that the student will be properly accommodated with board and lodging arrangements with private families or hotels. Establishments seem likely to be finally preferred, in which buildings erected by the College will be used, having the general appearance of large domestic houses, and containing a respectably furnished drawing-room and dining-room for the common use of the students, together with a sufficient number of private rooms to accommodate from twenty to forty lodgers." (PFLO VI: Olmsted, Vaux, "Report Upon a Projected Improvement of the Estate of the College of California, at Berkeley, Near Oakland, June 29, 1866.")

In Olmsted's scheme of things, civilization grew from and sustained domesticity — his idyllic perception of the family and of New England village life spreading out from hearth and home. It was from this deeply honored concept that Olmsted postulated:

The relative importance of the different provisions for human comfort that go to make up a residence is proportionate to the degree in which, ultimately, the health of the inmates is likely to be favorably influenced by each, whether through the facility it offers to the cheerful occupation of time and a healthful exercise of the faculties, or through any more direct and constant action.[7]

A house offered its inhabitants more than shelter; a home — the place dedicated to the well-being of a single family — was the building block of community and of communicativeness. Thus, Olmsted wanted to provide the dwellers in the residential area he designed with the fresh air and sunshine he believed essential for good health and cheer, and with placement that knit individual houses into a community. For Berkeley he planned houses with easy access to the out-of-doors and plantings natural to the topography and climate.

He also planned for privacy and for community. Berkeley was intended to be an upper-middle-class neighborhood of private houses situated on five-acre lots. Olmsted provided for the availability of services and goods that such a community would expect and for the leisure that affluence assured. He laid out walkways to encourage women and children to stroll within the community, to meet and talk with one another.[8]

Throughout his plans for Berkeley, Olmsted resisted the gridiron pattern, by then a commonplace plan for western towns and communities. Instead, he designed pleasant curving roadways to discourage traffic and trade, to take advantage of views and the existing topography, and to create an atmosphere of leisure and security, rather than one of commerce and efficiency.

The campus, too, encouraged a quiet life of scholarly reflection rather than one of worldly activity. He laid it out on slopes between two hills, giving prominence to an artificial plain created to provide a long view of the ocean. He sited two buildings — one for assembly, the other for administrative records and instructional collections — to anchor the terrace. Dormitories were to be small, he stipulated, resembling houses and containing both public and private areas, and thus promoting the virtues of domesticity. In his scheme, academic buildings were also to be of a residential scale and situated to encourage solitary study and thought as well as informal gatherings for discussion and civilized conversation. His program called for the architect to design all buildings as detached and individualistic entities, each fitting into an overall design, and each contributing to the campuswide sense of serenity and quiet work.

Olmsted's fee of two thousand dollars in gold was paid, and the plan published.[9] But the idea of developing a community was soon abandoned. The trustees of the then-private college sold it to the University of California, and Olmsted's plan was first ignored by the gardener who actually laid out the campus that became the University of California at Berkeley and then was lost.

🌿 *Massachusetts*

The trustees of the Massachusetts Agricultural College at Amherst, a public institution born of the Morrill Act of 1862, first hired Vaux and Boston architect Joseph R. Richards to design the initial and principal campus building. Vaux and Richards proposed a large stone building and recommended its site. But the trustees ignored the suggested placement of the structure and plunked it down in the middle of the vast farm that was to be the college campus. Having thus established the Vaux-Richards building as a major element in the design of the campus, the trustees called in Olmsted to lay out a road leading to the structure.

At the time they invited Olmsted's participation in the planning of the campus, the trustees were far from unified in their vision of the institution. In the end, Olmsted's report drove them further apart — insulting some, like prominent businessman D. Waldo Lincoln, to whom Olmsted wrote, insisting that the "individuality of an agricultural college lies in its agriculture, not in its building, which is a mere piece of apparel to be fitted to the requirements of the agricultural trunk." [10]

When he began to think about the campus near Amherst, however, Olmsted was not content to delineate merely a roadway leading from a thoroughfare to a large stone building standing solitarily in the middle of farmland. Rather, he approached the assignment as if nothing existed, and as if he had been invited to instruct the trustees on the creation of an agricultural college.

Since the time he spent with his brother at Yale, Olmsted had been interested in colleges and regretted throughout his life that he never earned a degree. He took a strong interest in the opportunities and ramifications of the Morrill Act, which, to his approval, required military training for students in the land-grant colleges, as well as preparation for useful work in disciplines related to agriculture and mechanics. Olmsted objected, however, to a separation of theoretical and applied curricula, and was opposed to what he considered to be egregious distinctions between the "gentlemanly" liberal arts students and the students in the less socially esteemed scientific disciplines. Thus, when invited to sketch a roadway for the Massachusetts College of Agriculture, Olmsted elevated his assignment and prepared to give the trustees suitable policies, as well as a complete plan for building and administering every aspect of the college.

He visited the Amherst site on May 23, 1866, talked with the building committee, and walked the three-hundred-acre college farm. When the building committee, which was worried about the cost of the proposed building, encouraged Olmsted to offer alternatives, he prepared a report, later published as *A Few Things to Be Thought of before Proceeding to Plan Buildings for the National Agricultural Colleges.*[11]

Olmsted ignored the trustees' preliminary guidelines and plans and used their invitation as a platform to proselytize for his own philosophy of education and for the approach to campus design he believed his policies required. Certainly aware of Thomas Jefferson's plan for the University of Virginia, Olmsted rejected the idea of a large central building and suggested in its place four smaller two-story buildings, each with its specific curricular

Olmsted consulted with officials at private institutions such as Madison University (now Hamilton College) and Amherst College, but little evidence remains of his attempt to shape these campuses.

function. The building for science should contain spaces for a laboratory, lectures, and a museum. Another building should consist of two lecture halls and two smaller rooms on each floor. A third would have a reading room and library. The fourth, a gymnasium and drill room, would contain spaces for general assembly, offices, and a boardroom.[12]

Olmsted argued that the college should promote social progress, acknowledge the farm-family and small-village lifestyle likely for its graduates, and effect a sense of community throughout its campus. Students should not only be instructed in the latest methods of scientific farming, but also induced to be patriotic and dutiful citizens as well as upright householders; and they should be prepared to engage in social intercourse with other professional men.[13]

His plan for an agricultural college, Olmsted advocated, would furnish examples of rural living that would encourage intelligent men to remain on the farm, to contribute to civilization, and to use leisure for aesthetic and spiritual improvement of themselves, their families, and their communities. The ideal rural neighborhood he thus proposed would resemble a New England village, with the military drill ground (required by the Morrill Act) serving as a public park surrounded by trees, paths, and natural vistas. He grandly insisted that the trustees of the Massachusetts College of Agriculture and Mechanics owed their students "education in the art of making a farmer's home cheerful and attractive." [14]

Toward his ends, Olmsted would have the leaders of the college live among the students, in model homes where grounds, household furnishings, and manner of living would teach students by example that the farmer's life included good taste, good manners, and luxury. Each house, Olmsted suggested, should be surrounded by a lawn, as well as such pleasant augmentations as birdhouses, icehouses, croquet courts. Olmsted concluded his report with the warning that he would consider any changes in his plan "as extremely undesirable." [15]

The trustees, after squabbling among themselves and after being criticized in the press for their confused management of the embryonic institution, paid Olmsted the $550 he asked for his report. Then they rejected the plan.

Maine

Olmsted's report attracted widespread attention in the press. In part, this was because at that time Olmsted served on the editorial staff of the *Nation*, a publication that gave special attention to the designer's philosophy of education. The widely read report impressed the trustees of the proposed Maine State Agricultural College at Orono, on the Penobscot River. In November 1866 the trustees invited Olmsted to visit the site of the future college and to advise them on planning the grounds.

The Maine institution necessarily embraced the goals set by the Morrill Act and by legislation introduced by Phineas Barnes, a Portland resident who would later become president of the college. As a land-grant institution, the college was expected to train students in practical skills and applied sciences to further the country's agricultural, industrial, and military well-being. But Barnes also wanted much of what Olmsted wanted in a college community.

Thus from the first discussions between Barnes and Olmsted, the college at Orono was envisioned as fostering among students a sense of morality and justice, truthfulness, patriotism, sobriety, frugality, chastity, moderation, temperance, and "all other virtues which are the ornaments of human society." It followed that the college, in order "to secure the best personal improvements of the students [would provide] as fully as may be practicable, that the internal organization of the college shall be on the plan of one or more well-regulated households and families, so that the students may be brought into relations of domestic intimacy and confidence with their teachers." [16]

The purpose of the college in Maine, according to Olmsted, was to offer "a liberal education to young men without unfitting them for or disinclining them to industrial callings." Acknowledging that graduates should be excellent farmers and workers, he also called upon the college to improve the "tastes, inclinations and habits" of its students as well. [17]

Olmsted arrived in Orono on December 21, 1866, to look at the property. He and several trustees walked over the wintery scene and discussed what the college should be. A month later, Olmsted filed his formal report. [18] Many aspects of it echoed features of the Massachusetts Agricultural College plan: individual buildings for specific functions, houses rather than dormitories, a village-style layout of buildings, and a conscious effort to use the college community as a model for the rural communities in which the students would later live.

In his plan for Orono, however, Olmsted laid heavy stress on military preparation for students. He recommended forming companies of forty students each, with units electing officers to serve for specified periods of time. Each company should be allotted a budget and required to run a commissary, office, kitchen, and mess room, with each student taking his turn as commissary officer. Olmsted's dismay at the lack of survival skills brought by volunteers to the Civil War showed in his hearty insistence on outdoor skills and on military preparation in the land-grant colleges.

The trustees who hired Olmsted paid his fee of $196. However, another board, elected in April 1867, rejected his plan for the site, for buildings, and for curriculum because, the board members decided, it placed too much emphasis on military training. Again, Olmsted's plan for an institution of higher education did not materialize; but again, the plan and the ideas reflected served to incite discussion about the purposes and nature of education in a democracy.

🌿 Gallaudet University

Edward Miner Gallaudet, then president of the Columbia Institution for the Deaf and Dumb (now Gallaudet University in Washington, D.C.) had begun work with Vaux and architect Frederick Withers on a building project for the campus. Gallaudet asked Olmsted, who had been his childhood neighbor in Hartford, to join the team shortly after he returned from California. Specifically, Gallaudet wanted Olmsted to lay out the site.

The resulting plan and report, submitted by the Olmsted and Vaux firm, included some of the ideas that marked Olmsted's plans for campuses in California, Massachusetts, and Maine. Although the campus was located in a city rather than on country farmland, and was much smaller than the land-grant colleges, Olmsted and Vaux laid out Gallaudet as a community, with common spaces, a chapel, and residences situated so as to protect campus life from the hurly-burly of the surrounding city.[19]

Olmsted urged Gallaudet to look to the future needs of the college and acquire additional land, pointing out that "it would be very poor economy to spare expense for necessary ground while undertaking considerable outlays for necessary buildings."[20]

When invited to lay out a road for the land-grant college of Massachusetts, Olmsted not only presented the board with a complete design for the campus, including a series of domestic-scale living units for students, but stipulated the mission and curriculum of the institution as well. His visionary plan exacerbated already vehement squabbling among the trustees, and it was rejected.

But a leading trustee of another New England land-grant college read the published plan and consulted Olmsted on the design of the Maine State Agricultural College at Orono. There — as he had for Massachusetts — Olmsted stressed the importance of military drill and discipline. Although land-grant colleges were required to provide military training, Olmsted, recalling the ill-prepared volunteer Union army of the Civil War, laid great stress on preparing officers and on organizing student life around armylike units of command.

Although the report from Olmsted and Vaux included advice on the college's program of study, the message bore the stamp of Yeoman's civilizing and educating hand:

In a well-regulated garden the sense of sight and smell are gratified in a most complete and innocent way, and there seems, indeed, to be no reason why the studies of horticulture, botany, ornamental gardening, and rural architecture should not be pursued to great advantage by your students if proper facilities are offered at the outset, and due importance is attached to that influential automatic education which depends entirely on an habitual daily contemplation of good examples.[21]

As a firm Olmsted and Vaux were consulted by other colleges and universities and applied to all of them the basic principles developed for the institutions in California, Massachusetts, and Maine. In these commissions, as in others, Olmsted worked directly with clients, while Vaux remained in the drafting room in the background, an apportionment of responsibilities consonant with each partner's personality, but one that resulted in Vaux's continuing to feel that Olmsted received too much credit for work done by the firm.

Still, representing the partnership, Olmsted urged Andrew Dickson White, the first president of Cornell University, to break with the quadrangle rigidity of the campus and to site buildings in a "[M]ore free, liberal, picturesque & convenient" manner.[22] He counseled William A. Stearns, president of Amherst College, to disengage the campus from the town growing around it.[23] And he preached his message to the president of Trinity College in Hartford, too, saying that a well-designed campus would encourage the "acquisition of the general quality of culture which is the chief end of a liberal education." Such a campus, enlivened by the faculty, he believed, would elevate civilization in America and would effect the values that he himself esteemed.[24]

Insane Asylums

Olmsted had met Dorothea Dix, head of the nurse corps, during the Civil War and, as a member of the Sanitary Commission, had agreed with her reports on the failure of the Medical Bureau to provide adequate care for wounded Union soldiers. Furthermore, he shared her dismay at the army's reluctance to accept the services of nurses in caring for the wounded, and then at the humiliating treatment of nurses (and other women) in the Union army camps and hospitals. Although another sanitarian, George Templeton Strong, referred to Dix as a "philanthropic lunatic," Olmsted respected her work on behalf of the insane and prisoners. Finally, he agreed with her humanitarian prescriptions for treatment — rather than incarceration, which resembled punishment — of the insane.

When Olmsted and Vaux undertook the design of several institutions for the insane — then universally called asylums — they created parklike surroundings to protect the patients and to encourage rest and recuperation. Their designs might have illustrated Dorothea Dix's requirements, so markedly different were they from the jail-asylums that had customarily confined the insane.

Before the Civil War, Olmsted and Vaux had advised administrators on redesigning the grounds of the Hartford Insane Retreat. In 1867 they designed the Hudson River State Hospital, north of Poughkeepsie, New York. While little is known about the actual plans for buildings and grounds, evidence suggests that Olmsted wanted a rural environment planned to promote serenity. And in 1872, Olmsted began work on the McLean Asylum, in Belmont, Massachusetts, arguing that "the most desirable qualities in the home grounds of a retreat for the insane are probably those which favor an inclination to moderate exercise and tranquil occupations of the mind." Patients, he said, should not be subjected to an environment which would "induce exertion, heat, excitement or bewilderment." [25]

Olmsted's designs for both campuses and hospitals are based on his strong commitment to community and to the values of both education and humanitarian treatment of all citizens. Every citizen — whether a student in an academic community or a patient in an institution of healing — would, Olmsted believed, benefit from peaceful and beautiful surroundings.

The Nation and the Political Man

During the years after the Civil War, when the partners Olmsted and Vaux had resigned from Central Park, Olmsted was close to exhaustion from work with the Sanitary Commission. Uncertain about the profession of landscape architecture, and uneasy about his future, Olmsted, perhaps harkening to his earlier celebration as a journalist, considered joining Edwin L. Godkin in publishing a weekly journal. Financial backing was not forthcoming, however, and Olmsted had gone west to amass a personal fortune.

But Godkin, with investments eventually promised, wrote to Olmsted in June 1865 about the Nation, the weekly magazine of their dreams. It would address many of the issues dear to Olmsted, and Godkin wanted Olmsted's editorial involvement in the journal. The journalist urged Olmsted, still very much a social reformer at heart, to return east and once again take up the journalist's pen.

When Olmsted returned east and joined Vaux in a secure commission to design and superintend work on Prospect Park, in Brooklyn, he also took an active role in the publication of the newly founded Nation. Further, despite his tight financial situation, he invested money in the fledgling publication, and, as an even stronger measure of his stake in the Nation, Olmsted spent much of his free time working without pay as an editorial assistant to Godkin. It was a labor of love.

Moreover, the relationship between Olmsted and Godkin was mutually beneficial. Godkin, who sometimes felt the sting of anti-Irish bigotry in America, believed Olmsted's name on the masthead would promote confidence in the publication. From his viewpoint, Olmsted saw the *Nation* as a vehicle for forwarding many of his social and political concerns: equal rights for all Americans, woman suffrage, international copyright law, protection of merchant seamen from tyrannical officers, and better training for military leaders.

During the first half of 1866, Olmsted participated vigorously in the *Nation*'s life, but his interest diminished after that time. Subsequently, although he seemed reluctant to take a public role in the *Nation*, he remained a financial backer until 1871.

The *Nation*, however, was destined to suffer financial insecurity, much of it born of the conflicting expectations and the political cross-purposes of its backers. With a hundred thousand dollars invested by men in New York, Boston, and Philadelphia, Godkin had to juggle opposing viewpoints on tariff reform and the welfare of freedmen, among other controversial issues of the day. Unwilling to dedicate the publication to a single issue, Godkin tried to build a magazine that would attract broader-based sales and subscriptions sufficient to cover its costs. But the *Nation* faced a precarious future.

Olmsted, a moderate Republican who was keenly interested in social issues, desired a stronger platform from which to advocate his policies for American civilization and, specifically, his concerns related to Reconstruction. He discussed and corresponded about such issues with friends, including Godkin, George William Curtis, Charles Eliot Norton, and Samuel Bowles — men who shared his vision of America, all liberal Republican reformists at heart, all concerned about the course of Reconstruction, the role of former Confederate states in the Union, and the welfare and future of freedmen. Moreover, they were leery of President Andrew Johnson's conservative bent and aware of the white South's lingering bigotry; they wanted no compromise for the South on ratification of the Fourteenth Amendment, a guarantee of civil rights for freedmen.

In 1866 Olmsted was heartened by Grant's appearance on the national political scene. Long an admirer of the Union general, Olmsted was quick to defend Grant against the reports of his drinking, which menaced his presidential campaign. Combining his convictions with his influence on the editorial policy of the *Nation*, Olmsted defended Grant in a letter published in that journal. He was pleased by Grant's election, but later repulsed by the corruption of the former general's administration.

Olmsted felt that the Republican Party had fought hard for a high moral ground during the Civil War and now seemed likely to lose its soul in dirty politics. When journalist Horace Greeley sought the Republican nomination for president of the United States, with support from Samuel Bowles, Olmsted was angry, believing Greeley to be too cozy with Tammany Hall and political corruption in New York. He preferred Charles Francis Adams, whom he believed to be upright and honest.

Throughout the Reconstruction period, Olmsted showed concern for humanitarian and philanthropic projects such as the Southern Famine Relief Commission — serving that organization as recording secretary for a brief time in 1867, then as chairman of its committee Business with the North. He edited circulars, and he used his connections with newspaper editors to publicize the work of the commission, much as he had done while heading the Sanitary Commission. By the time he wrote a final report in 1867 for the Southern Famine Relief Commission, Olmsted demonstrated an amicable attitude toward the South.[26]

Other problems related to social change in America captured Olmsted's attention. He speculated on the influence of immigration on the American character and on American civilization. His interests in social pressures and change impelled him to become an early member of the American Social Science Association, founded in Boston in 1865 to promote the then new disciplines born of rational and measured study of humankind. In 1870 Olmsted presented a paper, "Public Parks and the Enlargement of Towns," to the professional organization fostering ideas similar to his own. The paper was published later in its *Journal of Social Science.*[27]

Olmsted had returned to New York to find the city and the country after the Civil War bustling with challenge, opportunity, and change. He threw himself into the affairs of the age, using the *Nation* as well as his reports to clients as vehicles for expressing ideas, urging change, and arguing for the values and institutions he believed basic to civilization. Olmsted's outspokenness on these matters doubtless led a maverick faction of the Liberal Republican Party to nominate him in 1872 for vice-president. Somewhat embarrassed, Olmsted insisted he had no political ambition and refused to campaign for the office.

Olmsted and Vaux, Partners Again

*I*n November 1865, Olmsted and Vaux reaffirmed their partnership and, as planned in their exchange of letters when Olmsted was in California, they re-newed work on Central Park and undertook a commission to design Brooklyn's Prospect Park. They could scarcely have imagined the influence their work would exert on American park, community, and urban design. Although their partnership would last only until 1871, when Olmsted would dissolve it, their work together established the standards by which parks have been designed and made since that time and set criteria for defining communities and evaluating the quality of life in cities. And despite the discom-fort the two men experienced in working together, the partnership enabled Vaux to work on projects Olmsted attracted through his network of social and political connections and through his outgoing manner; and it captured Olmsted's imagination, focused his energies on the social good to be achieved through park and urban design, and caused him to mature as a landscape architect, to see and celebrate the artistry of the profession.

When Olmsted returned to New York to take up his partnership with Vaux, he must have anticipated also the resumption of his role in Central Park. But he had lost significant credibility — as well as manifest power and authority — to Andrew H. Green. Olmsted, who found Green's treatment of him to be humiliating, would hardly have returned to certain frustration and failure at the hands of his old tormentor. Despite the anxiety he expressed to Vaux, Olmsted must have expected to join his partner in a renewed influence on Central Park, and he must have dreamed of working again in the comparative freedom and heady excitement of the early days of Central Park. In reality, however, Olmsted, Vaux and Company never regained the power it had initially enjoyed in shaping and administering Central Park.

Nonetheless, as the two men resumed their partnership in 1865, Olmsted had high hopes. His time in California had left him in good health physically and financially. While reluctant to commit himself irretrievably to the profession of landscape architecture when Vaux urged him to return east, Olmsted was unable to let pass an opportunity for responsibility for Central Park.

Straightaway after resuming the administration of the park, Olmsted and Vaux turned their attention to the boulder-filled expanse of land from 106th to 110th Streets, a parcel of land added to the northern boundary of the original Central Park. There, they designed a rustic realm of paths and bridges, foliage-secluded interludes in the rural landscape, and romantic vistas featuring picturesque outcroppings of rock or masses of foliage.

Moreover, Olmsted was quickly captivated by the Prospect Park project, and, prodded by Vaux, he finally accepted landscape architecture as an art, and as his destined profession. Thus unself-consciously, Frederick Law Olmsted entered into the most creative period of his life.

Prospect Park

Central Park had prepared the partners to invest their ideas and creative energies in the development of Prospect Park in Brooklyn. Their enthusiasm grew when they discovered that the Prospect Park project was free of many of the corrosive and abrading political frictions that had plagued their days at Manhattan's great park.

While Olmsted was still in California, Vaux had laid a fine professional foundation for the Brooklyn park by establishing good communication with the park commission and by defining the actual space that would become Prospect Park. He had understood the pride of the Brooklyn citizens, at a time when that community was still an independent town, not yet joined to New York City. He understood that Brooklynites coveted a park that would rival Central Park, an ambition that invited Olmsted and Vaux to dream of grand plans.

Olmsted returned to New York in 1865 and found the port city bustling with postwar trade, having experienced a steady increase in population.

Vaux was also aware in 1860 that seven possible locations for an urban pleasure ground had been identified, and he understood that, as the Civil War neared its end, Brooklyn leaders proudly anticipated growth of their city. When they engaged Vaux to advise them on the possible treatment of a specific site, he convinced them to do what turned out to be the right thing.

Heavily traveled Flatbush Avenue divided the plot shown to Vaux into two unequal portions, a configuration the architect found inappropriate. He suggested that the smaller (northeastern) portion be sold, and that the larger (southwestern) portion be retained and augmented by the purchase of adjacent lands. Upon learning of Vaux's concept, Olmsted agreed with his partner and joined him in preparing a plan and writing a report to convince the Board of Commissioners of Prospect Park. The plan, presented in January 1866, persuaded the commissioners to locate the park where Olmsted and Vaux recommended, on the east side of Flatbush Avenue.

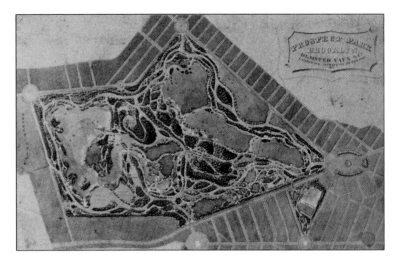

"From many points of the drives, rides and walks," Olmsted promised of plans he and Vaux proposed for Prospect Park, "the eye will range over a meadow-like expanse, wherein the first definite obstruction or break in the turfy surface will be at least half a mile away, sometimes considerably more than that, and in which tree tops will be seen in rising perspective, fully a mile away. These views will not offer merely peeps, but will comprehend quite broad and well-balanced pastoral landscapes, free from any object which will suggest the vicinity of the city, from which it is the primary purpose of the Park to give the means of a ready escape. Views will be had over water surface of equal breadth and distance. The visitor will feel the sense of freedom and repose suggested by scenes of this character, and be impressed by their breadth of light and shadow, all the more because they will be enjoyed in alternation and contrast with the obscurity of the thick woods already established, through the seclusion which he will be occasionally led." (PFLO VI: Olmsted, Vaux, *Report of Landscape Architects and Superintendents* to Brooklyn Park Commission, Jan. 1, 1869.)

The suggested change gave Olmsted and Vaux space for a large lake, rural scenery, and the curving paths and passageways that they deemed essential to an urban pleasure ground. It was to be a park in which the designers combined grand general sweeps with minutely configured details. It was to be a masterpiece of park design.

Olmsted and Vaux attacked the Prospect Park project with the same level of enthusiasm and creativity that had made Central Park a monument of civility and serenity in an urban setting. Prospect Park, though less celebrated, stands today as Central Park's equal in design and as a testament to the Olmsted and Vaux partnership.

Olmsted was forty-three when he joined Vaux in the Prospect Park project. It was an easier site than Central Park and offered the partners a more pliable and responsive topography than that which they had transmogrified into

Central Park. Unlike the spiny and infertile ground that became Central Park, the Prospect Park site consisted of gently rolling, richly wooded acres of fertile soil.

In May the commissioners adopted the plan proposed by Olmsted and Vaux and appointed them landscape architects and superintendents for the Brooklyn project, allocating to their firm eight thousand dollars a year. Olmsted was soon deep in the work he loved, hiring and directing men to move earth, shape paths, and set vegetation according to plan. His enthusiasm was not blunted by bureaucratic delays, and he and Vaux enjoyed freedom from the kind of political interference that had plagued them throughout their work on Central Park. Instead of the headstrong and interfering Green to obstruct their efforts at every turn, they appreciated the enlightened leadership of the chairman of the commissioners, James S. T. Stranahan.

The plan for Prospect Park included an expansive meadow, a rolling woodland, and a large lake — three ingredients Olmsted and Vaux thought essential to the urban park. They created what is now known as Grand Army Plaza at the juncture of Prospect Park West and Flatbush Avenue. This oval design device served as a symbolic separation of park from city, but another sensational feature actually shielded the park from urban bustle, muffled the noise, and secured the rural atmosphere. It was a mound of densely planted earth that ran just inside the walls encircling the park.

As a result of certain attributes of its original site, the mound-buttress against the intrusion of the city, and the masterful amalgam of open and planted areas, Prospect Park may be more successful as a rural park than Central Park. Untroubled by the crosstown traffic or the existence of city reservoirs that were necessary in Central Park, Prospect Park was a compact, well-defined mass of land. Its plantings were easily maintained and the paths for different forms of traffic well defined.

Olmsted and Vaux renewed a dream that had hatched first during their work on Central Park: they envisioned a vast chain of parks and landscape parkways linking the entire metropolitan area, reaching north into Westchester County, uniting Manhattan and Brooklyn, linking Staten Island, and extending into New Jersey. Their scheme for a connected park system, though never realized, underlay the work the firm accomplished in numerous designs for the region.

They designed the greenbelt Eastern and Ocean Parkways, with pleasure drives for carriages and pedestrian paths, as well as throughways for commercial traffic, as potential elements in their overall scheme for the growing urban area.

Olmsted and Vaux's 1868 report to the commissioners of Prospect Park mirrors Olmsted's increasing awareness of the role parks might play in urban design. Still with the sound of Yeoman in his voice, he outlined the history of street systems from the Middle

Ages, stressed the theme of democracy in cities, and argued that parks should influence the placement of streets and should serve as common meeting ground for all classes. He wrote,

> *We regard Brooklyn as an integral part of what today is the metropolis of the nation, and in the future will be the center of exchanges for the world, and the park in Brooklyn, as part of a system of grounds, of which the Central Park is a single feature, designed for the recreation of the whole people of the metropolis and their customers and guests from all parts of the world for centuries to come.*[1]

By the time Olmsted and Vaux undertook the design and development of Prospect Park, they were recognized as the leading park designers in the United States. By the beginning of the 1870s Olmsted, Vaux and Company could be seen influencing the park systems of Chicago, Buffalo, the District of Columbia, Philadelphia, Newark, Albany, Providence, and New Britain, Connecticut, and other towns and cities as well. They were

Strollers and carriage drivers enjoyed separated wide paths flanked by tall trees, an experience intended to contribute to the enjoyment of nature in a busy city.

"The influences [of any rural park in an urban setting] most desirable to be exerted on the mind," wrote Olmsted, "are the reverse of those from which the much confined, stimulated, and overworked inhabitants of large towns are habitually suffering, and from the wearing and disorganizing effects of which they most need to find conditions favorable to recreation." (PFLO VI: Olmsted, Vaux, *Architect's Report* to the Board of Commissioners of the Newark Park, Oct. 5, 1867.)

Rustic architectural features, such as trellises, were included in the design.

In order to add to the rural character of Prospect Park, Olmsted and Vaux arranged space for a herd of sheep.

often consulted for advice, and they often submitted formal proposals to design and superintend specific parks. In numerous instances — Philadelphia, Providence, and Newark, for example — they were not selected to design the parks, but those who did design and manage the parks showed the influence of Olmsted and Vaux.

Parks

Olmsted and Vaux would sever their partnership in 1871–1872, continuing to work together as a project required. But Olmsted exercised the profession of landscape architect, thereby instilling the material evidence of his social thought in four especially notable instances: Chicago, Buffalo, Montreal, and Boston.

Chicago

When commissioned to design a park system for Chicago, Olmsted addressed the particularly challenging topography of South Park; its Lower Division (later known as Jackson Park) contained the dunes and marshy edges of Lake Michigan; the Upper Division (later Washington Park) consisted of flat, treeless, uninflected prairie.

Taking advantage of the flatness, Olmsted and Vaux defined and perfected a hundred acres of open turf, one of the largest parade and games grounds in the United States. They used dense masses of foliage in an irregular border, defined meadows, created vistas, and enlivened the landscape into a picturesque rural pleasure ground.

South Park offered the visual advantage of Lake Michigan, a vast expanse of water that let the eye reach uninterrupted toward the horizon. In order to emphasize the presence of the lake, Olmsted and Vaux proposed cutting canals into the marshy acres, draining the land, mounding the soil to support trees and other foliage, and creating a peaceful lagoon. All the ingredients taken together, they believed, would produce an effective park.

Moreover, they planned to cut canals to connect Washington and Jackson Parks, an innovation with both aesthetic and social advantages, one that made dry ground available for attractive suburban living and, simultaneously, rid the area of unhealthy stagnant waters.

In 1871, just five months after Olmsted and Vaux laid their plan before the Chicago park commissioners, the Great Fire consumed much of the city. Work on the proposed parks was halted temporarily and, when resumed, was no longer supervised by Olmsted and Vaux. Rather, Horace W. S. Cleveland took over, but Chicago finances prevented him from following the Olmsted and Vaux design. The site was not reshaped and the canals not dug that would connect Jackson and Washington Parks. But the drier parts of South Park were developed. In 1893, however, Olmsted would return to the site and design the lakeside for the World's Columbian Exposition.

Buffalo

An affluent and influential Buffalo man, William Dorsheimer, consulted Olmsted in 1868 about a park project in the upstate New York city. Unlike most American cities at that time, Buffalo was a planned city, its streets having been laid out by a L'Enfant follower, Joseph Ellicott. Like L'Enfant's Washington, D.C., Buffalo was organized on streets radiating from a central point, Niagara Square; unlike Washington's streets, Buffalo's followed to some degree the topography of the land.

Buffalo was growing rapidly. Dorsheimer and other leaders were proud of their city and determined to have the conveniences and refinements that other cities displayed. Buffalo, no less than Manhattan, should have a park.

Concerned that growth was promoting chaotic development along the edges of the city, the Buffalo men invited Olmsted to advise them. Where should they place a park? And how should they integrate the park into the existing design of the city?

Dorsheimer took Olmsted driving on a Sunday afternoon and pointed out the sites he and his colleagues thought potential parks. Finally, reaching a hill that provided a view of Buffalo, Olmsted announced, "Here is your park, almost ready made." [2]

The two men were looking at land that would become Delaware Park, then gently hilled farmland with a creek that, to Olmsted, promised a large lake surrounded by romantic scenery. Moreover, it was within easy commuting distance of the city. Olmsted listed the advantages of the property for Dorsheimer and received the civic leader's promise of enthusiastic endorsement.

Later, Dorsheimer collected a group of influential and affluent men, presided over by former president Millard Fillmore, to hear Olmsted describe the large park he envisioned for Buffalo. Without much ado, Olmsted's plan was accepted and the land acquired.

Delaware Park, 350 acres of lakeside, meadow, hills, and artistically deployed paths, was only the first of Olmsted's work for Buffalo. He designed a total of about 600 acres of park system for the city, including the Front, a park with a panoramic view of the Niagara River and of Canada on the far side. Harking back to his memories of the Hartford militia drilling in the city of his youth, Olmsted also provided Buffalo with the Parade, a public park with an enormous expanse of level ground for military parades, games, and leisurely strolls.

Olmsted went further. He connected Buffalo's parks, using more than seven miles of tree-lined parkways and turfed walkways. Thus, in Buffalo, Olmsted realized the essential concept he had promoted unsuccessfully for the area around New York.

Montreal

The park commissioners in Montreal, an elected body without the experience and cohesion of their counterparts in Buffalo or Brooklyn, hired Olmsted in 1874 to design and build Mount Royal Park. In actuality, it was not a mountain but a 735-foot-high hill on a plot of land measuring a mile in length and half a mile in width, totaling about 430 acres. It was rocky and, it seemed to Olmsted, offered only poor prospects for becoming a distinguished park.

Nonetheless, Olmsted undertook the job and set about executing his usual methodical procedure of study, analysis, and design to promote specific activities or to create singular visual experiences. In accordance with the professional procedures he and Vaux had established, Olmsted required a topographical map and stipulated that it be supplied by his clients prior to his beginning work on a project. The commissioners, months late in ob-

Vaux designed several landmark buildings in New York, including the Jefferson Market Courthouse (1877). At the time Sixth Avenue (now Avenue of the Americas) supported an elevated rail system as well as horse-drawn trolleys.

taining the map, urged Olmsted to proceed without it to design a carriage drive, a scheme to provide work for the unemployed of Montreal but not one that was likely to produce the best park design for a difficult site.

Olmsted reluctantly acceded to the commissioners' wishes, but, after work on the carriageway was in progress, he received the topographical map and discovered that the city did not own all of the land designated for the park. From the onset of the project until May 1876, Olmsted replanned the park three times, each time in response to dramatically changed information from the commissioners.

Difficulties notwithstanding, Olmsted's imagination quickened to the problems of the site, and he soon felt that he could turn disadvantages into engaging features. He divided the plot into eight areas, identifying their characteristics with idealistic names: the Crags, the Upperfell, the Brackenfell, the Underfell, the Piedmont, the Côte Placide, the Glades, and the Cragsfoot.[3] As he envisioned the park, he emphasized existing natural features, creating dramatic vistas and picturesque spaces for contemplation of nature. He resisted suggestions for decorative planting and stressed the importance of deftly achieving and maintaining a natural look.

Olmsted further proposed to stimulate the perception of pristine nature — however artfully achieved — by laying out carriage routes and pathways that followed meandering routes and afforded places to stop for leisurely appreciation of the city below or the foliage nearby. Again, however, he encountered the mind-set of the commissioners. They saw the roadways as practical means for ascending and descending the hill and insisted that he lay out straighter and more direct carriageways. Olmsted modified his design, losing a measure of the experience he had hoped to foster with the slowly ascending and curving roads, that of "successive incidents of a sustained landscape poem, to each of which the mind is gradually and sweetly led up, and from which it is gradually and sweetly led away, so that they become a part of a consistent experience." [4]

More Parks

In the decade following the Civil War, enlightened civic leaders responded to the social problems generated by increasing urbanization in a number of ways. One of the most visible — and therefore most politically advantageous — was to build rural parks in cities. New York's Central Park had already attracted international attention, and, despite the political shenanigans that threatened its integrity, it served as a model. Moreover, its designers, who had been praised in press and public gathering, were widely sought to create similar oases in other cities.

Olmsted's sundry reports to clients and trustees on potential design products place him in the ranks of those we today identify as social engineers. Believing fervently in the power of physical surroundings to affect human behavior and nature, he set about *designing* or *forming* or *administering* the ingredients of human society so as to effect communicativeness, his term for the highest expression of human society, the responsible give-and-take among humans that lifted them from barbarity to a state of civilization.

Before the Civil War, Olmsted observed to a friend that Central Park exerted "a distinctly harmonizing and refining influence upon the most unfortunate and most lawless classes of the city — an influence favorable to courtesy, self-control, and temperance." [5]

Community Design: Suburban and Urban

Olmsted and Vaux never saw parks as isolated entities within urban settings but, rather, as areas designated to serve particular functions in the improvement of life for city dwellers. As the partners worked on designs for Central and Prospect Parks, they dreamed of extending greenswards and landscaped roadways into communities surrounding Manhattan and Brooklyn and of influencing the design of suburbia.

Moreover, laying out college campuses had heightened Olmsted's interest in designed communities. His attitude was unequivocally Ruskinian: the human being could be changed by surroundings; a spiritually elevating habitat could be expected to improve the morals, politics, and aesthetics of those who dwelled in it.

When given the opportunity to design a suburb surrounding an academic community, Berkeley, Olmsted sought to align his vision of civilization with his sense of community. Although the design for the suburb and the campus was never implemented, the exercise in programming and planning gave Olmsted important grounding in the fundamentals needed for designing suburbs. A series of commissions took him to the heart of the concept of suburban living.

Long Beach

In 1866, wealthy Howard Potter and real estate developer Louis B. Brown asked Olmsted to design a 150-acre stretch of oceanfront property in Long Beach, New Jersey. The clients wanted to subdivide their land into a fashionable resort enclave, which they intended to call Blythe Beach Park. Rather than sell the lots adjacent to the shore at high prices for immediate gain, Olmsted argued, Potter and Brown should preserve the land along the shore as common ground and the entire community should be designed to ensure every member access to the ocean. This, he maintained, would guarantee the lasting value of all the building sites in the whole community.

Olmsted further proposed that the community be defined by curving streets and that the natural features of the land be emphasized. He stressed the importance of vistas and sea breezes, as well as the commercial opportunities to be found in providing facilities for enjoyment of the shore. Potter and Brown dropped plans for developing Long Beach by the summer of 1867. Potter, however, turned to Olmsted to design walks, drives, and plantings for his own cottage at Long Beach.[1]

Meanwhile, early in 1867, Charles Eliot Norton had hired Olmsted to subdivide his family estate, Shady Hill, near Harvard University in Cambridge, Massachusetts. Olmsted proposed again that a common public green be preserved as the meeting area for the community. As further enhancement of community identity, he also advocated preserving existing trees — large and shade providing — and roads connecting the suburb to Harvard.

Riverside

The country's interest in suburban living was increasing in 1868, when Olmsted and Vaux were commissioned to design a residential suburb near Chicago. The designers were familiar with New Jersey's Llewellyn Park, generally considered a financial and social success. In laying out the community of Berkeley, Olmsted had concluded that certain design features — some of them evident in the West Orange, New Jersey, suburb — contributed to the good life of affluent suburban dwellers: a balance of private and public spaces, sufficient distance between houses to give their inhabitants a sense of privacy, paths to encour-

Charles Eliot Norton

Born in 1827, Charles Eliot Norton became a prominent member of the Boston-Cambridge intellectual aristocracy and a well-known Harvard professor, translator, editor, and critic. He traveled extensively and developed close contacts with writers and scholars in both Europe and the United States. He edited the *North American Review* and helped found the *Nation*. ❧

age strolls and leisurely encounters among neighbors, and roadways to provide easy but discreet access for suppliers of goods and services.

It was against this background that Olmsted, after visiting developer Emery E. Childs in Chicago, reported to Vaux:

> The [Riverside] enterprise is a big speculation. Childs does not want to pay one dollar down, but would be willing to pay us fairly in stock. . . . He wants to put 2000 men to work within a week & wants us to manage everything except "financiering." . . . The Chicago operation is to make a suburban village out of the whole cloth on the prairie & connect by a parkway with town. There will probably be a large demand upon us for cheap little cottages growing out of it, wood chalets — also for spring houses, arbors, seats, drinking fountains &c.[2]

Vaux and his wife were traveling in Europe at the time. When they returned, he joined Olmsted in the project to design a full village on the 1,600-acre site nine miles from Chicago. Their design for Riverside, however, did not feature "cheap little cottages" or "wood chalets," but included large lots for building, augmented by parklike rural scenery. Well-drained roadways were laid out in undulating curves conforming to and emphasizing the topography of the land and the path of the Des Plaines River.

The designers stipulated that houses were to be built within strict specifications, each at a minimum distance from the roads and approached by a private drive. Shade trees were placed irregularly beside the roads and, with similarly natural plantations of masses of foliage, created shady parks and communal greens echoing the New England villages of Olmsted's youth. The designers designated recreation areas, including a dammed section of the river to be used for boating and skating. The partners believed they had met the goals for a modern suburb that Olmsted had noted to the Riverside Improvement Company. In their judgment Riverside combined "urban and rural advantages" and promoted "the most attractive, the most refined and the most soundly wholesome forms of domestic life, and the best application of the arts of civilization to which mankind has yet attained," including the availability of "abundant artificial conveniences." [3] For Olmsted, Riverside furthered his idea of civilization: it promoted "domesticity . . . the essential qualification of a suburb" and offered its inhabitants "secluded peacefulness and tranquility." [4]

Although the directors of Riverside seemed pleased with the design, they suffered financial setbacks that jeopardized the project. When they failed to pay Olmsted and Vaux for their services, the designers agreed to accept lots in lieu of cash. By the fall of 1869 Olmsted and Vaux were convinced that the Riverside venture was an unethical operation and that the speculators would not carry out the plan for the Edenic suburb west of Chicago. Nevertheless, many of the features suggested by Olmsted and Vaux — including the well-graded, well-drained, well-built roadways — found their way into Riverside, making it an early triumph in design of suburbs. Eventually, it also proved a successful financial venture.

Tarrytown

Olmsted and Vaux had a better experience in designing Tarrytown Heights, a nine-hundred-acre area of rich vegetation and varied topography about twenty-five miles north of Manhattan. In October 1870 they commenced planning the suburb, earlier celebrated by Washington Irving in "The Legend of Sleepy Hollow," as an attractive site for home-owners and a profitable venture for speculators.

The same philosophical outlook that had shaped the Riverside plans impelled Olmsted and Vaux in their treatment of Tarrytown Heights. Again, they wanted to provide a combination of community and privacy, of rural picturesqueness and urban convenience, in proximity to a great metropolitan area.

The newly constructed railroad granted easy access between the designed community and Manhattan, and the closeness of the Tarrytown project to the offices of Olmsted and Vaux allowed Olmsted to assume a leading role in shaping every aspect of Tarrytown Heights. In 1872 he wrote the prospectus extolling the virtues of residence in the community, and he edited other publications advertising Tarrytown Heights. His enthusiasm for the project led him to accept eighty shares in the development company as recompense for the work of his firm, this despite the losses suffered at Riverside as a result of a similar agreement. [5]

Staten Island

In July of 1870 Olmsted responded to expressions of concern by citizens of Staten Island and to the establishment by the New York state legislature of the Staten Island Improvement Commission by writing a letter to the editor of the *New York World*. Since the 1850s Olmsted had been a citizen of that community and knew its problems well. He believed the island had failed to grow because "its public works have been formed by citizens of the most unquestioned probity and common sense but utterly ignorant of and incompetent for the duties they have assumed." Staten Island, he said, needed professional help. He indicated his willingness to serve and called for the establishment of a commission to study ways to improve Staten Island.

Henry Hobson Richardson

One of the most innovative American architects of the late nineteenth century, Louisiana-born (1838) Henry Hobson Richardson grew up in New Orleans and, after graduating from Harvard College, studied at the École National des Beaux-Arts in Paris. In Paris and out of money at the outbreak of the Civil War, Richardson worked in France and learned French attitudes and discipline regarding rational and restrained planning.

When he returned to the United States, Richardson established himself as a competent designer with such works as Grace Church (1867) in West Medford, Massachusetts, and the State Asylum for the Insane (1871–1881) in Buffalo, New York. But in his later works, combining a Romanesque taste for massive and simple masonry with minutely conceived plans, Richardson showed genius. Trinity Church (1877) in Boston, Sever Hall (1878) at Harvard in Cambridge, Massachusetts, and the library in North Easton, Massachusetts, show Richardson to be well versed in European styles but strongly American in his use of materials and simplification of plan.

His monumental work — such as the demolished masterpiece, the Marshall Field Wholesale Store (1885–1887) in Chicago — influenced later architects, including Louis Sullivan and Frank Lloyd Wright. Richardson's death in 1886 at the early age of forty-seven is still reckoned to have been one of the great losses to American architecture. ❧

Within months a group of Staten Island businessmen approached Olmsted for further advice and, indeed, appointed a committee consisting of Olmsted, architect Henry Hobson Richardson, and public-health expert Dr. Elisha Harris, to prepare a plan for the island. The businessmen wanted to improve the still spottily populated suburb of New York by creating a better environment for people and by planning business opportunities based on recreation and exposition.

Olmsted immediately identified some of the conditions that impeded the island's progress: poor transportation connecting it to Manhattan, dismal roads joining the various communities of the island, and swamps that posed problems for health and sanitation. As chairman of the committee, Olmsted approached the project of planning for Staten Island with his usual systematic analysis of problems, and with his overriding philosophy of community and civilization.

While visiting bustling centers of commerce such as Albany (seen here), Olmsted came to recognize the importance of public spaces for informal gatherings.

The report he and his colleagues presented called for reaching "the hidden treasure" of the island through improvement in transportation, drainage of stagnant water from the swampy areas, and the cultivation of a suburb "furnished with urban public conveniences and associated with permanent and generally available advantages of landscape and sylvan beauty, all accessible with regularity and comfort from the business quarter of New York, and all preeminently healthful." [6]

In addition to setting forth a program to improve the infrastructure and living conditions of Staten Island, Olmsted and his committee urged careful administration of their plan and special attention to protect the still-rural island from greedy land speculators. But the plan languished as individual villages failed to agree and showed no inclination to work together, and as funds were never appropriated.

Albany

Frederick Law Olmsted worked on the landscaping of the New York state capitol in Albany, and on the Capitol of the United States in Washington, D.C., during the decades of 1870 and 1880. Both brought him again into abrasive situations with politicians, but the Albany capitol swept the hapless Olmsted into extensive and bitter controversy and caused him considerable personal anguish. While his wife in later years told his biographer that he had little responsibility for the project, "except [to] back the others, and arrange the jardinieres,"[7] he was deeply involved in the project. And regardless of how he or his wife remembered the events, Olmsted supported the plan that brought about a vicious controversy within the profession of architecture.

Begun in 1867 the new state capitol at Albany was designed by Thomas S. Fuller from Italian Renaissance inspiration. In fewer than ten years, the still-unfinished building had exceeded its original four-million-dollar budget by another million dollars.[8] Architecture critic Montgomery Schuyler could find no indication that the architects had attempted to design a coherent, functional building. It was a design, he said, that could only result in a "huddled and confused" structure based on "the wonderful wilderness of things into which it was meant to break out on top — rows of round dormers in metal, eight little copper-covered towers in the style of Sir Christopher Wren, Greek pediments, Louis XIV pavilions hung with cast iron festoons and crowned with iron balustrades, and crestings wherever they could be squeezed in."[9] If anything, Schuyler found the interior to be more of the same hodgepodge, with a similar disregard for order, utility, and beauty.

In an attempt to solve the design deficiencies and stanch the leaking budget, the legislature appointed a new commission to review the project and to steer it to completion. William Dorsheimer, now lieutenant governor, was named chairman. Dorsheimer, already familiar with the work of Olmsted and Henry Hobson Richardson and personally fond of the two men, named them, along with well-known New York architect Leopold Eidlitz, to serve as advisers to his commission.[10]

Olmsted knew Eidlitz from the architect's Academy of Music in Brooklyn and from his Produce Exchange and Continental Bank in Manhattan. With these and other works, Eidlitz had demonstrated his gift for monumentality and detail. Richardson, then working on Boston's Trinity Church, was widely regarded as highly talented and creative and as possessing the technical competence and artistry needed by the style he was promoting — a picturesque, energetic, and massive version of Romanesque.[11]

Richardson, moreover, was probably Olmsted's most compatible collaborator. When the two men first met, after the Civil War, Olmsted was delighted by Richardson's assertion that until a building was "in stone [and] beyond recovery" it should be regarded as in

Richard Upjohn

English-born (1802) Richard Upjohn moved to the United States in 1829. Devoutly Episcopalian, Upjohn devoted his architectural talents mostly to the design of churches, including New York's Trinity Church (1839– 1846), a leading example of the Gothic Revival style. His book, *Rural Architecture* (1852), extended his already considerable popularity as an architect of small rural churches, often constructed of wood. Upjohn also designed houses in a variety of eclectic styles. 🦋

a state of flux and that the architect should keep at hand his tracing paper and India rubber, along with his willingness to experiment, test, and throw away drawings. Olmsted, too, was a perfectionist who would work and rework designs on paper, then continue to change lines and masses and textures — even ideas — until the project was completed. Both men loved natural beauty as well as their work.[12] It was as if they had been destined to work together.

By the time Richardson and Olmsted were appointed to the advisory committee, they had collaborated on aspects of the Buffalo State Hospital and grounds and Niagara Square in Buffalo.[13] Olmsted, perhaps because of his history of managing large public programs, was the principal author of the report of the advisers, submitted in 1876. While they found no malfeasance lurking behind the cost overruns, they were of the strong opinion that the building had already cost more than it was worth and that it would not be a good building even if finished. The advisory board duly noted the problems plaguing the capitol: it was poorly sited; work had so far been badly supervised; its interior was flawed to favor inconvenience over utility; and its exterior was as vulgar as Schuyler had suggested.[14]

In their advisory capacity to the New York state legislature, Olmsted, Richardson, and Eidlitz recommended a bold move: leave the structure, but abandon the Italian Renaissance style and replace it with a new Romanesque exterior. In that pre-Sullivan-and-Wright period, architects more or less adhered to the canons of a known style, modifying details timidly if at all and thereby continuing the widely accepted idea that historical styles properly dictated all architecture. The American architect of the 1870s and 1880s was not an experimenter or seeker of new form and style; contrarily, he was the professional adherent and promulgator of established canons of good taste. Architects and critics of architecture buttered their daily bread with the lubricant of those canons. Such was the conventional wisdom of the age, and of the architects who designed for it.

Nonetheless, Olmsted, Richardson, and Eidlitz joined in the opinion that the building could not be completed; they proposed a radical treatment of the capitol in midconstruction, a change that called for the destruction of another architect's work and for a repudiation of it in the superseding plan. Only by such a treatment, they argued, could the capitol be imbued with clarity and dignity; only then could a piece of "bad" architecture be transmogrified into "good" architecture. Olmsted wrote Charles Eliot Norton that the capitol could only be salvaged by a radical change.[15] And there is nothing to suggest that he gainsaid the solutions designed by Richardson and Eidlitz to effect the changes recommended.[16]

Leading architects of the day — Richard Morris Hunt, James Renwick, and Richard Upjohn among them — quickly and vehemently took up arms against the proposal. It was outrageous, they contended, that one building combine two styles — especially Romanesque and something else, and especially when the prevailing styles of the day were Gothic and Renaissance! The attacks and counterattacks were fierce, with the opposition firing salvos unrelentingly at Richardson and Eidlitz.

In an unprecedented action, the New York chapter of the American Institute of Architects chastised the New York state legislature for defiling the work of one architect with that of others. The New York AIA loftily asserted that mixing Romanesque and Renaissance styles was bad architecture, a judgment that was also released to the press.[17] Richard-

Richard Morris Hunt

Richard Morris Hunt, born in 1827 in Brattleboro, Vermont, was the first American to attend the École National des Beaux-Arts. After studying and working in Europe from 1843 to 1854, Hunt returned to the United States to practice architecture. The Studio Building, on West Tenth Street in New York, was one of his first important commissions (1857) and became the site of his French-style atelier, where his students included George B. Post, Charles Gambrill, and Frank Furness.

Hunt's style embraced rational planning as well as eclectic historicizing and resulted in such modifications of French romantic architecture as the (demolished) Lenox Library (1869–1877) in New York City; the (demolished) Vanderbilt Mansion (1877) on upper Fifth Avenue; the Vanderbilt Marble House (1892–1895) and the Breakers (1890–1892) in Newport, Rhode Island; and Biltmore (1892–1896), near Asheville, North Carolina.

Hunt's administration building for the World's Columbian Exposition (1893) fostered the popularity of the academic classical style in American architecture. Among the finest examples of Beaux Arts style in America is the Fifth Avenue facade and Great Hall (1902) of the Metropolitan Museum of Art in New York, Hunt's last major work.

Hunt was one of the founding members of the American Institute of Architects in 1857.

son and Eidlitz, both members of the professional organization, felt wronged: they had been attacked, and they had been given no opportunity to present their side of the controversy. Olmsted, an honorary member of the chapter, did not feel the compulsion his colleagues did to remain silent. He wrote angrily to Hunt, protesting the chapter's statement, one that was "apparently intended and certainly adapted to destroy all confidence in our taste and professional judgment." [18] The chapter ignored Olmsted's complaint. Indeed chapter members published their statement in pamphlet form and disseminated it widely among architects in other areas of the country.

Hunt, abetted by architects George B. Post, Napoléon Le Brun, Henry Dudley, and Detlef Lienau, visited the Albany site and issued statements that appeared in a number of publications, including *American Architect and Building News*. They blasted Eidlitz and Richardson, saying that their plan was evidence of one of two things: either the original design was flawed and the building could not be completed in the Renaissance style in which it had been begun, or Richardson and Eidlitz were unable to meet the demands of designing in Renaissance style. To rebut their first proposition, the architects exhibited pictures of monumental European buildings in the Renaissance style as evidence, they argued, that style was not the problem. If Eidlitz and Richardson could not attain the professional competence required by the canons of Renaissance style, sniped the Hunt contingent, or if "their narrow-mindedness and blind devotion to a favorite style had led them to neglect all considerations of aesthetic propriety," they should resign. [19]

The architects' slugfest added to the legislature's confusion, a condition brought about, Olmsted judged, not so much by aesthetic sensibilities as by its inability to find patronage in the new program to build the capitol. Olmsted noted Dorsheimer's agreement with his assessment. The lieutenant governor, brushing aside the architects' shrill polemics about style, acknowledged that the politicians were unhappy "not because of our plans, that is only a pretext, not because of our administration that has been unprecedentedly economical and efficient and everybody knows it, but simply because no one thinks we have given him as much patronage as he ought to have." [20]

When the uproar subsided, the board's plan was accepted, and Richardson, Eidlitz, and Olmsted were charged with bringing building and grounds to satisfactory completion. By this time, Olmsted was deeply involved in and associated with every aspect of the project, the building as well as the grounds. [21]

When they began work on the new capitol in Albany, Eidlitz and Richardson divided the task, with Richardson redesigning the interior and exterior of the south section of the building and Eidlitz reworking the north side. Their division of labor gave Richardson the senate chamber and Eidlitz the assembly chamber and great tower. [22]

The legislature kept watch as Romanesque began to overcome Renaissance. When Eidlitz's north side was finished in Romanesque style, the legislators decided that, after all, they preferred the Renaissance fashion. Montgomery Schuyler wondered if the legislators could characterize Renaissance style and jested that they should be required to submit definitions of it along with their votes. Richardson's response suggests he may have agreed with Schuyler about the legislature's erudition. He completed the upper stories of the south facade in a freely interpreted version of already bastardized Renaissance style.[23]

Although still unfinished, the building opened officially in 1879. The *American Architect and Building News* summed up the effect: "[W]e have a work of vigor, individuality and artistic power which, in spite of a forced conformity to an original scheme that does not suit with it, and that involves many shortcomings in the final result, will give it a place of permanent honor."[24]

The Profession

The Albany project highlighted some of the major issues shaping the profession of architecture in America at that time and suggests some of the criteria for professional credentials that have subsequently been defined and accepted. Richard Upjohn had been one of the founders of the American Institute of Architects in 1857, and its first president. Keenly aware of defining and maintaining professional standards, he played an important role in Richard Morris Hunt's suit against a client, Dr. Eleazer Parmly, in 1861. Hunt sued Parmly for fees owed him for his part in designing Parmly's son-in-law's house, the T. P. Rossiter House, in New York. In the course of the trial, Upjohn was called to clarify a major professional concern: Is an architect paid by a client for his concepts, or does a client buy drawings representing those concepts?

Under court examination Upjohn, speaking as a leading architect and as the embodiment of professionalism in the field, stated that he charged a fee of 1 percent for preliminary sketches and insisted that clients return those sketches to him if they did not use them. To make his point Upjohn reminded the lawyer of his own professional practice: "You as a lawyer, when you give your opinion, do not charge for pen, ink and paper, but for your opinion."[25]

As practiced by Olmsted, landscape architecture, even less evolved as a profession than architecture, was almost entirely conceptual. He used drawings to enlighten clients, and he often deviated from the approved plans as he oversaw the planting and shaping of land. He had objected strenuously when his concepts for Central Park and other projects had been altered or violated or nearly vandalized by others, and he had insisted steadily that professional opinion was superior to amateur caprice.

The Albany experience could not have been a happy one for Frederick Law Olmsted. But it had few lasting consequences in Olmsted's life or in the field of architecture. When the dust settled and tempers cooled, Fuller was again cordial to Eidlitz and Richardson, and Olmsted later worked successfully with Hunt on the Biltmore Estate.

But in 1879 Olmsted listed for a client the architects with whom he would choose to collaborate: Richardson, Eidlitz; his old partner Vaux and his associates, Withers and Rad-

Born of work by several important architects, the Capitol had been slow to come into being. It was a mammoth building that required time, money, and skill to produce, and its progress was interrupted by the Civil War. Moreover, the building was begun before modern machinery made hauling and lifting easier. The columns for the dome, made of fluted cast iron, had to be pulled by horses and lifted into place on the building by teams of men.

ford; McKim Mead and Bigelow; and Farnsworth and Sullivan. Certainly aware of Hunt's reputation and his client list at the time, Olmsted omitted him from the list for reasons other than professional competency.[26]

Washington: The Grounds of the United States Capitol

Olmsted found work on the grounds of the Capitol building in Washington more challenging and more congenial than the Albany project.

From its planning and through its several phases of building, the Capitol had been well conceived and well executed. Dr. William Thornton, Benjamin Latrobe, Charles Bulfinch, Thomas U. Walter, and Edward Clark, all sensitive and adept architects, had given the

Capitol loving care and had seen to its construction and maintenance. But the grounds, under the minimal care of a gardening staff, had never been planned or systematically kept and replenished. After eighty years of semineglect, augmented by the ravages wrought by Washington's climate and traffic, the land surrounding the massive Capitol was nearly derelict. The soil itself was poor, dust under the sun but easily provoked into sticky mud

The Capitol dome required extensive scaffolding, as well as skilled labor.

by the slightest fall of rain. Natural growth included scrubby oaks and a bristly thatch of coarse weeds.[27]

In 1873 Vermont senator Justin Morrill, originator of the land-grant bill, acting in his official capacity as chairman of the Senate Committee on Public Grounds, turned to Olmsted for advice on the Capitol's recently extended grounds.

A year later, in 1874, Congress appropriated two hundred thousand dollars for improvement of the fifty-acre site, and Olmsted was appointed landscape architect to the United States Capitol. He had first seen the building in 1839 when he visited Washington with his father. With his eye for landscape and urban design, and his abiding interest in parks and green spaces in cities, he must have been aware of the sorry history of the Capitol grounds.

Shortly following George Washington's death, the grounds had been fenced and the perimeter circled by a carriageway. When the Capitol was burned in 1814, any improvements that had been made to the grounds were lost, and no effort was made to improve them throughout the period of its rebuilding. A wall and iron railing defined Capitol Square by 1820, establishing the site for landscaping. But, again, nothing was done to improve the grounds, and by 1826, according to the commissioner of public buildings, the area surrounding the Capitol was littered with shops and stores of materials.

The topography of the Capitol was all but ignored from the beginning. The architects as well as government officials anticipated the growth of the city to the east of the mighty building. The western quadrant of the site, a slope downward to the Tiber Creek, was largely ignored until Bulfinch decided to hide the exposed west basement wall behind a gentle and ample terrace. This architectural element not only provided a stunning view of the Potomac, but defined another guide for the design of the grounds. Between 1825 and 1840, John Foy's supervision of the grounds consisted mostly of laying out and planting rectangular flower beds, keeping walks cleared, and establishing a dense inner "fence" of closely planted shrubs and trees. The result was that of an inflated cottage garden, cheerful enough in good seasons, but without the cohesion of a rational design based on proper management of soil, appropriate planting, and systematic management.[28]

When summoned to Washington in the spring of 1873 to confer with Senator Morrill and architect of the Capitol Edward Clark, Olmsted must have seen the challenges of the site, just as he must have entertained doubts about undertaking a job of such proportions. Looking with a professional eye upon the pitiful results of the few efforts made to beautify the area, he recognized that bringing clarity and serenity to the fifty acres surrounding the Capitol would not be easy.[29] Moreover, he was a sick man, suffering from an eye ailment that made it impossible for him to write or draw by artificial light or to read comfortably, and plagued by chronic neurasthenia. He had already reorganized the routine of his office to accommodate his reduced productivity.[30]

But by March 1874, when Congress appropriated the funds for renovation of the grounds, Olmsted was well enough to accept the appointment.[31] Within a month, he visited the Capitol grounds twice and formed the strong opinion that the area should not be dealt with in isolation, but should be designed as part of an overall spatial scheme that stretched to the White House, and included such important government buildings as those for the Departments of State, Justice, Treasury, Agriculture, Navy, and War, and the Smithsonian Institution. Never one to plan on a small scale or to accept facets of a given situation as immutable, Olmsted sought to design Washington so as to draw the functions of government into a cohesive unit and to symbolize the *union* of the nation. He would

Olmsted was also commissioned to landscape the grounds of the Washington Monument. After $1.3 million and thirty-six years, the Washington Monument was finally completed in 1884. "It is George Washington's finger pointing to the sky," said British ambassador Cecil Spring-Rice of the 555-foot-tall stone monument. Olmsted believed that large expanses of green spaces in cities provided visual pleasure and, as in Washington, areas for formal displays of celebrations.

create for government a setting of grace and dignity; he would symbolize and actualize a "federal bond." [32]

Olmsted suggested that a committee of important American landscape architects — including H. W. S. Cleveland and William Hammond Hall — should be assembled to examine his proposal for the Capitol grounds, "it being one which in my judgment concerns the credit of the profession and the honor and dignity of the country." But Congress was not convinced and rejected Olmsted's big plans. He was to confine his efforts to the Capitol grounds, to undertake the project alone, to be paid fifteen hundred dollars for the design and compensated for his travel expenses; assistants hired to help prepare the design or to set stakes for surveying and making topographical maps would also be paid. [33]

Olmsted turned his attention to the aesthetic and utilitarian aspects of the acreage assigned to him and the goals set by Congress. In his mind, the first purpose of the grounds was to enhance the heroic Capitol building, to intensify its dignity and power, and to strengthen its symbolic portent. In order to facilitate the work that occurred within the great building, he calculated that he needed to lay out a total of forty-six pedestrian and carriage entrances to the grounds, contributing thereby to a proliferation of pavement. To overcome the heat of the pavement and the commotion of scurrying traffic, he planned to organize masses of shrubbery and trees to provide shade and a feeling of serenity and to offer cool respite from Washington's brutally hot summer days. He planned to use plants and trees that remained low and thick to allow the Capitol to rise above them visually from every angle. In the shady areas, he avoided hard-to-maintain grass and planted gently curving expanses of ground cover, again vegetation that would remain low and grow in lush thickness.[34]

No amount of planting, however, could overcome the fragmentation of the grounds caused by the numerous walkways and carriageways, the overwhelming intrusion of pavement. He might have solved the problem by resorting to a more formal, less verdant, style of design. But his political and philosophical values, as well as his aesthetic preferences, led him to his characteristic "natural" design.[35]

To support the lush growth and greenswards he desired to create on the Capitol grounds, Olmsted worked literally from the ground up. He attacked the flimsy soil by adding topsoil peeled from old gardens and vacant lots and tilling and harrowing wagonloads of street manure into the soil. He knew the budget. And he knew that he would exceed it. "I should hardly like the Ways and Means to know," he wrote his friend George Waring, who had worked on Central Park, "that I mean to have $60,000 spent for the improvement of the soil, but I don't see how a tolerable condition can be hoped for at much less cost than that, do you?"[36]

He also made certain that members of Congress would not have reason to assume the work was nearing completion, causing them to forgo additional appropriations. He informed the foremen who worked for him that no section of the ground was to be completed before winter and the end of the working season. "Besides the general objection that premature and incomplete finish always creates misconceptions and diminishes ultimate popularity," he wrote, "the more chaotic the ground looks until the rougher preliminary and foundation work is out of the way, the better it will be thought of and the less will be the loss through damage and misuse of the final surfaces."[37]

By late 1874, Olmsted was pleased with the progress being made on the project and reported to the public by means of a letter published in the *New York Tribune*. He described the sweeping away of old and inferior aspects of the space, the removal of old pipes for sewer, gas, and water, the laying of new systems for utilities and drainage of the land; he noted work on gutters and curbs, the removal of old trees and the planting of new ones, and the foundations being laid for walks and roads. At that point, he told the public, work had not begun on the west side, but a plan was under way and soon to be submitted.[38]

The western slope, the approach to the Capitol from the Mall, was not likely to submit to a design solely of lawn, shrubbery, trees, and ground cover. Olmsted invented an expansive marble terrace wrapping the north, west, and south sides of the building, which was reached from the west by a double flight of steps. The architectural addition would give the Capitol a more substantial base to balance the visual weight of the recently enlarged dome and would yield an overall grandeur to the building.[39]

Congress accepted Olmsted's architectural concept, but did not include appropriations for it in the 1875 budget. Money to build the terrace was not appropriated until 1884, but before construction could commence Senator Henry L. Dawes of Massachusetts suggested changes in the plan. He proposed piercing the walls of the terrace with windows to allow use of the interior space created by the large addition. Olmsted, offended by the senator's tampering with his design, secured help from his friend Richardson in organizing opposition to Dawes's proposal and in stressing that the intrusion of windows would destroy the unity of the design. Congress compromised: windows were admitted to the west side between the stairs.[40]

Over the years, Olmsted made frequent trips to Washington to consult with the men he had hired to carry out his plans, from whom he also received regular reports. While he considered work on the grounds of the Capitol to be his most important project by 1879, his attention was shifting toward efforts to restore the natural beauty around Niagara Falls.[41]

Niagara

In 1857 Frederick Edwin Church's heroic painting *Niagara Falls* [42] attracted considerable attention on both sides of the Atlantic. About a decade later, Calvert Vaux heard the artist lecture to the Century Club on the impending ruin of the scenery around the falls. Church's lecture further spurred discussion that had been growing slowly since 1834 when Reverend Andrew Reed and Reverend Thomas Mattheson, two Scottish ministers, visited Niagara Falls and made the then-unprecedented suggestion that the great scenic vista "should be deemed the property of civilized mankind; and nothing should be allowed to weaken their efficacy on the tastes, the morals, and the enjoyment of all mankind." [43]

Frederick Law Olmsted, during a visit to his uncle in Geneseo, had also visited the falls in 1834. Forty-five years later Olmsted, having earned distinction in the field of landscape architecture, was as awed by Niagara Falls as he had been when he was a boy. He responded to "[a]ll [the] distinctive qualities, the great variety of the indigenous perennials and annuals, the rare beauty of the old woods, and the exceeding loveliness of the rock foliage" on Goat Island, which he believed to be "a direct effect of the Falls, and as much a part of its majesty as the mist-cloud and the rainbow."[44]

But, like Church, Olmsted was dismayed by the hucksters and signs, icehouses and hotels, fences and gatekeepers that packed the banks of the river, preventing serene contemplation of the falls. Vast numbers of nineteenth-century Americans had been visiting Niagara Falls for years, their presence and money spawning some of the major threats to the beauty of the surrounding area. Businessmen, quick to capture the great power generated by the river for their mills, contributed further to the creeping ruin around the falls. By 1860, Americans were admitted to the few places from which the falls could be observed only after paying a fee.[45]

Since his initial visit to Niagara, Olmsted had been awed by Yosemite and had come to consider that his professional duty as a landscape architect was to protect the natural environment; he had developed his own ideas, parallel to those of the Scottish ministers, about government conservation of natural beauty. Neither Yosemite nor Niagara should be prostituted by the greed and commercial interests of a few, but should be protected and preserved in a natural state, to provoke feelings of wonder and spirituality in many people. To Olmsted's way of thinking, the government had an obligation to reserve such properties and, further, to educate citizens to full appreciation of them.

Olmsted had argued passionately for government management to perpetuate the natural state of Yosemite, becoming recognized as an ardent spokesperson for himself as well as the group of influential men around him who were advocating the reservation of scenic grandeur under federal auspices. Samuel Bowles heard Olmsted deliver his plan for Yosemite in 1865 and was inspired to write about the importance of nature as part of his observations throughout his travels. When he returned to western Massachusetts, where he edited and published the *Springfield Republican*, Bowles promoted the concept of reservations such as those at Yosemite and the Mariposa Big Tree Grove and urged that similar programs be created for Niagara Falls and the Adirondacks.[46]

Olmsted solicited the interest of other influential friends as well, including Richardson. During their work together in Buffalo, the two men and their wives vacationed at Niagara Falls in August 1869. Olmsted carefully arranged to take his friend and collaborator on a long, meandering carriage ride on the first day of their stay at the resort. They relaxed and talked, but did not see the falls. The next day, however, Olmsted thought Richardson sufficiently relaxed and mentally removed from his urban cares to view the great falls. Only through such gradual preparation, Olmsted insisted, had Richardson "caught the idea of throwing curiosity aside and avoiding amazement, and was willing to sit for hours in one place contemplatively enjoying the beauty, saying little of what was before us . . . but taking quiet pleasure and laying up pleasure." [47]

And that, to Olmsted, was the point of preserving nature. In a pamphlet he wrote several years later, he summarized his philosophy: "I felt the charm of the Yosemite much more at the end of a week than at the end of a day, much more after six weeks when the cascades were nearly dry, than after one week, and when, after having been in it, off and on, several months, I was going out, I said, 'I have not yet half taken it in.' " [48]

Frederick Edwin Church

Born in Hartford, Connecticut, in 1826, Frederick Edwin Church became one of the most important members of the Hudson River school of painting. After studying with Thomas Cole (1844–1848), Church combined his interest in art with his passion for scientific observation, often using multiple perspectives to dramatize panoramic views of monumental vistas.

In expeditions to Colombia and Ecuador in 1853 and 1857, Church found dramatic and exotic subjects in jungles, waterfalls, and volcanoes. Such paintings as *Heart of the Andes* and *Niagara Falls* drew crowds in New York and in Europe.

In 1867, while visiting Europe and the Near East, Church sketched Mediterranean landscapes and ruins, producing a series of lively, intense small pieces that evoke the grandeur of his earlier and larger masterworks.

During the last twenty-three years of his life, his right hand crippled by arthritis, Church worked very little but lavished attention on creating his estate, Olana, near Hudson, New York. He died in 1900. ❧

During the Niagara vacation, Dorsheimer joined Olmsted and Richardson, and the three men explored the riverbank on the American side, visited Goat Island above the falls, and speculated together on what might be done to improve the area. Olmsted's plan was unfolding to his satisfaction; the next phase brought Vaux and several others into their discussions the next day. Although Olmsted and his friends continued to discuss the need to improve the riverbanks and to protect the scenery around Niagara Falls, they took no action.[49]

It was not until the end of 1878 that the campaign to save the falls began. Presumably at the instigation of Church, the governor-general of Canada took the lead.[50] Evidently Olmsted had not known of Church's concern for the falls and had not heard his lecture at the Century Club. It is possible, too, that the governor-general, Lord Dufferin, may have arrived at his concern independently.[51]

Lord Dufferin shared his concern with New York governor Lucius Robinson shortly before September 1878, when he broached the subject in a speech to the Ontario Society of Artists. He suggested that Ontario and New York join forces to develop an international park around Niagara Falls. He insisted that it should not "be desecrated, or in any way sophisticated, by the puny efforts of the art of the landscape gardener, but must be carefully preserved in the picturesque and unvulgarized condition in which it was originally laid out by the hand of Nature." [52]

In response to Lord Dufferin's proposal, Governor Robinson recommended to the New York legislature in January 1879 that a commission be appointed to work with Canadian representatives in the formation of a plan to protect Niagara. The commissioners of the New York State Geological Survey were then directed to undertake the assignment, a fortuitous circumstance for Olmsted. He knew several of the commissioners, among them Dorsheimer, George Geddes, and Frederick A. P. Barnard, president of Columbia College. Moreover, the State Survey Commission was headed by James T. Gardiner, who mapped Yosemite in 1865 with his partner, Clarence King. The commissioners turned naturally to Olmsted for advice he was well prepared to offer.[53] After his first visit with Gardiner to Niagara, in May 1879, Olmsted wrote Norton, "The general outlines of a scheme which I presented was fully approved by all." [54]

The principles of landscape architecture that Olmsted articulated for the group proved to be the smaller portion of his contribution to the project. The enlightened and progressive New Yorkers and Canadians agreed on the need to restore the riverbanks to a pristine state and to preserve the natural qualities of the site. They agreed that the park should include strips of land on either side of the river for planting and development of walkways and carriageways, and that it should include the islands above the falls and extend to a bridge below the falls.

Financing the project, however, would be difficult and would necessitate appropriations from the governments of Canada and New York State. When the commissioners decided to enlist the support of "weighty names," Olmsted took the lead. With help from Dorsheimer, Charles Eliot Norton, and Church, as well as others, he directed the collection of signatures of influential men from several countries. By March 1880, Olmsted and his colleagues presented a report endorsed by more than seven hundred people, including all the justices of the United States Supreme Court.[55]

In the interim, however, New York had elected a new governor, Alonzo Cornell, who did not share the sentiments of the commissioners. In their report they had contended that contemplation of the beauty and grandeur of Niagara would "draw together men of all races, and thus contribute to the union and peace of nations." [56] Cornell saw the plans for the park only in terms of its drain on the state coffers.

The great natural wonder Niagara Falls exists on the boundary of the United States and Canada. Goat Island separates American Falls and Horseshoe Falls (on the Canadian side). Discovered by Father Louis Hennepin in 1678, the scenic marvel became a major tourist attraction in the nineteenth century, and its hydropower was harnessed in 1882 and used to light the streets of Niagara Falls, New York.

Abetted by H. H. Richardson, Olmsted and leading businessmen of the day strove to have the scenic beauty of the falls protected by means of government creation and management of a park.

Faced with Cornell's "contemptuous opposition," Olmsted realized that the state of New York was unlikely to protect the falls. Moreover, matters on the Canadian side of the border were equally unpromising. In order to overcome public apathy and to prod government officials to take action, Olmsted and Norton again joined forces to organize a publicity campaign on behalf of the preservation proposal. Olmsted put forward a copy of the report he had prepared on Yosemite that Ashburner had suppressed; Norton thought that it stated the case for Niagara in principle; and Olmsted and Norton recast the Yosemite report as the rationale for saving Niagara.

But in order to reach a large segment of the public, the men decided to follow an initial attention-getting newspaper story with a series of articles, to keep the issues simple and alive, and to build public sentiment. In the spring of 1880 the *Springfield Republican* and the *Boston Advertiser* published letters supporting the project, but they were soon followed by the fierce editorial opposition of the *Niagara Falls Gazette* and proprietors of a big wood-pulp mill operating on the river shore.[57]

As the price of riverbank land increased, the likelihood of legislative action decreased. Norton and Olmsted maintained their campaign. When the bankers' convention met at the falls in the summer of 1881, they approved a statement prepared by Norton and Olmsted endorsing the park plan. Immediately after that gain for their side, Olmsted and Norton commissioned two gifted young men — Henry Norman, a young Englishman recently graduated from Harvard, and Jonathan Baxter Harrison, a Unitarian minister who had become a journalist — to visit the falls and write a series of articles for New York, Boston, and Buffalo papers. Under steady supervision from Olmsted, the journalists succeeded; after wide publication throughout the country, their articles and letters were collected and published in pamphlet form, which also was distributed broadly.[58]

By 1882, the men working to create an international park around the falls, Olmsted and Norton among them, no longer believed that plan possible. They decided to concentrate their efforts on persuading New York State to buy land on its side of the river for a state reservation. In 1883, at Olmsted's instigation, supporters of the Niagara reservation movement met in New York City and formed the Niagara Falls Association. The new organization charged Harrison with a renewed campaign of letters, articles, pamphlets, and petitions. The information blitz soon roused public opinion throughout New York State, influencing the assembly and the senate to pass the Niagara bill in 1883. Grover Cleveland, then governor of New York, appointed one of his chief advisers, Dorsheimer, as president of the Niagara Commission.[59] The grounds of what would become the park opened officially to the public in July 1885.[60]

In the campaign for the preservation of Niagara, Olmsted displayed his passion for preservation, as well as his daunting skill as an organizing force behind a public relations campaign. Harrison, having served as Olmsted's lieutenant in the campaign, understood the older man's contribution to the success of Niagara. "Success was obtained by the co-operation of multitudes," he pointed out, "but the indispensable factor was Mr. Frederick Law Olmsted's thought. He was the real source, as he was the true director, of the movement, and but for him, there would be no State Reservation at Niagara today." [61]

Olmsted had not finished his work for Niagara, however. In 1886, he and Vaux — despite efforts on the part of Olmsted's old enemy Andrew Haswell Green to prevent it — were commissioned to plan the layout and planting of the state reservation. [62] In 1887 they reported that, in planning for large crowds of visitors, they had accepted the need for shelters, picnic facilities, and other artificial constructions, recognized the need to restore eroded areas, but had rejected anything of "an artificial character . . . on the property, no matter how valuable it might be under other circumstances and no matter for how little cost it may be had: their design had one purpose alone: "the provision of necessary conditions for making the enjoyment of the natural scenery available." [63]

Olmsted and Vaux were no more friendly toward fancy gardening than they had been when they designed Central and Prospect Parks or when Olmsted argued for the conservation of Yosemite and the Mariposa Big Tree Grove in their pristine natural state. They resisted changes in their plan that would have placed a fancy restaurant on Goat Island or made it possible for visitors to view the falls without leaving their carriages — features more consonant with an urban than a rural experience. Intent on heightening the natural character surrounding Niagara, the partners insisted that the special leisure experience offered by the park could best be experienced by pedestrians. A deeply spiritual experience in nature, they believed, should not be diluted by the presence of commercial enterprises or intrusive carriage traffic. [64]

The "Unpractical" Man

When Frederick Law Olmsted returned to New York to resume his partnership with Calvert Vaux, he had spent the first four decades of his life largely supported by his father as he plunged into a series of high and low adventures, each of which received his intense concentration and commitment for a brief period. Entering his middle years, Olmsted was zestful but not robust, physically small, frail, and nervous. He had amassed varied experiences, but had not found a vocation farming in poor conditions on the Connecticut shore or gentlemanly farming on Staten Island. He had cut a fine figure at *Putnam's Magazine* and in the literary world of Manhattan, walked through the English countryside and pondered nature, class, and the rudiments of social engineering.

He had explored the southern country and the meanness of slavery, designed and managed America's first large urban park, and administered volunteers in the context of governmental bureaucracy. He had tried his hand among the "careful capitalists" he admired and tried to wrest profit from a failing gold mine on the California frontier.

His return to New York did not end his penchant for adventure, but it forced him to consider economic, social, and professional reality. In his midforties, with a wife and children, he had to earn a living, and he wanted to do so in an occupation that would bring him the attention and respect — as well as power and wealth — that he desired. His curriculum vitae included praise for his writing and for his administration of Central Park, the Sanitary Commission, and Mariposa; it also included a record of overworking to near collapse, temperamental displays when he did not get his own way, and erratic dealings with subordinates and superiors. Neither the Olmsted Papers — collected, saved, and given to the Library of Congress by his family — nor his biographers provide a full and clear view of the man's complicated personality or the roots of his egotism and muleheadedness. Olmsted's letters to friends like Charles Loring Brace and to his family are dotted with glimpses of his ambition and impatience with disagreement, as well as his generosity of spirit and intelligence. But while it is evident that his association with Vaux was not always smooth, the full story of their partnership has eluded Olmsted's biographers. Similarly, his emphasis in his papers on the importance of domesticity overshadows the faint references to his own and his children's emotional turmoil.

A self-designated "unpractical man," Olmsted filled his years in New York with a heavy burden of work and the compensatory pleasures of domesticity. Unable to transpose to New York the grand style of life he and his family had enjoyed in California, he nonetheless continued to stress the importance of home life and family and of his loving but authoritarian role in rearing and educating the children.

After living in expensive rooming houses and briefly at the Staten Island farm (then officially owned by John's children and under the care of hired managers), Olmsted and his family settled in a town house in Manhattan, where the household was organized around Olmsted's work, intermingling the affairs of his office with the daily activities of Mary and the children. Marriage and fatherhood undergirded Olmsted's sense of himself, his position in society, and his thinking about civilization.

This was due in part to his relationship with his father, a patient, self-effacing, and supportive man. After his return to New York, Frederick found frequent opportunities to travel through Hartford and stop for a visit with John Olmsted and his family in their house on Asylum Street. As John aged, Frederick and his half brothers quietly assumed greater responsibility for Mary Ann.

Shortly after Christmas, 1872, John Olmsted arranged a meeting with Frederick and his half-brother Albert Henry. In his usual orderly and meticulous manner, the old man explained his business affairs and instructed his sons as to the handling of his estate. "All with great cheerfulness, kindliness, and some pleasantry," Olmsted told Frederick Kingsbury, a friend from his youth, "I felt the greatest respect for his character, meek, dignified & sagacious." [1]

In January 1873 Olmsted received news that John had fallen and broken his hip and that he was ill, rushed to Hartford, and, satisfied that John was resting well, returned to his work in New York. The next day, however, Alfred summoned him to Hartford. Olmsted sat with his dying father until the old man woke and demanded, "Air — give me all the air you can!" With that, John Olmsted died on January 25, 1873.

"He was a very good man and a kinder father never lived," Olmsted told Kingsbury. "It is strange how much of the world I feel has gone from me with him. The value of my success in the future is gone from me." [2]

Olmsted's attention to his children owed much to the example John had set as a father. In answering a letter about Sabbatarianism from Kingsbury, Olmsted railed against that bit of piety but also described the joys he found in his family. Olmsted had no use for the strict Puritan Sundays practiced by childhood neighbors in Hartford, he hotly told Kingsbury, and still remembered them with anger and indignation. He was outraged, he said, at the suggestion that laws might now be passed to inflict such deprivations on the population at large. "I realize with some difficulty that you still remain essentially in a position from which I have drifted so far," he wrote. "I am in the ranks of the 'enemies of the Sabbath' fully and unreservedly." In fact, he continued, providing a picture of his home life:

[I make] no distinction between holy and unholy work — secular and sacred. I recognize nothing of the kind. I undoubtedly greatly overwork myself . . . [But] I do try to get a little more rest also on Sundays of a certain kind, but it is mainly antiSabbatarian rest. I lie longer in bed, I am longer in dressing, I am longer at breakfast. . . . I read two Sunday newspapers. I smoke after breakfast as I usually do not. Being on the coast and near shipping I reciprocate their courtesy, and pay the day the compliment of hoisting my ensign or seeing that the children do it. I play with the children more. Generally late in the day I go out with some of them — in summer we go rowing — sometimes drive back in the island — go to the Brewery and I treat them to a sangaree or a little beer; in winter I have been to the skating ponds with them. My wife generally goes with us. She has often been — at least more than once or twice — to the brewery. Sometimes we go picnicking either by boat to the Long Island shore or to the high woods by wheels. I wish these excursions were more frequent, but I rarely get through or get too tired to go on further with my work till near sunset, and it is too late for anything but a row. I have taken the boys to a beer Garden concert. I never took them to a church. . . . Mary and the other ones play cards, I never had head for cards. . . . I should be very angry with

William Marcy Tweed

As the Democratic boss of New York City, Tweed (1823–1878) ran one of the most corrupt political machines in American history. A bookkeeper who became a foreman of a volunteer fire company in the 1850s, Tweed mastered the systems of political patronage and kickback as he negotiated himself up the power ladder. Allied with the corrupt political organization Tammany Hall, he served as alderman (1851–1855), U.S. representative (1853–1855), and a member of the board of supervisors and school commission (1856). Until 1861, Tweed and his cronies controlled and corrupted Tammany Hall and New York City government.

Elected to the state senate in 1868, Tweed and his ring began to acquire power in New York State politics. During his years of ascension in political ranks, Tweed amassed a fortune, estimated to be at least $2.5 million in 1871. In addition to a personal fortune acquired through theft and influence peddling, Tweed and his protégés are believed to have stolen from $40 million to $200 million in public funds.

Newspaper stories in 1870 about Tweed's dishonesty led to the investigation of Tammany Hall and conviction of Tweed in 1873 of fraud. In 1875 he escaped prison and fled to Spain, but was returned to New York, where he died in jail. ✿

the man or men who prevented me from having my newspapers, my boat, my conveyances, my wine or my cigar or my Robinson Crusoe. If the Times should drop its Sunday edition, I should drop the Times, as I should drop my cook if she dropped my Sunday breakfast.[3]

But domesticity for Olmsted was simply the first step toward civilization. Driven also by passion for social reform and for shaping American civilization in accordance with his values, Olmsted spoke out on issues and took an active role in effecting change. He had criticized the rigid grid pattern of New York as conducive to tenements and had advocated intelligent urban design as a method of improving society. He had visibly opposed the Tweed Ring and its impact on Central Park, had worked on relief committees to aid the South during Reconstruction, and had fought to instill liberal and humanitarian goals in the Republican Party. While he may have been an "unpractical man," Olmsted was never apolitical, and while he had not run for elective office, he had a background in civil service. With the disintegration of Tweed's power in 1871, Olmsted served as president of the Board of Commissioners of the Department of Public Parks and as a member of the Board of Audit and Apportionment.

Olmsted's political and reformist actions were in part outward manifestations of his inner convictions regarding civilization, but they also indicated the degree to which he wanted recognition for his philosophy of civilization. The Republican Party, embroiled in turmoil surrounding its role and purpose in the rapidly changing and industrializing post–Civil War country, splintered in 1872. A group of "liberal" voters, unhappy with Grant and impatient for social change, proposed Olmsted as candidate for the vice presidency. To many who knew him, Olmsted seemed an obvious — if not altogether willing — candidate for political office. But in 1920 Mary Olmsted recollected that

> *the Fifth Avenue Convention nominated Groesbeck of Ohio for President . . . [and] Mr. Olmsted for Vice-President. When Mr. Olmsted heard of it, he hid, so that when the reporters came . . . Mr. Olmsted was nowhere to be found. The "Nation" was much amused at the incident but Mr. Olmsted's friends kept the matter rather quiet because it made him [he thought] ridiculous.*[4]

The park maker may not have sought public office or been willing to serve if elected, but he was deeply interested in the political life of the country and mightily offended at the nomination of Horace Greeley to oppose Grant in 1872. During the Civil War, Olmsted had been impressed by Grant. Later, and only reluctantly, he had acknowledged the corruption that surrounded President Grant. Even so, Olmsted insisted to Samuel Bowles, Grant was a superior man to Greeley. "A thousand years of Grant, say I, before one minute of Greeley." Olmsted characterized Greeley as an impostor — a man who masked his sophistry with the persona of a simple farmer, affected disinterestedness in his appearance when he was actually a "fop," and pretended to be a man of the people when he was driven by ambition for glory and power. "I know [Greeley] is an imposter, Olmsted fumed to Bowles. "You knew he was an imposter before you went to Cincinnati . . . but now you soberly ask me to help him impose on the country. If I do I'm damned. If all the world went for him and I stood all alone it would be the unforgivable sin to my moral nature to have any patience with such an outrage to it. . . . When such a man can have the countenance of such a man as Sam Bowles in asking to be made President of the United States it is the darkest day I have known. Bull Run was bright to it . . . am I mad, or are you?"[5]

Sympathetic to Greeley's strong antislavery sentiments, contribution to the founding of the Republican Party, and long-standing progressive journalism, Bowles all but ignored Olmsted's attack on the man he supported. "You are certainly laying yourself open to suspicions of having positive views on the subject," tempered Bowles. "I am not so terribly earnest on the other side as to feel inspired to wrestle with you in behalf of brother Greeley." Then he added in a jocular vein, "Clearly you need the cooling presence of the country. Come out here, and we will figure out Greeley's defeat, and the country's salvation on my back piazza."[6] Bowles wrote from Springfield, Massachusetts, where he led his influential newspaper in opposition to Grant and his corrupt cronies.

Despite their conflicting political views, Olmsted found Bowles a good friend. In seeking refuge from the stress (however self-imposed) of his work, he confided to Bowles that

Horace Greeley

On the hundredth anniversary of his birth on February 3, 1811, Horace Greeley was lauded by the *New York World* as "probably the greatest political force this country has ever known except Thomas Jefferson." The son of a poor family in New Hampshire, fifteen-year-old Greeley was apprenticed to a printer in Putney, Vermont. Self-educated, he developed a passion for politics and social reform. In 1831 he went to New York to work as a printer; ten years later he founded the *Tribune* and dedicated it to airing differing opinions, covering important news, and reaching Americans throughout the country. "Uncle Horace's" paper soon became popular in rural America.

Greeley's mosaic of causes — all presented forcefully — included promoting equality for women in education and employment while opposing women's suffrage and liberalized divorce laws. With similar inconsistency he wrote with equal conviction in support of agrarianism and industrialization; free trade and protective tariffs. His targets for denunciation, however, were clearer, including monopolies, liquor, tobacco, capital punishment, the theater, and slavery. He exerted considerable influence before and during the Civil War.

A founder of the Republican Party, Greeley was a delegate to the 1860 convention and was instrumental in securing the nomination of Abraham Lincoln. During the Civil War, Greeley often criticized Lincoln and, through the *Tribune*, took a number of unpopular viewpoints. During the 1863 draft riots, mobs stoned the newspaper's building.

At the end of the Civil War, Greeley supported universal amnesty and male suffrage as the cornerstones of Reconstruction and personally contributed to bail for the release of Confederate president Jefferson Davis.

Greeley's leadership of the *Tribune* fostered the talents of journalists and editors such as Charles A. Dana, Margaret Fuller, Bayard Taylor, Henry J. Raymond, George Ripley, Albert Brisbane, Carl Schurz, John Hay, Whitelaw Reid, Henry James, and Charles T. Congdon; for a time the paper published articles by London resident Karl Marx.

Greeley's political life brought him less success than he sought. He rarely won an election, but served in Congress to fill a vacancy (1848–1849); twice ran unsuccessfully for the Senate (1860 and 1866); and twice for the House (1866 and 1870). In 1872, bitterly opposing President Grant's corrupt administration, Greeley led a splinter group from his old party to help found the Liberal Republican Party, becoming its nominee for president. Although endorsed by the Democrats, Greeley was resoundingly beaten, winning only six states to Grant's thirty-one.

Physically and mentally exhausted from the campaign and from nursing his sick wife who died just before the election, Greeley's health broke; he became deranged, and died at the end of November 1872.

---

he was tired, ill, worried about money, and unhappy in his partnership with Vaux. Bowles urged Olmsted to sever the relationship with Vaux and establish himself as a consultant.[7]

"You write in view of one horn of my dilemma," Olmsted answered. "I must have more assistance and even if there were no ties of sentiment and obligation I have not courage enough left to dispense with Vaux's cooperation. I feel myself so nearly desperate that I have to school myself against the danger of some mildly foolish undertaking — such as putting all I can together in a farm, cutting the world and devoting myself to asceticism.

But against extreme lunacy in this way my wife makes a pretty strong bar. But I say to my-self ten times a day that I positively must find some way of living in the country and es-caping this drive. I cannot live another year under it."

Bowles encouraged Olmsted to chuck the fetters of the city and join him in the tran-quillity of the Connecticut River valley. He offered to sell his farm in Massachusetts to Olmsted.

By the end of the seventies, his work for Central Park apparently ended, Olmsted was often tired and frustrated. He and his associates had more work than they could do, and it fell to him to maintain contact with clients and direct supervision of as many projects as possible. Moreover, his family responsibilities were enormous. All of his children — three stepchildren and two of his own — were still dependent on him. Seventeen-year-old Mar-ion focused her energies largely on her devotion to her father; Owen, twenty-two and a recent graduate of Yale, had resisted entering his father's business and, instead, gone west to become a rancher; and twenty-four-year-old Charlotte, recently married and living nearby, had begun to exhibit symptoms of severe mental illness. At twenty-six years of age, John was only beginning to leave behind years of rebellion against his stepfather and to settle into Olmsted's business. "Take good care of your father," Mary wrote to John from Cambridge in the summer of 1879, "and don't contradict him; he is not such a fool as you think him!" [8]

Although Olmsted had taken John into the business and was learning to depend on him for routine management of the office, his adoring attention was fixed on Frederick Law Olmsted Jr. Named Henry at birth, called Boy until he was about four years old, the child's name had been legally changed, and his father had determined that his son would carry both his name and profession into the future. Called Rick, he was not yet ten years old, but was the center of the family's attention and the brightest star on his father's horizon.

Stanford

In the 1880s Olmsted's office faced a mountain of work, including public, private, and institutional grounds such as Easton's Beach and the Frederick Vanderbilt place at New-port; Lawrenceville School, at Princeton, New Jersey; a series of parks for Rochester, New York; and Downing Park in Newburgh, New York, a work commemorating the man Olm-sted and Vaux regarded as mentor and colleague. [9]

Toward the middle of Olmsted's seventh decade, in 1886, Senator and Mrs. Leland Stanford hired him to lay out the grounds of a college. During the Civil War Stanford had served as Republican governor of California and had kept that state in the Union. He ac-

Leland Stanford

Born in Watervliet, New York, in 1824, Leland Stanford read law and was admitted to the bar in 1848. He practiced in Wisconsin, then went west to join his five brothers. After establishing himself as a merchant in California, he served as Republican governor of that state (1861–1863) and United States senator (1885–1893).

In 1861 Stanford and his partners started the Central Pacific Railroad; in 1870 he founded the Southern Pacific Railroad. With a grant of twenty million dollars in 1885, Stanford created Stanford University. He died in 1893. ❦

cumulated wealth as a railroad builder, first as a founder of the Central Pacific and then president of the Southern Pacific, and continued his political career as a United States senator (1885–1893).

Intending to commemorate their young son who had recently died in Europe, the Stanfords envisioned a New England–style campus. Stanford University was to grow on a seven-thousand-acre site in the San Jose Valley, near the Menlo Park home of its founders, about thirty miles south of San Francisco. In their minds, a college campus consisted of broad green quadrangles, Georgian buildings of red brick with white wooden trim, verdant lawns, and venerable trees. But Olmsted had other ideas for a campus in California. He was familiar with the arid landscape and the climate that differed markedly from that of his native New England. Olmsted advised the Stanfords instead to be guided by the architecture and landscape of the Mediterranean countries.

After Richardson's death, his firm had been succeeded by Shepley, Rutan and Coolidge, a group of architects. Hired by the Stanfords to design the buildings for the college, they proposed a style of architecture consonant with Olmsted's approach to the site. When the designers began work on plans for Stanford University, they faced a vast rural setting. Olmsted saw it — as he had seen Berkeley earlier — as an opportunity to create a coherent community of teachers and learners, a microcosm of civilization. Combining California mission and Mediterranean Romanesque with Richardson's attitudes about mass and detail, they presented plans for low buildings arranged around quadrangles and connected by shade-providing arcades. Olmsted spread wide his search for suitable plants, acquiring specimens from Spain and the North African coast, and creating an overall landscape that would survive the dry season of California.

For a landscape architect who had propounded the virtues of the English style of garden design, the Stanford campus was not only a bold departure in style but evidence of Olmsted's creative ability to meet the requirements of a given situation. He was flexible. He could change his materials without compromising an overall philosophy of design.

Olmsted's young partner Henry Sargent Codman, a nephew of Charles Sprague Sargent, had brought the Stanford project to the office and prodded Olmsted to set a fee of ten thousand dollars for the preliminary plan. Olmsted hesitated to ask for such a grand amount, but then followed his younger colleague's advice. Governor Stanford agreed without argument.[10]

Veteran of the Mariposa Estate, Olmsted knew the importance and scarcity of water in California. Governor Stanford, he realized, was less convinced of the significance of that fact. "I find Governor Stanford," Olmsted griped mildly in a letter to his young partner Charles Eliot,

> bent on giving his university New England scenery, New England trees and turf, to be obtained only by lavish use of water. The landscape of the region is said to be fine in its way, but nobody thinks of anything in gardening that will not be thoroughly unnatural to it. What can be done I don't know, but it will be an interesting subject of study.[11]

Late in August of 1886, Olmsted, his son Frederick, and Henry Codman headed for California. Traveling via Minneapolis, they called on H. W. S. Cleveland, who was supervising the city's parks. Olmsted viewed the parks with Cleveland and the head of the park commission and, rather than writing a critique in response to the latter's request for his opinion, offered advice on the role of the commissioners in park development and maintenance. It was the duty of men entrusted with parks to create rural scenery in urban settings. All else, he insisted, was subordinate to this goal. Perhaps recalling his own suffering at the hands of Green and other New York park commissioners, Olmsted also indicated that the commissioners were fortunate to be guided by "so experienced and so excellent a professional counselor" as Mr. Cleveland.[12]

From Minneapolis the travelers made their way to Portland by rail, caught a stagecoach for their journey to San Francisco, and completed their trip with yet another rail trip and another by stage. At the end of their long and tiring journey, they joined Senator Stanford in his Menlo Park residence. The senator had also invited General Francis A. Walker, president of the Massachusetts Institute of Technology, to advise him on building the proposed college. Charles A. Coolidge, a young architect from the firm Shepley, Rutan and Coolidge, was there to get the architectural commission for his group.[13]

Stanford's site for the university included a large expanse of flat land with a gentle rise into foothills.[14] As Olmsted and Coolidge examined the site, becoming familiar with the topography as well as the vegetation — oak trees on the lowlands, forests with sturdy conifers on the higher ground — Olmsted recommended that Coolidge place the buildings on the higher planes. But Senator Stanford had other ideas. He remembered young Leland's joy in riding over the plain, and there, he insisted, was where the buildings should rise to memorialize his son who died just a few months short of his sixteenth birthday.

Olmsted set aside his preferences in deference to Stanford's feelings and notified John, then managing the firm's office in Brookline, that the site had been selected. He assigned a local engineer to oversee the fieldwork and ordered a topographical map of the eight hundred acres involved in the landscape design project, and he instructed John to prepare the office for the enormous undertaking.[15]

When Olmsted returned to his office in Brookline in October, work progressed on a zoological park for Washington, D.C., the Niagara plan, and the Stanford project. But even as Olmsted sought appropriate plants for the site, he worried that he and Stanford had not agreed fully on the essential style of the design. Convinced that the environment should be allowed to dictate the kinds of plants and their placement and maintenance, Olmsted tried to dislodge dreams of New England greenery from the senator's mind. The hot and often-dry climate of California was no place to attempt to create a greeny leafdom of New England shade trees, Olmsted insisted. "If we are to look for types of buildings and arrangements suitable to the climate of California," he advised Stanford, "it will rather be in those founded by the wiser men of Syria, Greece, Italy and Spain."[16]

By the end of 1886, Stanford had accepted Olmsted's concept of the landscape design and had agreed with the architects' proposal that the initial buildings include a memorial church and a dozen low buildings, all to be constructed of stone, and all to be arranged around a generous and thoughtfully landscaped quadrangle.[17]

Stanford, in recollection, ignored his earliest directions to his designers and credited himself with the choice of architectural style. "When I suggested to Mr. Olmsted an adaptation of the adobe buildings of California," declared Stanford with understandable pride, "with some higher form of architecture, he was greatly pleased with the idea and my Boston architects have skillfully carried out the idea, really creating for the first time an architecture distinctly Californian in character."[18]

The Stanford University buildings designed by Coolidge's firm resulted in a rational marriage of suggestions made by both Stanford and Olmsted. Combining aspects of California mission architecture and Mediterranean Romanesque with an overall Richardsonian sensibility, the buildings, connected by protective arcades, embraced the paved quadrangle with its ornamental palms. Protected equally from rain or blistering sun, students and faculty could move serenely among the academic areas or could socialize informally in the protective arcades.[19]

But when Coolidge carried the plans to California in April 1887, the Stanfords' suggestions for "improvements" threatened the integrity of the collaboration between architects and landscape architect. Coolidge wrote Olmsted that Stanford, insisting on his own way, had declared that "a landscape architect and an architect might be disappointed but he was going to have the buildings the way he wanted them." Noting that Stanford's demands substantially changed Olmsted's plans for grading, Coolidge backed down. "[W]e did the best we could to preserve your plan as intact as possible," he assured Olmsted.[20]

The Stanfords had other demands, too. Rejecting the quiet and modest campus entrance proposed by the architects, they insisted on a large memorial arch. Moreover, in their eagerness to break ground on the day that would have been their son's nineteenth birthday, they left no time for the plans to be returned to Olmsted, modified, and sent back to California.

While Olmsted accepted the Stanfords' broadax changes to the design, he told an architecture critic, "There is a story to be told about the Stanford University. . . . The matter is not going well but not ruinously."[21]

Olmsted continued to deal cordially and patiently with the Stanfords for the rest of his professional life, but he sometimes found their arrogance daunting. In the summer of 1888, for instance, Olmsted recommended that they commission sculptor Augustus Saint-Gaudens to create a frieze for the monumental arch at the entrance of the college. Olmsted arranged a meeting between the sculptor and the prospective patrons. The Stanfords seemed impressed with Saint-Gaudens and directed him to prepare sketches for them to see on their return from Europe in October. Discerning that the Stanfords knew nothing of Saint-Gaudens, Olmsted discreetly sent them an article about the talented sculptor. Mail between Olmsted and Stanford crossed, however, and, before the senator had seen the article on Saint-Gaudens, he wrote to tell Olmsted he had changed his mind. "Mr. De Gordon" should not prepare a design for the arch, he said, but declared that he and Mrs. Stanford would return from Europe with drawings "of about what we think we would like to have."[22] In the end, the Stanfords commissioned Saint-Gaudens to decorate the arch, but his work was ruined in the 1906 earthquake.

Although the Stanfords' second thoughts and capricious ways did not deter Saint-Gaudens's work on the arch, they did threaten a project dear to Olmsted. Once it was determined that the university would be built on the flatlands, Olmsted planned to create a forest on the hills and an arboretum at their foot. He hired a forester, planned a nursery to support experiments in propagation and planting, and established a system of record keeping that would provide important information "to aid investigation in schools of Dendrology, Horticulture, and Botany." [23]

By the spring of 1889, Stanford changed his mind. He no longer favored the arboretum and related planting. Olmsted was dismayed.[24] Codman learned of Stanford's change of mind while he was in Europe collecting information on trees suited for the California site, and concurring with Olmsted's reaction to the situation, the young partner wrote that he regarded Stanford as "a very uncertain man." [25]

But on a day-to-day basis, Stanford was anything but uncertain. Each decision or idea that came to him immediately fell as a command before those he had hired. And commands changed very quickly indeed. To save money, he directed that only Chinese helpers were to be employed to work on the grounds. Unable to read or write English, however, they ignored plans and set plants randomly in the earth if not closely supervised.[26] This problem, along with the threat of eroding changes being made to the plan, prompted Olmsted to make several visits to California to examine work in progress and to offer advice.

Olmsted's association with Stanford ended in 1890, leaving the landscape architect disappointed. At the onset of their association, Stanford had rejected the idea of a written contract between them, but verbally agreed that Olmsted would have authority to follow his usual procedures: Olmsted would hire and direct a supervising staff — an engineer, a forester, a gardener, and other men with special skills required by the job — and Stanford would pay them directly. Thus, following his usual practice, Olmsted hired local engineer J. G. McMillan and Scottish forester Thomas H. Douglas and authorized them to work under his firm's direction to complete the grounds.

But Ariel Lathrop, Stanford's manager, insisted on controlling all work done on the campus. When Lathrop fired McMillan without consulting Olmsted, the landscape architect penned a polite and professional letter, attempted to explain the policies and procedures appropriate to the practice of landscape architecture, and sought to clear away any lingering misunderstanding about his firm's role in building the grounds of Stanford University. As an experienced landscape architect, Olmsted placed his trust in men who could execute his plans. He could not, he said, merely complete drawings and call a project finished. Moreover, he stated, Stanford had agreed to employ and pay the men Olmsted chose to "act cooperatively with, and under the general direction and supervision" of his firm.[27]

Lathrop was not persuaded by Olmsted's letter but, indeed, insisted that Olmsted's only business with the university was to supply drawings. Olmsted appealed to Stanford. "Imagine," he said,

a sculptor attempting to produce a statue, through workmen and by processes which a stone-cutter would use, throwing overboard all that he had learned of his profession beyond what a stone-cutter had learned; imagine this, and it may give you some idea of the position in which I feel that Mr. Lathrop demands that we shall place ourselves. We do not offer our services to be rendered under such conditions, and you have no right to put us, or let us be put, in such a position.[28]

But Leland Stanford rejected Olmsted's argument for the role of a professional and backed Lathrop. Olmsted soon realized that Stanford had effectively removed him from participation in the project. Since there was no written agreement, Olmsted's resignation was a mere formality. When he read of the opening of the university in 1891, however, Olmsted wrote to praise and congratulate the Stanfords.[29]

Stanford University was a palpable departure from Olmsted's earlier landscape designs. The success of the campus is attributable in large measure to the collaboration of architects and landscape architects. The result manifested ideas that had surfaced in Olmsted's earlier efforts to create a community of connected but discrete buildings in a landscape conducive to learning. To support that community of scholars, Olmsted also planned a residential community that became Palo Alto, a railroad station, and a system of roadways linking them.[30]

Biltmore

George Washington Vanderbilt, grandson of the commodore, invited Olmsted in 1888 to visit his huge expanse of land near Asheville, in the Great Smoky Mountains of North Carolina, and to advise him on developing the great gentleman's estate he had in mind. The Biltmore Estate was to be one of the last great works by Olmsted, and a project on which he remained keen until his withdrawal from practice in 1895. Olmsted was already working on two other designs for Vanderbilt — his family's mausoleum in the Moravian Cemetery at New Dorp, Staten Island, and his summer home in Bar Harbor, Maine.[31] When he first inspected the two-thousand-acre expanse of land on the French Broad River, with its spectacular view of Mount Pisgah, he understood that Vanderbilt envisioned for himself an enlarged version of a French château, an estate with a deer park and formal gardens, perhaps a vineyard or some other agricultural enterprise appropriate to a man of wealth and breeding. Olmsted listened patiently, then offered avuncular advice to Vanderbilt and persuaded him to set aside about 250 acres for a formal garden surrounding the grandiose French château being designed for him by Richard Morris Hunt. The remaining land, Olmsted argued, should be cultivated as a managed forest. However friendly Olmsted's advice, it was also solidly professional. First, Olmsted noted, the quality of the soil and the mountainous topography of the region would not support a formal garden; but second, and more important, the United States had no program for forest management and replenishment. Since Olmsted felt that the government was not likely to undertake a program like those already well established in European countries, he challenged Vanderbilt to serve his country while enjoying a useful occupation suited to his scholarly and poetic nature.

Over the remaining working years of his life, as he attended to the grounds of the United States Capitol and the development of the Columbian Exposition in Chicago, Olmsted was drawn to Biltmore. He enjoyed working with Vanderbilt and often visited the estate several times a year, traveling when he could with Vanderbilt in his private railroad car. Of all of his projects, Biltmore is perhaps the only one that challenged the affection Olmsted held for Central Park.

This doubtless was evoked in part by the social life of Biltmore. While at the estate, the aging Olmsted stayed in the Brick House, where he complained of the cold in winter, of the food in all seasons, and of the servants — "good, big, blundering forgetful, thoughtless children." [32] But he enjoyed life as Vanderbilt's guest and enthusiastically joined the evenings of conversation and whist after long days of hard work.

There is no doubt that Olmsted was fond of the twenty-six-year-old George Washington Vanderbilt, still a bachelor, described by Olmsted as a "delicate refined and bookish man, with considerable humor, but shrewd, sharp, exacting and resolute in matters of business." Vanderbilt, the son of Olmsted's farm neighbor on Staten Island William H. Vanderbilt, had first visited Asheville with his mother, found the climate bracing and the air healthful, and found the views as splendid as anything he had ever seen in his extensive travels. After days of long horseback rides and carriage drives through the backwoods region, young Vanderbilt determined that he would like to live there. He knew better than to advertise his wishes, however, and in 1888 began purchasing land through an agent.[33]

At the time Vanderbilt began to acquire property in one of the poorest sections of rural America, he was single-mindedly pursuing his own pleasure. Subsistence farms, one-room log cabins sheltering entire families, and a small community of African Americans and their church and cemetery were bought on his behalf, as Vanderbilt prepared to build the grandest country estate in America at that time. Today Vanderbilt's development of what became the country's first scientific forestry program may mitigate somewhat history's harsh view of his insensitivity to the suffering of his neighbors.

However, as he began planning his elaborate château and its numerous dependencies, his formal gardens, his pastures and barns, and even his gentlemanly dabbling in dendrology, Vanderbilt was primarily concerned with a setting for himself. Biltmore's opulence exceeds even the prevailing standards of the age, and only the serenity and rationality of Olmsted's landscape design save the estate from vulgarity.

Plans for Biltmore included a lavish house designed by Richard Morris Hunt, the architect who had traveled with Vanderbilt and tutored him on the beauty of French châteaus. The palatial edifice, following Hunt's recommendation, would be constructed of Indiana limestone, brought six hundred miles by railroad, which culminated in a private spur linking the local depot with Vanderbilt's site.

Hunt, a staunch Francophile, had studied at the École National des Beaux-Arts in Paris and returned to his native America to build a career as favored architect to the country's newly rich tycoons. Hunt's clients sought visible symbols of their wealth and social status and were usually as eager to display their sophistication as they were able to pay for the construction and maintenance of enormous and lavish European-style castles, châteaus, and feudal manors.

Olmsted had enjoyed collaborating with Richardson, with whom he shared pleasure in picturesque and rural designs based on informal and often robust treatment of materials, whether Richardson's Romanesque public buildings and shingle houses or Olmsted's parks of craggy glens and unceremonious greenswards. But by the 1880s, when Olmsted began work on Biltmore, American tastes had shifted toward the classical style practiced by Hunt.[34]

Accepting Vanderbilt's choice of architect, Olmsted put aside his history and animosity with Hunt and entered a professional working relationship with the architect who had so bitterly attacked the Albany project. In March 1889, after viewing Hunt's drawings, Olmsted expressed approval and offered several suggestions to improve the views and surroundings of the steep-roofed, many-turreted, and gabled castlelike structure. To take advantage of the view, Olmsted suggested building a terrace on the southeast and, to protect strollers from the sometimes cutting winds, recommended designing a sheltered ramble below the terrace. He proposed adding to the north end of the house an arm of stables and offices and a walled courtyard.[35]

As Hunt proceeded with the plans, access roads were laid and the Brick House, an existing structure, was refurbished to provide housing for Vanderbilt and his numerous guests, as well as Olmsted, Hunt, their assistants, and others who visited the project for significant periods of time. As stakes and scaffolding marked the dimensions of the house, Olmsted checked to make sure the best views were visible to the future inhabitants.[36]

Augmenting a topographical map by taking extensive horseback rides to investigate the special features of the property, Olmsted worked on a complicated plan for the entire Vanderbilt property. He reserved about 250 acres of land for a park around the house and proposed a program of soil improvement and cultivation to include the meadows sloping gently downward from the house to the French Broad River. Olmsted saw the Biltmore project as an opportunity to carry out some of his most cherished ideas about forestry and, apparently without conscious intention, seemed in time to appropriate the estate and to look upon his plans for soil improvement, reforestation, and forest management as the reasons Vanderbilt employed him. While Vanderbilt had accepted Olmsted's initial argument for a forestry project,[37] he probably did not comprehend the degree to which his landscape architect would call on the Vanderbilt fortunes to achieve his personal and professional goals.

Olmsted had lost the possibility of building the arboretum he desired for the Stanford campus. But he could achieve such a scientific model on Vanderbilt's property and simultaneously provide his client with scenic vistas beyond his dreams. The best thing about the land Vanderbilt bought may have been its scenery, its views and vistas, the presence of mountains and mists rising to the tops and sinking into the valleys. But to Olmsted's professional eye, the soil was weak; the woods had been cut mercilessly until only scrub and saplings remained; and the topography was unsuitable for the English country squire's seat envisioned by Vanderbilt.[38] Olmsted told his rich young client:

> Such land in Europe would be made a forest; partly, if it belonged to a gentleman of large means, as a hunting preserve for game, mainly with a view to crops of timber. That would be a suitable and dignified business for you to engage in; it would, in the long run, be probably a fair investment of capital and it would be of great value to the country to have a thoroughly well organized and systematically conducted attempt in forestry made on a large scale. My advice would be to make a small park into which to look from your house; make a small pleasure ground and garden, farm your river bottom chiefly to keep and fatten livestock with a view to manure; and make the rest a forest, improving the existing woods and planting the old fields.[39]

Vanderbilt can be forgiven for knowing little of forestry.[40] The Europeans understood the need to replenish forest growth and to manage plantations for a steady supply of wood. But in America, where the supply seemed endless, woodsmen cut and harvested centuries-old hardwood forests and moved on to the next patch of woodland. Virgin forests had already been depleted along the eastern seaboard of the United States. Olmsted knew from his travels in the West, and from long familiarity and agreement with colleagues such as H. W. S. Cleveland, that failure to replenish forests imperiled the environment. He also knew that businessmen, eager to capture profit, would not be persuaded easily to spend money replanting trees in anticipation of financial returns that

Olmsted was an aging and respected landscape architect when George Washington Vanderbilt invited him to design his vast estate near Asheville, North Carolina. From 1888 until he retired from his practice, the father of American landscape architecture visited the palatial private home and expansive acreage several times a year. In addition to laying out the grounds to include both formal gardens and informal rural parks, Olmsted designed a nursery for the propagation of rare and useful indigenous plants. He also persuaded Vanderbilt to underwrite the first scientific forestry program in the United States.

suaded easily to spend money replanting trees in anticipation of financial returns that could only be realized a hundred or so years later.

As early as 1871 Olmsted had expressed concern in the *Nation* for the country's water supply, sharing Cleveland's and Charles Sprague Sargent's fears about the deforestation of the country. Olmsted had called for a limited program of forest management on the slopes of the Stanford University campus. Moreover, with Sargent, Olmsted had helped found *Garden and Forest,* a periodical devoted to dendrology and horticulture, and the two men had worked together on the creation and design of the Arnold Arboretum of Boston.

Given an opportunity to build an arboretum for a client of seemingly unlimited financial resources, Olmsted unleashed his imagination. He laid out the proposed arboretum on a generous expanse of property, running from the mansion and along the tributaries of the French Broad River into the next valley to the south. He planned to cull the less-significant trees and shrubs and add to the varied soils and growing conditions of the area a distinguished collection of trees and shrubs.[41]

Olmsted also planned a nursery for propagating plants for the arboretum and the grounds. The gathering and nurturing of local shrubs and trees, he assured Vanderbilt, would prove more economical than buying needed plants from commercial sources.[42]

To supervise the nursery Olmsted hired Cornell University graduate Chauncey D. Beadle, and in 1891 he added Gifford Pinchot, a young forester with a Yale degree, to his on-site staff. Both men added considerable professional depth to the running of the Biltmore enterprise: Beadle displayed a knowledge of horticulture that amazed Olmsted, and Pinchot's passion for forestry paralleled Olmsted's.

After graduation from Yale in 1889, Pinchot had gone to France to study forestry and had become familiar with forestry practices in England, Germany, and Switzerland as well as France. When he returned to America, Pinchot traveled in the South and West to explore forests. Stopping in Asheville on his way home from one of his trips, Pinchot, though a rich man, had been appalled by the Vanderbilt mansion rising so close to the poor cabins of mountain farmers; he had also been intrigued by the possibilities the estate offered for developing a model for forest management in the United States.[43] In the summer of 1890 Pinchot understood what Olmsted's plan presaged for forestry in the New World. Here he saw six thousand acres as a laboratory; he saw a scientifically run nursery with forty thousand trees and shrubs; and he examined Olmsted's "Project of Operations for Improving the Forest of Biltmore," a document on which Olmsted had sought Sargent's expert advice.[44] After several sessions with Olmsted, Pinchot was chosen to manage the first large-scale experiment in forestry in the United States. "The conception," he recalled, "was of course Mr. Olmsted's, but it was George Vanderbilt who put it through." [45]

In what is one of his most magnificent works of landscape architecture, Olmsted developed the park surrounding the mansion. In order to dramatize the house and its unsurpassed vistas, Olmsted created a dramatic approach road. Alongside deeply creviced land he laid out a long winding road climbing slowly from the gate of the estate to the great house. Establishing pull-offs for carriages, often with water sources for the horses, Olmsted wanted the arriving guests to partake of the drama of numerous carefully chosen views of massed flowering shrubs beside quiet pools, of streams tumbling over artfully placed rocks, or of secluded glens. He withheld distant views until the roadway curved finally and entered the open, expansive grounds of the house. Then, simultaneously, the visitor would behold the majestic views of distant mountains and the towering great house itself. Olmsted wanted to deliver the stunning effect when "the visitor passed with an abrupt transition into the enclosure of the trim, level, open, airy, spacious, thoroughly artificial Court, and the Residence, with its orderly dependencies, breaks suddenly and fully upon him." [46]

Then leaving the carriage and approaching the house on foot, stepping onto the terrace, the guest would be presented with the serene expanse of quiet field and nobly situated plantations. The experience was styled to underscore the grandeur of the landscape and wealth of the landowner.[47]

Olmsted designed drives throughout the property, adhering to the character of the topography and creating scenic vistas for the visitor's enjoyment. He also laid out footpaths for leisurely strolls and intimate appreciation of plantations and secluded passages of nature. One such path took the stroller gradually from the civilized to the wild, from the large conservatory at the south end of the house, down several tiers of terracing, through a formal garden and then onto more rustic paths. Another cushion between the cultivated and the wild was the Vernal Garden, now densely planted in azaleas. This scheme of moving concentrically from the formal to the natural allowed Olmsted to balance his style of rustic design with Hunt's grandiose structures.

Once he had completed an elaborate design, Olmsted hired engineers to oversee the grading, paving, and bridge building; to monitor workers building culverts, drains, and dams; and to supervise the preparation of soil and setting out of trees and shrubs. Each field supervisor reported to Olmsted on progress made and answered to him for the quality of work completed; all were paid directly by Vanderbilt through his estate manager, Charles McNamee.

George Washington Vanderbilt had inherited ten million dollars, a modest portion of his father's great wealth. But in a time when the Goelets, Belmonts, and Astors were building conspicuous monuments to their riches, young Vanderbilt conclusively outstripped the competition with his palace, and then he surrounded himself with evidence of wealth and taste — a ceiling painting by Tiepolo, Gobelin tapestries, thousands of rare books, and Napoleon I's chess set. With encouragement from Hunt and Olmsted, Vanderbilt did not confine his extravagance to his house and private land, but soon began planning a village for workmen between the estate and Asheville and a group of more expensive dwellings in the adjacent hills.

This profligate display of riches among people who worked hard merely to survive did not go unremarked. The local people, many of whom rationed their stores of cabbages and turnips to last through the winter, stared in wonder at the opulent mansion, the extensive gardens, and the other evidences of wealth, including Vanderbilt's three-mile-long spur railroad built, at a cost of $77,500, to carry building materials to the construction site. "When he considered that the building of this road was a measure of economy," noted a journalist, "the average Tar Heel begins to comprehend something of what it is to be a millionaire." The same journalist quipped that the "unthinking spectator seeing [the Biltmore mansion] for the first time, might mistake it for a hotel, although people of education and taste would by no means fall into such an error." [48]

In 1893 Olmsted assured his partners that Biltmore was the firm's most important work for an individual client; it was "the most distinguished private place, not only of America, but of the world, forming at this period." [49] Olmsted no longer spoke in Yeoman's voice but in the cadences of a man who savors the privileges of class and riches when he advised his son:

> Seek the best society. Seek to enjoy it. Seek to make yourself desirable in it. Make yourself well-informed on matters of conversation of the best and more fortunate sort of people. [50]

Today the Biltmore Estate, owned by Vanderbilt's heirs but open to the public, is the best-preserved example of Olmsted's work. In 1914, after Vanderbilt's death, his widow gave a substantial segment of the original forest to the government to form Pisgah National Forest. [51]

 ## Chicago

> The damage wrought by the World's Fair will last for half a century from its date, if not longer.
> — Louis Sullivan
> The Autobiography of an Idea

Until very recently, Sullivan's damnation of the architecture of the Columbian Exposition of 1893 has gone unchallenged. His firm, Sullivan and Adler, had contributed to

Chicago's claim to having the most innovative architecture in America at the end of the nineteenth century. And in a clear break with other architects of the period, Sullivan believed that a new order was in the making and viewed the Beaux Arts style of the buildings of the fair as a nearly immoral affront to the art of architecture.[52]

Sullivan, like the critics and historians of architecture who have followed him until recently, viewed the Columbian Exposition as a celebration of all the worst features of architectural taste of the past, including wasteful grandiosity, decorative silliness, and out-of-scale monumentality. Until the recent manifestation of postmodern and deconstructivist architecture, it has been agreed that the overall employment of a Beaux Arts style all but denied the talents of some of America's best architects. Rather, the White City, as the fair came to be known, consisted of a group of dull and mercifully temporary buildings of little merit other than classical pretentiousness [53] — with the exceptions being Louis Sullivan's Hall of Transportation, Chicago architect Henry Ives Cobb's Fisheries Building, executed in the Richardsonian manner, and skyscraper innovator William Le Baron Jenney's Horticultural Building. Sullivan's building, removed both symbolically and actually from the other architecture, was an extravaganza of color with its spectacular gold-leaf-covered grand entrance and arabesques in yellow, orange, and red stucco.[54]

The architecture of the Chicago exposition is no longer so easily dismissed. With the recent changes in public taste, and a widespread willingness to look critically at the development over the years of an implicit rigidity and formulaic morbidity in the International Style of architecture, the architecture of the Columbian Exposition emerges as an important display of fantasy and an honorable solution to the problem of melding disparate tastes in design with a variety of functional requirements. As a designed community, it raises issues regarding urban design, the relationship of individual buildings to an established architectural scheme, and the significance of landscape design in defining the character of such a prescribed architectural district.

Moreover, if the exposition did not nurture seeds of architectural avant-gardism of the period, it did reflect the excesses of America's Gilded Age. And, in retrospect, it renews intellectual speculation on the relative merits of design undertaken within established constraints as opposed to design as expression of individual creativity. For good and bad, the fair was the child of committees, and it reflected the compromises and triumphs of opinionated men accustomed for the most part to controlling their own work.

Long before it opened to hordes of curious and pleasure-seeking Americans, the fair served to gather and focus the attention and efforts of some of the most prominent architects and artists of the period, among them Frederick Law Olmsted. And although the architecture of the World's Columbian Exposition was of a style Olmsted had avoided when possible, his professional reputation was capped by his contribution to the celebration of the four-hundredth anniversary of Columbus's landing in the New World.

As both a senior professional and a reasonable man with long experience in administering large public projects, Olmsted leavened the plenary sessions of the proud men assembled to design the physical aspects of the exposition. He negotiated and mitigated, replacing confrontation with collaboration and compromise. At a time in his life when he might have been forgiven for feeling his own ideas to be superior to those of other professional men, Olmsted showed himself to be an ideal committee member and team player.

The committee developing the exposition, which was to be an international display of the benefits of the industrial revolution, hoped to rival the five previous world's fairs. In 1851, Prince Albert had organized the first fair, the Great Exposition, and under his auspices Sir Joseph Paxton had created London's famed Crystal Palace. In 1889, Gustav Eiffel's tower rose against the Paris skyline in celebration of the Exposition Universelle.

The Chicago fair was to be the first of the exuberant international expositions to be staged in the New World. After a period of disagreement over its location, the commission consulted Olmsted in August 1890. He and Codman examined the proposed sites and, after consideration of transportation and other factors likely to contribute to the effectiveness of the fair, recommended Jackson Park.

Although it was the same site that Olmsted and Vaux, twenty years earlier, had treated as an integral part of their design for the Chicago park system, very little of their plan had been realized. When Olmsted began work on the fairgrounds in 1890, the five hundred acres on the shore of Lake Michigan still consisted largely of swampland and scrubby growth. A primary design feature of the earlier plan had been a series of lagoons connected by canals, a program that served utilitarian concerns by draining the swamp and aesthetic ones by emphasizing the view afforded by the water. The basic program, Olmsted decided, would serve the needs of the exposition. Buildings could be erected on sandspits, making approaches to them possible by either land or water, and giving the whole area a flavor akin to that of Venice.

To the contemporary mind, Central Park stands as Olmsted's signature work. As envisioned and developed by Olmsted and Vaux, Central Park was a romantic rural interlude in an urban context, an artificial public park through which a visitor (much like a visitor to a museum or theater) could suspend attention to the hustle of the city and imagine himself or herself to be in a bucolic country setting: the visitor to Central Park, Olmsted believed, could escape the harsh sights and sounds of the city and find serenity in a created rural experience. On the other end of his career, Olmsted worked on the design of public grounds to produce an almost opposite sense of place. The Chicago fairgrounds, as Olmsted defined the project, was to bring people into contact with one another and with architecture, to lead them efficiently and comfortably from the steady sway of rail or water transportation, along pleasant walks through handsome grounds, to the interiors of great exhibition halls: the visitor to the Chicago fair was led from rural and suburban informality to the formality of Beaux Arts architecture and educational exhibitions.[55]

The fair was intended to show off industrial products, evidences of scientific progress and of prosperity, from all around the world. But in anticipation of crowds of visitors, Olmsted from the first imagined the exposition to be a vast pleasure ground, rather more an urban than a rural park. While politicians and tycoons might entertain the notion that humankind would be united through industry — a frequently played theme of the fair — Olmsted's mind-set led him to concern for comfort and pleasure. Walkways should be level and easy to use, with enough curves to seduce the stroller into a restful and amiable state. Plantations should be massive and conducive to serenity, not colorful and jarring. Boats should glide slowly and gently on the waterways, and waterfowl should be abundant, entertaining, and restful to watch. Olmsted saw the fairgrounds as an opportunity to elevate strangers into a state of communicativeness, by gentling them and drawing them together through the design of their shared surroundings.

Once the site was settled for the Chicago fair, Olmsted and his colleagues were required to think about design in a manner to which they were unaccustomed. In contrast with the usual practices of designers, the approximately 150 buildings of the fair had to be planned for eventual dismantling, with the exception of the Art Gallery, which had been copied from a Prix de Rome model and was destined to become the Art Institute of Chicago.[56] The grounds, however, had to be designed for life beyond the fair. Their ultimate use notwithstanding, the grounds could not be planned as a conventional park or parklike area surrounding a great house; rather, Olmsted had to think in terms of laying out walks, establishing conveyances and conveniences, and providing access and pleasure for masses of people intent upon visiting exhibitions in the various buildings, and all of this had to be effected within an overall scheme that would settle eventually into being a lakeside park.

Olmsted considered the needs of the project in the shadow of recollections about his earlier work on a design for Jackson Park. His initial evaluation of the poor land, for example, did not change. His original plan involved separating the firmament from the waters and was based on a layout of lagoons separated by mounded earth dredged from the shallow stagnant water that covered much of the acreage. He had enlivened the plan with a circular road system, a bridge of land between the lagoons and the lake, and a long pier. The basic plan for Jackson Park, Olmsted believed, could serve as the blueprint for the

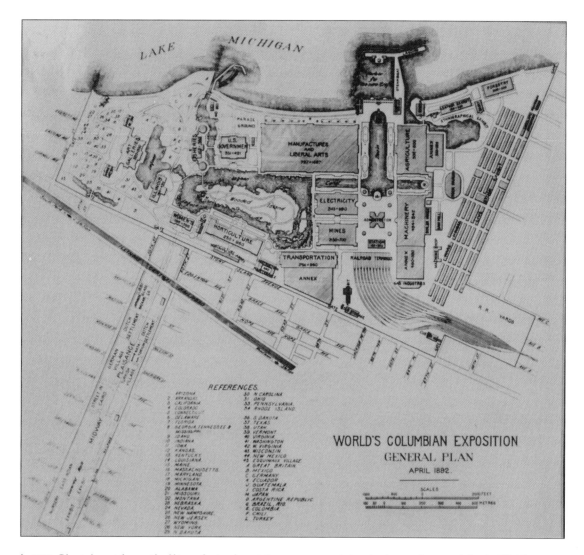

WORLD'S COLUMBIAN EXPOSITION
GENERAL PLAN
APRIL 1892.

In 1890, Olmsted — at the zenith of his professional reputation — was commissioned to lay out the grounds for the World's Columbian Exposition in Chicago, which opened in 1893. He recommended use of Jackson Park, a site on the shore of Lake Michigan, for which he and Vaux had earlier designed a unit of a large park project that was never completed.

grounds of the Columbian Exposition. But in order to accommodate and emphasize the role of architecture on the fairgrounds, Olmsted narrowed some of the lagoons, making them into canals and defining them with geometric edges that transformed the landmasses between the waters into plinths for the fanciful Beaux Arts buildings that would rise above them. By this means, Olmsted conceived of making the exhibition buildings accessible by water and land and allowed them their individual identities as well as membership in the overall scheme. In addition, in what would now be thought of as the introduction of a related series of superblocks, he laid out connecting pathways and a circling trolley line that connected with the rail system. His dynamic program for moving people through and around the fairgrounds minimized the sense of crowding and encouraged a restful and cheerful mood.[57]

With his general plan in mind, Olmsted and Codman began work with Daniel Hudson Burnham and his partner, John Wellborn Root, two of the most powerful and successful architects in Chicago. The firm of Burnham and Root played the leading role in the architectural planning for the fair, with Burnham serving as chairman of the board of consulting architects, landscape architects, and engineers at work on the fair. Olmsted's plan was not immediately accepted, he told his son. Only by persuasive argument did the landscape in his plan prevail to tie "the Fair to the Lake." The question, Olmsted observed, was "chiefly of what people called taste and in which they hold that argument is out of place. . . . [W]e carried it simply by argument, it is a triumph."[58]

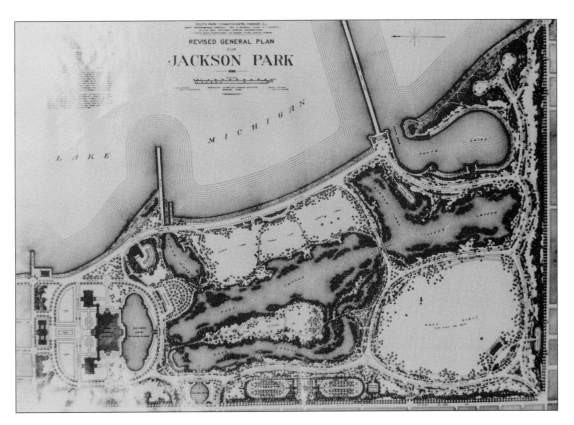

Olmsted decided that the original design for Jackson Park was adaptable to the needs of the great Chicago fair. Using a series of dredged lagoons and built-up land spits, Olmsted produced a complicated scheme for placement of the numerous white Beaux Arts buildings to be used for exhibition of the world's industrial and technological progress.

Augustus Saint-Gaudens

Irish-born Augustus Saint-Gaudens (1848–1907) reinvented portrait sculpture in America. His style combined technical skill and aesthetic simplification of naturalism and suggested heroism and monumentality.

He became interested in sculpture as a child when, shortly after arriving in the United States, he was apprenticed to a cameo cutter. After studying at Cooper Union and the National Academy of Design, Saint-Gaudens went to Europe in 1867, where he mastered the French Beaux Arts style and developed a strong appreciation for the Italian masters Ghiberti and Donatello.

Saint-Gaudens returned to the United States and undertook a commission that assured his reputation: the bronze full-figure portrait of the courageous Admiral David Farragut (1878–1881) for Madison Square Park, New York City.

Saint-Gaudens also created the bronze memorial portrait of Abraham Lincoln (1887) for Chicago's Lincoln Park. The president, gaunt and gangly, stands before a chair, apparently thinking before beginning to speak. The monument is both expressive and elegant.

The sculptor invested the same qualities, along with a deep sense of solitude and reverie, in what is considered his masterwork: the 1886–1891 bronze figure of a shrouded, seated woman, in Rock Creek Cemetery, Washington, D.C. Commissioned by Henry Adams for his wife's grave, the sculpture is Saint-Gaudens's most abstract work.

He is also celebrated for his last great work (1897–1903), the equestrian sculpture of General William Tecumseh Sherman at the Fifty-ninth Street entrance to Central Park in New York City. The heroic bronze piece, washed in gold leaf, combines the sculptor's talent for portraiture with a sense of physical movement and energy. His Robert Gould Shaw Memorial, a high-relief work opposite the State House in Boston, was seen in the movie *Glory*. 🎺

After agreement on the basic orientation of the fair, Root drew a quick and rough preliminary plan for the placement of the various buildings. The national committee accepted the combined ideas of Olmsted and Root, setting entrances to the grounds by water at the east end and by rail at the west. The administration building was to be placed on a large open paved area, one of the plinths created by a hard-edged jut of land separating two lagoons. Several larger buildings would also be placed on the paved area. Other buildings, all accessible by both land and water, would be set artfully around the lagoon system. A large central lake with an island would serve to unify the various lagoons.

Burnham, though committed to the Beaux Arts style, selected architects from outside Chicago, including McKim, Mead and White; Peabody and Stearns; Van Brunt and Howe; George B. Post; and Richard Morris Hunt. Olmsted had been on the receiving end of the attack on the Albany project by Hunt and Post, but had subsequently worked peacefully with Hunt on the Biltmore Estate. He had listed the other firms as those with whom he would like to collaborate. In addition, Burnham added to the participating architects two Chicago men much admired by Olmsted, Jenney and Sullivan.[59] Following a meeting of all of the architects (save Root, who had died suddenly of pneumonia) and Olmsted and Codman, Olmsted wrote Henry Van Brunt, "I feel with you warmly that the meeting at Chicago was a most happy, useful, and promising occasion and I look forward with much pleasure to others to follow." [60]

Two of the compromises that issued from the committee — whether authored by Olmsted or merely the result of dead-end disagreements — contributed to the visual failings of the exposition. As the artists and architects met to confer on the physical elements necessary to give the buildings and grounds of the exposition coherence, they were unable to agree on the colors the buildings should be painted and settled on a glaring and uniform white (again, Sullivan's building alone excepted). They also agreed to design all buildings with conforming cornice lines, a decision that added to the sameness of the architecture. [61]

In addition to architects and landscape architects, Burnham turned to Francis D. Millet to enlist the energies and talents of painters and sculptors, including mural painters like Kenyon Cox and Edwin H. Blashfield and sculptors Augustus Saint-Gaudens and Daniel Chester French. Addressing a problem that was decidedly peripheral to their artistic role in the project, Millet and his artists, dubbed the "Whitewash Gang" by Burnham, devised a method of spraying white paint on all the buildings. The result was a blinding, miragelike image shimmering on the shore of Lake Michigan, which earned the fair its nickname, White City.

The cooperation among artists, architects, and landscape architects led Saint-Gaudens to remind Burnham, "Look here, old fellow, do you realize that this is the greatest meeting of artists since the fifteenth century." [62]

The fair was a dramatic success and an overwhelming crowd pleaser. The elaborately designed and decorated buildings, uniform in their whiteness, astonished visitors by day and night. In the sunshine the white buildings seemed to be of overwhelming size and dazzle; by night, outlined by the still-new electric lighting, they were a thrilling combination of technological miracles and aesthetic derring-do. Daniel Chester French's sixty-five-foot female figure of the Republic as well as Frederick MacMonnies's colossal fountains added to the splendor of the Court of Honor, a vast space at the heart of the fairgrounds surrounded by buildings facing the water. Visitors arriving from east or west, by boat or train, would pass through the Court of Honor and onto the lagoons and spits of land supporting other buildings. [63]

Olmsted's work in Chicago was not all smooth sailing, however. Committees are not favored clients for architects. By the beginning of 1891 Olmsted and Codman worked to please "our hundreds of masters," Olmsted told a friend.

Divided into several organizations, commissions, directors, committees, there is no one who will give us any exact instructions upon cardinal points, such as the extent of floor room there will be wanted for any department or subdepartment of the show. We keep making tentative plans, but the most liberal of these would not allow a tenth part of the aggregate space which we are unofficially advised will be wanted for their special state exhibit. We think two acres would be an extravagant allowance etc. In general we are allowing 25% more space than was used at the last French Exposition.[64]

Even while away from Chicago and at work on other projects in his Brookline office, Olmsted insisted on being informed fully of every progress or alteration in his plans. Dutifully, Codman let him know that plans were afoot to build a music hall on the island. This use of the island ran opposite to Olmsted's plan for the island to be reserved from "all the splendor and glory and noise and human multitudinousness of the great surrounding Babylon," and that it be maintained as a point of visual rest and serenity. He instructed Codman to make his protest known to the committee, but to accept defeat gracefully if that became necessary.[65] Olmsted was defeated. A Japanese temple and horticultural exhibits were placed on the island, and, after the fair opened, a space he had hoped to keep a peaceful preserve became a bustle of crowds.[66]

In addition to the problems inherent to working efficiently with committees, the site itself presented serious challenges to the landscape architects. Olmsted had three growing seasons in which to plan, plant, and bring to desired density the ground covers, shrubs, and trees he specified for the grounds. All plantations had to succeed with minimum maintenance, withstand heavy human traffic, and contribute to the beauty and restfulness of the plan. Olmsted fretted over the selection of plants for the edges of the lagoons, seeking specimens that would hold the earth, appear natural, and subtly affect the character of the grounds. In addition, he wanted to introduce picturesque water plants to emphasize the relationship of land to water. He planned to develop natural-seeming foliage on the island and to create a mass of greenery on which visitors could rest their eyes from the glaring white of the architecture all around them.[67]

Ever attentive to details, Olmsted stressed the aesthetic importance of waterfowl and boats in the water surrounding the fairgrounds. The boats at the exposition would ferry people, of course, but their major role, like that of the fowl, was to add a moving visual motif to the design, to give people something to look at as well as to use. Olmsted recalled:

The effects of the boats and the water fowl as incidents of movement and life; the bridges with respect to their shadows and reflections, their effect in extending apparent perspectives and in connecting terraces and buildings, tying them together and thus creating unity of composition — all this was quite fully taken into account from the very first; and the style of boats best adapted to the purpose became at once, a topic of much anxiety and study.[68]

The Dairy Building from South-east

During the three years of work on the world's-fair grounds, Olmsted enjoyed the company of other leading artists and designers. He lavished attention on all details of the fair, including the style of the boats used to transport people, the shoreline plantings, and even the selection of decorative waterfowl.

In addition to offering educational exhibitions and programs, the Chicago fair introduced the Ferris wheel, Cracker Jack, and the hoochee-koochee dance to Americans.

Agricultural Building from North-east

Olmsted's letters to Burnham in December 1891 suggest that Burnham may have been hard to convince as to the aesthetic importance of the boats. Olmsted insisted that the presence of both boats and waterfowl was to contribute to the serenity and beauty of the grounds. For him the boats, as well as the waterways and waterfowl, were design elements, with an important role to play in the grace and elegance of the setting for the exposition. The boats, he repeated several times, should be small and light; they should run low to the water, and quietly. After writing several letters and not receiving the response he apparently desired, Olmsted shifted into another gear: the boats, he declared, were second only to the water in importance to the design of the fair.

Olmsted prevailed and found exactly the boat he wanted for the fair.[69] In England on an extended vacation, he cruised the Thames in an electric launch. It was, he wrote his partners, the silent small boat, with jolly awnings and furnishings, that should be used at the exposition.[70] Fifty of the electric-powered launches were purchased for the fair and, along with gondolas from Venice and full-size reproductions of Columbus's three ships, provided color and merriment for the waterfront.[71]

Olmsted contributed greatly to the appearance and functioning of the White City. In addition to selecting the site, he and his firm received a fee of $22,500, significant in itself, to supervise all aspects of the landscaping.[72] In his work on the Columbian Exposition, Olmsted showed flexibility and inventiveness that might have been more expected in a younger artist. From 1890 until the opening of the fair in 1893, he played a major role in setting the tone of its physical properties.

Considering Olmsted's association with *Garden and Forest*, it may be assumed that he agreed in the end with that publication's opinion that "[t]he efficient cooperation of these allied professions [architecture and landscape architecture] is one of the most happy results of the Exposition. It is greatly to the credit of both, and of excellent promise for the future of all art in this country."[73]

His pride in his work did not exist in a vacuum. Others, too, realized that something important had happened in the design of the Columbian Exposition. One instance of recognition occurred when guests gathered for an elaborate banquet in New York, in March 1893, to applaud Daniel Burnham's leadership of the fair project in Chicago. Olmsted was traveling at the time and unable to attend. When given the floor, Burnham deflected the praise aimed at himself and told the gathering:

Each of you knows the name and genius of him who stands first in the heart and confidence of American artists, the creator of your own parks and many other city parks. He it is who has been our best adviser and our common mentor. In the highest sense he is the planner of the Exposition — Frederick Law Olmsted. No word of his has fallen to the

ground among us since he first joined us some thirty months ago. As artist, he paints with lakes and wooded slopes;
with lawns and banks and forest-covered hills; with mountainsides and ocean views. He should stand where I do
tonight, not for his deeds of later years alone, but for what his brain has wrought and his pen has taught for half a
century.[74]

Frederick Law Olmsted was an aging and ailing man when the exposition opened to the public on May 1, 1893. Nearly half a million people pressed into the architectonic space of the Court of Honor to hear President Grover Cleveland speak. But Olmsted, avoiding the dignitaries' dais, wandered anonymously around the edges of the crowd to check on the details of the fair. In the days and weeks following the grand opening, he continued to observe the visitors to the fair. He wrote Burnham a series of suggestions for improving the experience. Noting that the visitors were too serious, Olmsted urged Burnham to add cheering and entertaining features — banjo players, lemonade sellers, and others in colorful dress — to lighten the mood.[75]

After the fair closed and most of its buildings were demolished, Olmsted finally had the park that he had envisioned for Chicago twenty-some years earlier. Olmsted could take pleasure in other achievements spun from the fair as well. He had been a part of a team of artists working to enliven civilization; in creating the White City, Olmsted and his colleagues had laid before visitors a vision of what design could do for cities.

Following the fair, civic leaders throughout the country led communities in building great public monuments, including state capitols and civic centers. Olmsted had participated in a successful experiment in education: Americans had learned from it that the elevated sensibilities of artists and the progressive ideas of business leaders could meet in commonweal.[76]

Boston and Brookline

After half a century of life, Olmsted's health began to deteriorate. Never robust, and always plagued with insomnia and a variety of stomach complaints, with middle age his symptoms intensified and multiplied. And, as in the past, his physical health was always stitched to his psychological state. Anxiety, frustration, and annoyance over specific projects such as Central Park or Mount Royal in Montreal exacerbated his insomnia and other complaints. Even a three-month tour of Europe, partly for rest and partly to study parks, did not fully restore him.

By 1881 New York no longer charmed Olmsted or promised him problems to solve as a landscape architect. He was sick of the political corruption and angry at the treatment he had received. His son later claimed that Olmsted chose Brookline during an overnight visit with Richardson, who was already ensconced in that fashionable suburb of Boston. One morning after a heavy snowfall, Olmsted looked out the window and saw a snowplow clearing the street. "This," he is reported to have said to

PLAN of
CHARLESBANK

Richardson, "is a civilized community. I'm going to live here." [77]

When he was dismissed from Central Park, he fortunately was able to turn his attention to projects in Boston. Indeed, he moved his family to Cambridge for the summer, where he began work with Charles Sprague Sargent on the Arnold Arboretum.

After several summers in rented houses around Boston, Olmsted first rented the Clarksted, a square farmhouse in Brookline, and eventually arranged to buy the congenial house on Walnut Street. He put his New York home up for sale and settled with his family in Brookline. He added a wing for his studio and office, built fireproof brick vaults for storing plans, but kept the forthright and honest appearance of the house.

The house in Brookline, like the house in Manhattan, held the comfortable mixture of home and office, with books and photographs, shelves holding reports and drawings, and large tables for spreading and reviewing plans. Olmsted designed simple drafting tables, placed near windows for maximum daylight.

Over the years, Olmsted had watched the urbanization and industrialization of America, revolutionary changes in the fabric of the country that directly influenced him and the

Olmsted undertook a series of individual parks that, when linked, formed Boston's Emerald Necklace. He wrote: "Parks have plainly not come as the direct result of the great inventions or discoveries of the century. They are not, with us, simply an improvement on what we had before, growing out of a general advance of the arts applicable to them. It is not evident that the movement was taken up in any country from any other, however it may have been influenced or accelerated. It did not run like a fashion. It would seem rather to have been a common, spontaneous movement of that sort which we conveniently refer to as the 'Genius of Civilization.' . . . Considering that it has occurred simultaneously with a great enlargement of towns and development of urban habits, is it not reasonable to regard it as a self-preserving instinct of civilization?" (FLO, *A Consideration of the Justifying Value of a Public Park* . . . [Boston: Tolman and White, 1818], 8, 18, 19.)

profession he was building. As transportation and communication had become easier and more rapid, living patterns changed. Congregating in cities, people lived in closer proximity to one another; not only did the number of people in

Olmsted's parks for the Boston area represent the designer's genius at its most accomplished, subtle, and profound. He combined turf and water edge, shade and sunlight, to create outdoor spaces that support human activities.

cities grow, the density of that population also increased. Despite the attendant rise in crime and other social problems, Olmsted saw the city as the true seat of culture, of learning and communication, and of civilization. But it was the suburb, for him, that held the real promise for the good life for affluent Americans. Cities around the world were spawning handsome suburbs where citizens combined the best aspects of both rural and urban living. Men of means and their families, settled in comfort on the outer edges of cities, would, Olmsted believed, contribute significantly to the prosperity of the cities. For instance, he wrote in 1879 that

> the metropolitan advantages of New York, and the profits of its local trade must be greatly increased by constantly increasing accession to its population of men who have accumulated means elsewhere, and who wish to engage in other than purely money-making occupations. Such men, living under

By the time Olmsted took a professional interest in the Boston parks, he was in a position to expand the city's tradition of urban pleasure grounds. The Common had been in use as a park, more or less, since 1725 when the city banned horses and carriages from the area. It also was an important informal gathering place for citizens of varied interests. By the middle of the nineteenth century, men gathered in a special section to talk and smoke. The Boston Common allowed large crowds to gather for celebrations, for military parades, and for promenades.

favorable circumstances and with capital and energies economically directed to matters of general interest, are the most valuable constituents of a city [author's emphasis]; and it is by their numbers, wealth and influence, more than anything else, that a city takes its rank in the world as a metropolis.[78]

These words came from the same "yeoman" who had so passionately advocated democracy in his youth. Casting suburbia as the natural habitat of the "most valuable constituents of a city," Olmsted forecast one of the great problems of twentieth-century life — the separation of people according to class and wealth, with the likelihood now of begetting a permanent inner-city underclass. Olmsted's view of suburban life, as reflected in this passage, drew him away from New York City and toward Boston.

It was not an abrupt move, but occurred over the years, beginning in the summer of 1878, when he and his family shared a house in Cambridge with his journalist friend Godkin and his family, and completed in 1881, when he moved his office and family to Brookline. At first, running his office out of the crowded shared house in Cambridge, Olmsted was drawn to Boston by his work with Sargent on the Arnold Arboretum and his project for the Fens.

At the same time Olmsted's commissions for work on the Arnold Arboretum and the Fens drew him toward Boston, however, he was working also on projects in other cities — among them Hartford and Albany — which offered no lure as new home sites. During a period when Olmsted's health was uncertain, his firm had a lot of work, which presumably would have permitted Olmsted to maintain his office in any location he chose.[79] That he selected Boston as he neared sixty years of age likely owed much to the friends he found there, men he considered his intellectual and social equals, including Sargent and Godkin, as well as Brookline neighbors Henry Hobson Richardson and Asa Gray, and nearby Quincy resident Charles Francis Adams Jr. Soon after he settled in Brookline, Olmsted was elected to the elite Saturday Club, a private organization of Boston-area men who considered themselves to be the intellectual (and possibly moral) leaders of the community. In Brookline, Olmsted found the form of communicativeness he most valued.

He had always prized the company of interesting and powerful men, never more so than when another important aspect of civilized life, domesticity, was changing sharply for him.

John all but ran his father's office and was a dependable colleague as well as dutiful son, and Rick amused his family with his capers and pleased them with his schoolwork. Crises concerning Marion, Owen, and Charlotte, however, disrupted the family.

Nineteen-year-old Marion, traveling in Europe with relatives, contracted a nearly fatal fever. Upon learning that Marion, after months of illness, would recover, Olmsted wrote to his half-sister Bertha, "I had felt before that she was very dear to me but I did not know how much of what of hopefulness in life is left to me depended on her." [80] Although Marion never regained her health, she was, according to Olmsted, "just the nicest girl — little old maid — possible; patient, happy, indefatigable." [81]

In late October 1881, the Olmsteds received word that Owen was dangerously ill. After graduation from Yale, the young man went west in pursuit of independence and fortune. Under the guidance of Clarence King, Owen had bought a cattle ranch and undertaken the grueling outdoor life of a cowboy near Little Powder River in southeastern Montana, west of the Black Hills. Owen wrote letters home about building a cabin and corrals with the help of only three hired hands, driving his herd of fifteen hundred cattle, and enduring the winter cold on the plains. Owen asked his brother John to send him warm clothes from Brooks Brothers, where he had left his measurements with tailors.

Upon learning of Owen's illness, John immediately went west to bring his brother home. But even that proved impossible. Owen was too ill to survive the long train trip and lapsed into a coma before Mary and Olmsted could board the train in upper New York State. "My poor boy got no farther East than Albany," Olmsted wrote a friend, "where his mother and I met him. But he was already unconscious when taken from the train and breathed his last the following day." [82] On November 21, 1881, twenty-four-year-old Owen died.

In March 1882 Mary reviewed the family situation in a letter to a friend. They missed Owen, she said, but consoled themselves in knowing that he had been happy in his life as a rancher. "Charlotte has a second son and is doing well. Marion is pretty well and Rick is *very* well." [83]

But twenty-eight-year-old Charlotte was not doing well. Married to physician John Bryant, living in Cohasset, Massachusetts, in a house by Richardson and grounds by her father, she was the mother of two small boys. Before her marriage, Charlotte had exhibited disturbing evidence of mental instability. After the birth of her third son, Charlotte suffered a breakdown and was hospitalized. In time Olmsted accepted the fact that she would never recover and would require care for the remainder of her life. She died in an asylum in 1908. [84]

Marion's health, Owen's death, and Charlotte's disability weighed on Olmsted's mind. While his office was prospering and his fame as a landscape architect expanding, he was aging and his health was deteriorating. Chronically plagued with episodes of dizziness, ringing in his ears, diarrhea, rheumatism, insomnia, and nervousness, Olmsted continued to extend his business. That, in his mind, included undertaking new projects and protecting the works he had completed.

Olmsted's attention to every detail of park design led him to give special treatment to creating rustic water fountains to furnish drinking water to park users, but he cloaked their function in artfully contrived natural surroundings.

Spoils of the Park

It was one thing to move to Boston, but it was unthinkable for Olmsted to abandon Central Park. Though still titular consulting landscape architect for the Manhattan park, Olmsted was all but ignored. A few commissioners pressed for his return, but Olmsted knew that his era with Central Park had ended. Even though he received, and responded to, letters from park staff and others associated with its operations, he made no move to return to the superintendency even when, shortly after his move to Boston, the position was open.

Olmsted had no recourse against a series of threats to the park. Under the new superintendent, extensive tree cutting

The Olmsted family settled in Brookline, Massachusetts, a suburb of Boston, in 1883. Olmsted refurbished the Clarksted, an old, square farmhouse at 99 Warren Street, to accommodate his office. Brookline combined the conveniences of city life with the space, air, and vistas of the country, all features that had made Olmsted an early proponent of designed communities and of suburban living. The tranquillity of Brookline and of work on the Boston parks differed in the extreme from the turbulence of life in New York City and the political pressures Olmsted had experienced in working on Central Park. In addition, he enjoyed the company of his neighbor, architect H. H. Richardson, as well as that of intellectual and influential men he joined in the exclusive Saturday Club.

to "open vistas" all but destroyed the screen Olmsted had built to keep the city out of the park. As nature abhors a vacuum, so promoters and developers itch to make profit on benign real estate. One group wanted to build a fast driving track — a carriage raceway — around the park; another group wanted to hold the 1893 world's fair in the park.

Olmsted wrote letters, using his influence with the journalism community, but saw little hope of saving the park from those determined to destroy it in the name of progress, fortune, political expediency, or common sense. In 1881, driven by frustration and presumably a modicum of bitterness, Olmsted wrote *The Spoils of the Park, with a Few Leaves from the Deep-Laden Note-Books of "A Wholly Unpractical Man."*

The pamphlet, though guarded and circumspect in tone, reflected Olmsted's experiences, fears, and hopes related to Central Park and to urban parks as a concept. Reformers and politicians, he observed, shared a tendency to meddle in park operations and to place inappropriate pressures on park administrators to corrupt the mission of the park and to dispense jobs as patronage. To counter prevailing tendencies, and to safeguard the role of the park superintendent against "that form of tyranny known as advice or influence, and that form of bribery known as patronage," Olmsted suggested that the governance structure of the park be defined by a law which would both direct and limit the commissioners' authority, and that professional administrators have clear power to meet assigned responsibilities.[85]

In a similar mood of reflection, analysis, and reform, Olmsted edited lectures he had delivered in Montreal. Neither his *Spoils of the Park* nor the published Montreal lectures incited press attention to what Olmsted saw as a distressingly increasing disregard for public parks. It is important to remember that Olmsted could not — would not — have so assertively lamented the perils surrounding park development and management in America if he had not harbored, even as he aged, an idealistic dream about the role of parks and of nature in human life. The move to Brookline had reaffirmed for him the importance of rural scenery and the power of natural beauty to elevate his soul. He wrote his old friend Charles Loring Brace, "I enjoy this suburban country beyond expression, and the older I grow [the more] I find my capacity for enjoyment increasing."[86]

The suburb, as Olmsted experienced it in Brookline, promised to support domesticity and communicativeness — civilization — in physical surroundings designed to preserve natural beauty. The proliferation of suburbs would also influence the way in which Olmsted conceived of parks, giving them an expanded role in urban design and heightened significance in civilized life, as proved to be the case in his development of the Boston park system.

Olmsted saw that the Boston parks, even more than Central Park, could define the city, increase the value of property within it, and elevate the lives of its citizens. Perhaps more than any other American city, Boston had both the topographical resources and common spirit to support a great park system, all the more so because of the suburbs radiating from the urban center. Further, Boston had a long and respected history of preserving public parkland. By the 1850s Bostonians, along with social reformists in other American cities, were discussing the need for public parks as a part of civilized urban life, but, unlike most other eastern cities, Boston already had open rural spaces within its confines: the Common, dating back to 1634, had evolved from shared cattle-grazing land into a park; the Public Garden, too, had become a shared public treasure. By 1867, when Harvard professor Charles Eliot Norton called on Olmsted for his professional opinion, Boston was ready to support the development of public parks. It was against this back-

ground that Olmsted, in February 1870, presented his paper "Public Parks and the Enlargement of Towns" to the American Social Science Association at the Lowell Institute in
Boston. Olmsted articulated his philosophy on city planning, including the role of parks in
promoting a civilized style of living in an urban environment.

When topography and space allowed, Olmsted created bodies of water large enough to accommodate boating and to supply a
varied shoreline for strollers. In winter, frozen ponds and lakes became rinks for skaters.

Olmsted's America had changed dramatically since his birth in 1822. He realized that
the industrial revolution was bringing about the country's future shift from rural to urban
concerns, and people would congregate densely in cities, which, in his view, fostered invention, transportation, industry, communication, education, and civilization.[87]

Optimistic about the city as the seat of civilization in the future, Olmsted also recognized the social problems that attended population density, including prostitution, alco-

holism, and crime. In Olmsted's vision of America's future, however, technological progress and scientific rationality would provide means for overcoming social ills.[88] The strife and danger of city life, according to Olmsted, could be mitigated by the rational creation of rural parks, thereby giving citizens an environment that provided recreation and induced a calm state of mind. Parks also, Olmsted believed, encouraged people of all classes to mingle and therefore strengthened democracy.[89]

Against this background of lofty observations and assertions, Olmsted focused his audience's attention on the future of Boston. The venerable city, he told a select group of its most influential citizens, did not have to grow haphazardly as its borders extended and its population swelled. Rather, he insisted, careful planning could turn future growth to the advantage of Boston. As one specific means for ensuring improvement of life for urban dwellers in Boston, Olmsted recommended the design and development of a rural park, a "simple, broad, open space of clean greensward," separated from the city, to furnish a place of calm and recreation for its citizens. He also recommended that serious study be undertaken to determine an appropriate site for such a park.[90]

Olmsted's remarks to the gathering at the Lowell Institute were circulated in pamphlet form, giving his message wide attention and doubtless contributing to public interest, which led, in 1875, to the passage of legislation to create the Boston parks.

That same year, at the request of the Boston park commissioners, Olmsted undertook the study he had recommended be prepared to aid in selecting park sites. He traversed the city and its environs and presented a scheme for an extensive park system for the area, including land along the Charles River, marshy areas of Back Bay, a large parcel around Jamaica Pond, and acreage in West Roxbury. The city council took no action for two years, until the mounting public pressure persuaded them to authorize acquisition of the recommended lands and to inaugurate a program to develop parks.

Arnold Arboretum

Olmsted did not have to wait for public support, however, to begin work on another front, having been engaged by Charles Sprague Sargent to help create the Arnold Arboretum in Boston. Although Sargent wanted the arboretum to be a part of the Boston park system, it was being developed on land owned by Harvard College and was being paid for with money from the city. President Charles Eliot of Harvard and the Boston city officials initially were reluctant to consider Sargent's suggestion that the arboretum be put under city control, but eventually agreed, in part because of Olmsted's innovative plan for bridging the best of both worlds by providing access to the public and materials for scientific study for the college.

Olmsted devised a legal solution to the problem. In 1882 the land of the Arnold Arboretum was condemned and designated a unit within the Boston park system; then the land, with the exception of the roadways and paths, was leased to Harvard College. The city maintained the roadways; the college managed plantings; the park was open to the public, but continued to serve as a laboratory for scientific study sponsored by Harvard.

Along with the Biltmore Estate, Arnold Arboretum today provides the most easy-to-read, and perhaps best-preserved, of Olmsted's numerous designs. Olmsted took great pleasure in designing Arnold Arboretum, in meeting the needs of scientists, horticulturists, and dendrologists who wanted plant material for study, and in creating a pleasure ground for people in the Boston area.

Wire frames were designed to support the growth of vines in Arnold Arboretum.

Both foot and carriage traffic through the Arnold Arboretum was limited, and spaces were laid out for masses of foliage as well as individual specimens or objects of unusual aesthetic interest.

The Fens

Olmsted held his nose and set about figuring a way to drain the stagnant water and sewage from the swampy Back Bay Fens. Unsightly, unhealthful, and the source of a god-awful stench, the Fens had to be drained in order to produce ground for a park, and in such a way as to prevent flooding when heavy rains caused water to back up from the Charles River and overflow into the Fens.

It was understood that the Fens project was to rid the city of a pestilent nuisance, but Olmsted accomplished more

In order to create the Emerald Necklace, Olmsted first had to devise a system of drainage and water control. He combined utility with decorative concerns, as in the case of certain portions of the waterways in the Back Bay Fens.

than this practical aim. He held the shape of the land with plantings, then built bridges and causeways that linked the two sides of the extensive Fens area. In a combination of imagination and practicality, Olmsted rid the area of a health hazard and established land high enough and dry enough to support the development of a park.

He devised floodgates to prevent water from the Charles River from inundating the Fens, then ordered a conduit be built to intercept the flow of sewage on the Boston side of the Fens and drain it away from the land. Anticipating the necessity of providing a temporary runoff for heavy rains into the basin of the Fens, he planned vegetation that would prevent extensive flooding of the surrounding grounds.[91]

Completion of the park was slowed by the inadequacy of appropriations by the park commission. Dredging produced narrow canals suitable for canoeing and attracting waterfowl; dredging also produced soil, which added height to the land. Cod grass and trees planted around the edges held the mud-flat and dry land in place. Olmsted established six entrances to the area, with drives, walkways, and a system of bridle paths.

Olmsted worked on the Fens in 1879–1880, keeping the larger project in mind. Boston would have a metropolitan-area park system linking the Common and Public Garden, Commonwealth Avenue, the Fens, Muddy River, Jamaica Pond, Arnold Arboretum, and an extensive rural park at West Roxbury. The proposed connections would create a continuous flow of parks, the seven-mile "Emerald Necklace" that would stretch around the city.

Boston Greenbelt Plan and Franklin Park

Benjamin Franklin honored his natal city by bequeathing a fund that, after a century of accrued interest, was used in 1881 to purchase five hundred acres. The West Roxbury site was soon named Franklin Park and became, along with Central and Prospect Parks, one of Olmsted's major triumphs. He began designing Franklin Park in 1885, finding the existing woods and pastures excellent material for the creation of picturesque vistas. After his usual careful preparation of the soil, Olmsted laid out six miles of carriageways, two miles of bridle paths, and thirteen miles of walks for strolling, allowing for a variety of movement through the large site. Different areas, given descriptive names by Olmsted, offered unique characteristics. The Playstead was designed to be a large and level central meadow; Ellicottdale, a slightly more lushly planted and curving area; and between the two, Schoolmaster Hill afforded long views from its rounded crest. Another rise in the landscape, Scarboro Hill, looked down over a bucolic pond on its south side. Woods were shaped around smaller and more private spaces, smaller-scale interludes in the overall grand scheme of Franklin Park. One architectural space, the Greeting, resembled Central Park's Mall. Olmsted wrapped a drive around the entire park, shading and defining it with thick plantations of trees, which also blocked the city's intrusion.[92]

The area he called the Country Park, a space about a mile long and three-quarters of a mile wide, appealed to those who wanted quiet communion with natural scenery. But Franklin Park, more than any park previously designed by Olmsted, set aside space for games, sports, and active recreation. Around Country Park, Olmsted laid out croquet and tennis courts and diamonds for baseball — sports favored by men and boys. Women and girls, of course, were expected to exercise by strolling in ladylike dignity on the paths provided.

Franklin Park has changed over the years and now includes a public golf course, a stadium, and a parking lot, as well as a greensward used by cross-country runners.[93]

The Boston park system was not completed until the 1890s. The banks of the Muddy River, acquired in 1890 after lengthy negotiations between Boston and the town of Brookline, allowed the closure of the Emerald Necklace.[94]

Olmsted's plan for the Boston park system followed the topography of the region and boldly incorporated areas destined to become suburbs. In basic concept the scheme resembled the idea Olmsted and Vaux had promoted in New York, a chain of parks and greenbelts that would have linked all corners of metropolitan New York from Westchester County and suburban New Jersey to all of the corners of the boroughs, with Central and Prospect Parks serving as epicenters of greenery.

Olmsted brought the dream to reality in Boston, where he also articulated fully the human needs that the modern park must support: circulation of traffic, recreation, and delight. With his work in Boston Olmsted established that great urban park systems should include large expanses of rural landscape, areas for picnics and relaxation, ponds or other bodies of water surrounded by appropriate landscape, and belts or bands of land containing roadways, walkways, carriageways, and bridle paths.[95]

After his experiences with the Central Park commissioners, Olmsted appreciated the atmosphere surrounding work on the Boston parks. He had been cast as a subordinate (if not servant) in New York; in Boston he was respected as an authority, an expert, and an intelligent professional of impeccable integrity.[96] Olmsted understood the importance of his work on the Boston parks from the beginning. He realized that it was a regional — rather than merely a city — design; and he grasped fully its importance to the future of landscape architecture as a profession. The Boston parks, he told his partners, were "the most important work of our profession now in hand anywhere in the world."[97]

In 1900, five years after Olmsted had ceased work, the Boston park commissioners honored him by voting to change the names of Leverett and Jamaica Parks to Olmsted Park.[98]

palm growing out of a jungle, but ...
overgrown by the creepers, is the ephemer...
... thirs... There are parts ...
Ramble where ...
have this result, ...
considerable dep...
In a few years ...
shorten... bring a few shrubs that will ...
the shade and the upper, low spreading
or artificially dwarfed trees, assisted by
I own doubt that in the interior of there
you would find spots where the ground
was killed by density of shade and the tr...
supported a canopy, or extended parasol
rendered complete and by the absence of shade above.
pervious by the vines. The theory of adap...
of varieties thus accounts for the palm li...
of so many tropical trees and shrubs or
trees. Our sassafras will grow in the sa...
... Ramble is a perfectly usef...

The
End of
a Career

Even as he aged Olmsted held himself to a grueling schedule of travel, supervision, and proselytism, on behalf of parks, urban design, and other embodiments of his concept of civilization. His proclivity to work himself to the brink of physical and emotional collapse, if anything, intensified as he aged. After hours of negotiation with the city fathers of Detroit in 1884, he retreated to a hotel, unable to digest food, "not even toast and milk." [1]

In his late years, Olmsted often enjoyed displaying his talents and his power. His physical distress in Detroit followed a jaunt on a ferryboat with businessmen and civic leaders to inspect progress on Belle Isle Park. Olmsted, exasperated by what he considered the captain's lack of skill, took the wheel, gave orders to the crew, and docked the vessel safely, boasting that he had made a "lead line of spun yarn and scrap iron." [2]

As Olmsted aged, his slight frame filled out, his hair receded, and a beard obscured the lower part of his face. His clear eyes, however, retained a youthful sparkle. He looked the part of the role he had chosen in his youth: he was a patriarch, a wise and influential man, an important and widely honored citizen.

In his sixties Olmsted often flaunted his intellectual and physical powers to strangers, clients, associates, and family members. Returning from his work on the Stanford project in California in October 1886, he visited Wyoming to inspect the ranchlands that Owen had left to him. "It was a high interest speculation," he wrote to John, "and luck has not been with us." [3] After completing a thorough examination of the property that would have challenged the physical stamina of a younger and stronger man, Olmsted eagerly shared his findings with his son in Brookline: "It has been reported that under close feeding the nutritious buffalo and bunch grasses die and worthless grasses take their place. I saw no evidence that the Company's ranges had at all deteriorated in this way. The number of antelopes indicated a wild and uncrowded condition." [4]

The aging park maker displayed more than physical stamina and intellectual acuity. He brandished his prestige and power wherever and whenever it suited him. A passenger on the Union Pacific railroad in 1887, Olmsted demanded that the train stop in the windswept high country of southern Wyoming. As perplexed passengers watched, Olmsted limped across the plain to inspect the Ames Monument, designed by Henry Hobson Richardson to commemorate the role of Oakes and Oliver Ames in building the transcontinental railroad.[5] Satisfied with what he saw, Olmsted returned to the train and let the journey continue.

Other passengers on the train could not have known that Olmsted was visiting the work of a dear and recently dead friend. Richardson had died in 1886. Olmsted and Mary, knowing that the architect's lifestyle cost more than he made, called on Richardson's widow, Julia, and offered help. Reassured that their friend could live satisfactorily on her small personal income, abetted by a friendly landlord's promise of modest rental fees, Olmsted turned his attention to establishing Richardson's reputation.

Fearful that Richardson's premature death at the age of forty-eight might truncate appreciation of his contributions to architecture, Olmsted and Charles Sargent commis-

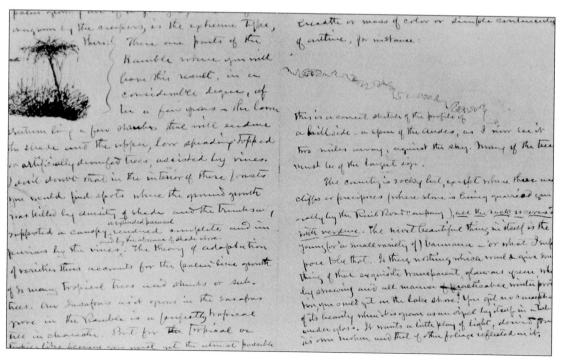

Olmsted wrote long and detailed letters to clients, associates, and employees, often describing aesthetic or practical matters related to landscape architecture and sometimes loftily putting forth political arguments or observations and theories about civilization. These documents constitute the most significant portion of the Olmsted Papers in the the Library of Congress.

sioned preparation and publication of Mariana Griswold Van Renssalaer's book on the in-novative designer. Olmsted instructed the author to begin work immediately on "a memo-rial book, giving some account of him and his works with illustrations . . . before his office is dismantled, his friends dispersed and while memories of him are fresh."[6] As Van Renssalaer embarked on the project, Olmsted wrote numerous letters to her, providing much of the material that appeared in the book. Later, Van Renssalaer would turn her at-tention to writing the first biography of Olmsted.

By the 1880s Frederick Law Olmsted reveled in his fame. Behind the public man — the progenitor of landscape architecture, urban designer, and social reformer — the "do-mestic" man was aging, suffering physical ailments, overworking, and trying to ensure the continuation of his name and ideas after his death. During the last of his working years, Olmsted continued to write letters, some to old friends like Charles Loring Brace, some to clients and associates, and many to his sons John and Rick.

He also continued to work himself to exhaustion and to flare up in impatience with those around him. His chronic poor health and his "hardened . . . habits," he said, lay be-hind his temperamental outbursts. Realizing he had distressed the architect of the United States Capitol, Thomas Wisedell, by his behavior, Olmsted wrote:

> *We are both of us invalids, both suffer from a similar form of nervous irritability, extremely provocative of impatience, and if your malady is the hardest . . . I am much the older man, more hardened in my habits and less tractable. There-fore as to mere expressions of impatience and petulance we have neither [of] us much to boast of, and between ourselves I don't think we need attempt to cast up accounts. If you do and find a balance against me, it can only be a case for forgiveness . . . and I ask your forgiveness.[7]*

A number of Olmsted's friends and associates died in the 1880s, including Bellows and Van Buren from the Sanitary Commission and Geddes, his farmer-mentor in upstate New York.[8] "You decidedly have had the best & most worthily successful life of all whom I have known," Olmsted reflected in a letter to Charles Loring Brace. Pointing out that he, too, had made an important contribution, Olmsted wrote that his work was

> *constantly & everywhere arrested, wrenched, angled, and misused & it is not easy to get above intense personal disap-pointment & mortification. The politicians & the reporters & the editors don't torture me as they once did but still not a little and I am older and don't bear what comes as well — or without greater agitation — than I once did for I never bore it well. I think it comes harder to an old man to be grossly insulted.[9]*

Olmsted assured Brace that he still worked "as close to my possibilities as ever," and added that John had taken more responsibility for the office, and other young men —

"pupils" — had been brought in to help in the business. Still, Olmsted felt burdened by "a great multitude of diverse concerns . . . & I get very weary of turning so often from one thing to another and of so many long & short expeditions. Perhaps I all the more enjoy my house & place & the bits of quiet work I am able to do in it." [10]

A few years later, in 1887, Olmsted mused again to Brace: "What a different world it is from those we used to know. I don't concern myself the least bit with speculations. I don't know and I don't care. I am occupied quite enough with 'the duty that lies nearest to you.' The most horrible waste in the world seems to me the waste of mind in what is called Theology and I repent of nothing more thoroughly than my own sin in superstitious maundering. I take pleasure in observing how perfectly healthy our children are in this respect, how completely uninterested they are in all that used to be such a terrifically cruel burden upon me." [11]

In 1890 Olmsted wrote to Brace, "If I have lost power in some ways, I have gained compensatingly in others, and it must be more so with you and your chances of living vigorously and, with your habits, a great deal better than mine. I never had more before me or less inclination to lay off than now, though my arrangements are such that nobody need be dissatisfied if I drop out tomorrow. . . . My office is much better equipped and has more momentum than ever before." [12]

Olmsted indeed had turned great responsibility for the business over to John. As he traveled, stroking clients and overseeing projects in process, Olmsted wrote continually to John, detailing aspects of their shared professional concerns and reporting on his health. Complaining of "choleric attacks," train travel, poor hotels, and a host of problems with projects, Olmsted also called on John for increasing support, and simultaneously he began to prepare Rick to carry on his name and style of landscape design. He sent John to job sites as his proxy and stoutly defended John when a client complained that, in effect, he had hired the father and got the son. "My son," he wrote the disgruntled client in January 1889,

has from early childhood been familiar with my works. He has lived with me on some of them. He has systematically taken lessons in our profession upon them. He has traveled thousands of miles with me while I have been inspecting and studying. He has been professionally educated under my directions, has studied abroad under my guidance. He has been at the head of my office ten years, has latterly taken an equal part with me in all my works, public and private. He is in the prime of life — a young middle-aged man. More than one of my clients after experience have requested that I would allow him to lead in their affairs, finding him apter than they found me. [13]

Following the death of Charles Brace in Switzerland, Olmsted wrote to Frederick Kingsbury. "His death was a shock to me (I heard of it while in Carolina) and the shock has been growing greater since." [14] But late at night and sleepless at Biltmore, Olmsted poured out his heart in a many-paged letter to Mrs. Elizabeth B. Whitney, a woman he had scarcely seen in decades, but whom he remembered as his youthful mentor, Elizabeth Baldwin. Nearing seventy years of age, grieving for his youth and his friend, Olmsted wondered what had happened to all of them since their shared youth. What had Charley accomplished? And what had he achieved? Olmsted recalled the hopefulness and purpose that Elizabeth Baldwin had kindled in him many years earlier in Connecticut. "I am thinking that of all the young men you knew," Olmsted confided, "I was the least likely to do what I have and that you cannot know or guess in what way I was led to it." He cataloged his feats for her: seventeen large public parks, scores of smaller ones, and numerous private developments and estates. After he and his associates had completed them, he told her, "they have in the majority of cases been more or less barbarously treated, yet as they stand, with perhaps a single exception, they are a hundred years ahead of any spontaneous public demand, or of the demand of any notable cultivated part of the people. . . . They are having an educative effect perfectly manifest to me — a manifestly civilizing effect. I see much indirect and unconscious following of them." [15]

To the parks, estates, and rural and urban developments, Olmsted added another accomplishment. "I know that I shall have helped to educate in a good American school a capital body of young men for my profession. I know that in the minds of a large body of men of influence I have raised my calling from the rank of a trade, even of a handicraft, to that of a liberal profession — an art, an Art of design." [16]

Olmsted wrote the truth to the former Miss Baldwin; he had indeed formed an elite corps of able young men in the field of landscape architecture. In addition to his son John, whom he had made a partner in 1884, he had brought Harvard president Eliot's son, Charles, and Charles Sprague Sargent's nephew Henry Codman to work in his office. Eliot, a Harvard graduate, worked for Olmsted for two years, 1883 to 1885, studied in Europe for a year, and, in 1886 opened his own office. Codman joined Olmsted immediately after his graduation from Massachusetts Institute of Technology, in 1884. In 1887, he went abroad with Sargent, worked in Paris under André for a while, and returned to a partnership in the Olmsted firm. Eliot and Codman, as well as John, took turns traveling with Olmsted, tending him as he lay sick in hotels in cities around the country, and stepping in to help him remember the names, places, and details of business that he forgot with increasing frequency.

During his last years of practice Olmsted assumed responsibility for the reputation of the profession of landscape architecture as well as for his standing within that discipline. Always a compulsive overworker, he drove himself particularly hard in his later

Olmsted placed high value on the role of parents in creating the domestic unit he believed basic to American civilization. His own father had exerted considerable influence on young Frederick, who, in turn, participated strongly in the rearing of his own children, stepchildren, and grandchildren.

years. As rich clients came to him for advice on Newport cottages, private estates, and country retreats, Olmsted seemed to intensify his interest in educating the public to the purposes and benefits of landscape architecture. He also wanted to expand the practice and to win commissions in the South. But time was against him.

Olmsted realized sometime in the spring of 1895 that his memory was unreliable. He informed his partners and told them that he planned to decrease his involvement in the firm's business. Over the next few years, however, he often reversed this decision, sometimes believed that his partners were plotting against him to keep him away from clients or, worse, that John was trying to control the business and prevent Rick from inheriting it.

Olmsted compulsively advised Rick on preparing for a career in landscape architecture. Rick, more than ever, became the center of Olmsted's life. Olmsted begged his son to protect him from embarrassment and to help him hide from clients "any confusion in my mind . . . as you conveniently can." In July 1895 he told Rick, "I have rarely felt so little master of myself." [17]

Mary and Marion took him to Deer Isle, in Maine, hoping that a rest away from the office might improve his memory and general health. But Olmsted spent the time fretting, suffered from insomnia, and wrote long letters to Rick, sometimes begging him for information on projects, sometimes pouring out advice, and always expressing his love for the son who would carry on his name and profession.

Mary admitted that Deer Isle had failed to soothe and restore her husband and, in consultation with John, decided to take Olmsted to England. In his more lucid moments Olmsted understood that his doctors were humoring him by pretending that he would get better, and he suspected that he was being sent to England to get him away from the office.

Rick, now a salaried employee of the office and assigned to the Biltmore project, was called home by John for a visit with their father before the old man sailed for England. At Mary's request, Rick sailed with them to England, sharing Olmsted's compartment and caring for him on the voyage.

In England, Olmsted deteriorated. Rick left his family and returned home; Mary and Marion, exhausted and anxious, placed Olmsted under a doctor's care in a country rest home. As Olmsted's condition worsened he sometimes became violent, depressing Marion so deeply that Mary feared she might suffer the same fate as Charlotte.

Although Olmsted had some lucid moments, his family decided not to tell him when Calvert Vaux died by drowning, either the victim of an accident or of suicide.

Mary, worried about Marion's state, and on the point of exhaustion herself, notified John and Rick that they would have to take over. Leaving Olmsted under their care, Mary took Marion sightseeing briefly before sending her home. Mary then went to Paris to shop and on to Nice to visit the grave of her first husband, John Hull Olmsted.

Meanwhile, John and Rick had hired William Ralph Emerson to design a cottage on Deer Isle, planning to establish Mary, Marion, and Olmsted there with nurses and others to see to their well-being. Once the family arrived at Deer Isle, they lived in a rented house until their cottage could be completed. Mary masterminded elaborate plans to entertain Olmsted — drives, walks, sailing, picnics, and visits to the cottage being built. Before they could move into the new cottage — Felsted — Olmsted's behavior alarmed Mary. In the past several months she had watched him shift rapidly from depression to agitation and sometimes become violent. When his violence was no longer confined to inanimate objects, but was directed toward the man and woman hired to take care of him, Mary fired the hapless nurses. But in the end she accepted Olmsted's senility.

In September 1898 Frederick was appointed his father's legal guardian, and Olmsted was committed to McLean Hospital in Belmont, Massachusetts. He lived there in a cottage on grounds he had designed, no longer able to recognize his family. Rick, who visited him regularly, was with him when he died at two in the morning on August 28, 1903.

Epilogue

rederick Law Olmsted designed, assisted in designing, or encouraged the design and development of a vast amount of land in the nineteenth century, causing speculation that he is "probably responsible for the betterment and preservation of more of the earth's surface than anyone else." [1] He is seen, too, as a major force behind today's ecological movement and credited with helping initiate the federal park system with the preservation of Yosemite. He helped to define suburbia and to articulate criteria for ideal communities and campuses.

For Americans today the genius of Olmsted and Vaux designs is best celebrated by the resiliency, flexibility, and generosity of their parks. For us, Olmsted's designs are far less marked by rigidity than are his ideas; his parks more democratic than he was; and his contribution to the health and well-being of city dwellers more profound and ubiquitous than he could have imagined.

Olmsted saw parks as civilizing influences in human society, and he had definite ideas as to what *civilization* meant. Strolling in a park, for Olmsted, was a means of escaping life's daily routine, putting the urban necessities and the roar of the marketplace in the larger perspective of nature. The park user's inner turmoil would subside in the presence of quiet glens or gently flowing water; cares would lose their urgency in view of grand vistas, mighty trees, and ancient rock formations. Scale and familiarity — but not essence — separated the experiences preserved in an urban park or in Yosemite or at Niagara Falls. Nature had the power to touch and rearrange the souls and minds of all human beings, insisted Olmsted, and thus the authority to remind all citizens of equality.

Olmsted's existing works — or, in most cases, patches of land identified as having been designed by him — hardly reflect the park maker's ideals or the homage we pay him in words. Most of them have suffered encroachments by automobiles, as is the case with the highways that now exist where once his carriage drives wound through Boston's Emerald Necklace. Use of his parks has veered from their original purpose of preserving a sanctuary of rural calm and peace in urban situations, as in Central and Prospect Parks — where Olmsted resisted installing gaslighting, which would damage foliage, and stipulated that in the interest of human safety only parts of the parks would be lighted and used at night — no longer conducive to strolling and contemplating nature, but now tempered by the visible and often menacing evidence of vandals, thugs, graffiti "artists," homeless and toiletless people, and urban aesthetes equipped with boom boxes.

Although he complained that his parks had been subjected to barbarous treatment during his lifetime, Olmsted could not have imagined them in the state in which we know them. In the first place, he would be hard-pressed to comprehend the human activities that fill the parks he designed for recreational strolling. But Olmsted's idea of leisure was far different from the contemporary citizen's passion for physical activity. A spiritual "high" did not result from heart-bursting pain-for-gain exertion, but from quiet time spent in nature. For him, contemplation of nature evoked a different kind of high, one akin to religious experience, and the purpose of recreation was to escape the clutter and clatter of urban life, find refuge and spiritual solace in a rural setting. He also envisioned some of the same benefits for the suburban dweller. It is ironic therefore that the middle-class migration to the suburbs has contributed to the radical change in the nature and use of American parks and, perhaps even more ironic, that the unchecked growth of suburban developments has proved a threat to both the leisurely contemplation of nature and the ecological system on which scenic beauty rests.

Affluent Americans today are more likely to contemplate nature from the confines of an automobile than on foot in an urban park and to use the park as a setting for outdoor exercise. The popularity of the automobile and increases in population are not the only factors exerting pressures for change on Olmsted's parks. When he designed Central Park, he did not reckon on the soon-to-develop widespread favor of sports and other forms of physical recreation. The playground reform movement in America took hold in the 1880s, and, over the years, Olmsted designed areas for sports activities. Prospect Park's Parade Ground, just outside the picturesque pleasure ground, accommodated sports. Buffalo's system included a special area on the south side of the city for sports. Boston's Franklin Park contained distinct areas for baseball and tennis.

As such social reformers as Jane Addams and Jacob Riis called for opportunities for outdoor play for children, park administrators diluted the purely aesthetic functions of parks by adding sandboxes, seesaws, swings, and even swimming pools. Numerous playgrounds now exist within Central Park.

When Olmsted urged the preservation of the scenic beauty of Niagara Falls and Yosemite, he predicted that the sites would receive millions of rapt viewers each year. He could not have calculated the impact, however, of exhaust fumes from the internal-combustion engines in automobiles, motorcycles, and campers, or the erosion, trash, and damage to natural growth caused by careless people. Indeed, he would have had difficulty in understanding the twentieth-century emphasis on the "rights" of individuals in the use of public spaces.

Olmsted only reluctantly acceded to Calvert Vaux's insistence that he regard himself as an artist. In the twentieth century an artist has almost unlimited right to express herself or to celebrate his individuality. Recent American artist Robert Smithson, who shaped land into works such as *Spiral Jetty*, recognized a kindred spirit in Olmsted.[2] The nineteenth-century park maker, like the contemporary earthwork artist, marshaled artistic talents and administrative skills to accomplish a plan; both "artists" directed others in the use of machinery to move and reshape tons of earth, rock, and vegetation. But while Smithson worked the earth to manifest a form or idea he desired to express as art, Olmsted insisted that it was the artist's duty to serve his client — not himself. The whole concept of self-expression would have been anathema to Olmsted. He was a nineteenth-century man, for whom self-expression would have appeared as self-indulgence, irresponsibility, or lack of discipline; at best, he would have seen it as evidence of a failure of acceptable codes of behavior among civilized people.

Olmsted was a man of his time — an affluent male thoroughly rooted in nineteenth-century America. He spent his childhood and youth in small-town and rural New England, where he absorbed a yeomanly array of skills along with a romantic and spiritual appreciation of nature. Conservative and reform-minded, he found in landscape architecture a means to improve civilization, and for him talk of such "social engineering" was not a political blasphemy but the responsibility of powerful men of his class.

Olmsted believed parks would educate and civilize citizens, that they would provide physical and spiritual benisons to people from tenements and sweatshops as well as those from Fifth Avenue mansions and Wall Street law offices. Moreover, he believed all people would meet and mingle in parks, thus overcoming the barriers of class and wealth. He believed unequivocally in what architecture critic Ada Louise Huxtable has termed "existential pastoralism."[3]

Olmsted's faith in the power of parks to elevate humankind, improve urban life, and promote spiritual reverie evolved, too, from his social position. Paternalism kept the wheels of democracy turning, and the elite dispensers of paternalism also controlled roles, responsibilities, and opportunities for all other citizens. Although tolerant of other races, immigrants, and people living in rude frontier circumstances, Olmsted saw diversity and pluralism as symptoms of social transition that were to be dissolved as quickly as possible in a single concept of American civilization. And, for Olmsted, promoting that common notion was the single most important function of education, including the education afforded by parks.

Olmsted's great parks may have been shoddily treated and may show the scars of abuse, but they still exert extraordinary influence in the lives of people in cities. Central Park embraces crowds far in excess of those it was designed to soothe, and it endures aspects of every imaginable urban ill and pressure. Yet it is of unquestioned popularity among New Yorkers and, as Olmsted intended it to be, an oasis in the urban pandemonium. Newspapers report Central Park's muggings, rapes, and murders; citizens recount to one another their experiences with outrageous and rude behavior but, with a practiced urban shrug, recognize the park as an integral part of the larger fabric of New York life. That's how it is. Dogs romp, children shout, skateboarders and cyclists whiz by; car horns blare and sound systems send suggestive throbs through the earth; couples stroll and caress one another; elderly people read, play cards, knit, or talk; and groups of artists organize and present plays, readings, happenings, and concerts. Central Park is alive, and its DNA has evolved along with the city.

In spite of appearances today, the great nineteenth-century parks have not been destroyed by society's changes or by treacherous and barbarous treatment by their stewards. Rather, almost like nature itself, the parks have shown themselves to be accommodating, even forgiving, of cataclysmic changes in treatment, management, and use. But should he see his parks today, Frederick Law Olmsted — opinionated, passionate, romantic, and "unpractical man" of the nineteenth century — might remark, "You may question if common sense is not liable to be at fault in the planning of parks. Reflect that common sense would never have given the world a good many things the world values." [4]

Notes

Abbreviations of sources frequently cited in the notes; for full references, see the bibliography:

PFLO I, II, III, IV, V, VI: *The Papers of Frederick Law Olmsted,* volumes I-VI.
LC: Olmsted Papers in the Manuscript Division, Library of Congress
DAB: *Dictionary of American Biography,* single volume
Forty Years: Kimball and Olmsted Jr., eds., *Forty Years of Landscape Architecture*

Abbreviations of persons mentioned:

HWB   Henry Whitney Bellows
CLB   Charles Loring Brace
EMG   Edward Miner Gallaudet
FJK   Frederick J. Kingsbury
JSN   John S. Newberry
FLO   Frederick Law Olmsted
JO   John Olmsted
JHO   John Hull Olmsted
MPO   Mary Perkins Olmsted
LS   Leland Stanford
GWV   George Washington Vanderbilt
CV   Calvert Vaux

Prologue

1. *Garden and Forest* 6 (May 3, 1893): 192.

One Yeoman's Beginning

1. PFLO I: Autobiographical fragment, "Passages in the Life of an Unpractical Man."

2. LC: John Olmsted journal (hereafter JO), Sept. 27, 1830.

3. "Unpractical Man."

4. Ibid.

5. Ibid.

6. PFLO I: Autobiographical Fragment A, Autobiographical Fragment B.

7. "Unpractical Man."

8. Van Rensselaer, "Frederick Law Olmsted," 860–67. PFLO I: Autobiographical Fragment B.

9. *Rode's New York City Directory*, 43, 260. LC: JO journal, Aug. 18, 1840; Mar. 11, 1842. PFLO I: FLO to Mary Bull Olmsted, March 20, 1841.

10. PFLO I: FLO to JHO, April 8, 1843; FLO to parents, Sept. 5, 1843. LC: JO journal, Apr. 23, 1843.

11. PFLO I: FLO to family, Mar. 10, [1900].

12. PFLO I: 190. "The Real China," essay written in 1856, presumably while FLO was en route to Europe.

13. PFLO I: 134. FLO, "A Voice from the Sea," *American Whig Review* 14 (Dec. 1851): 526.

14. PFLO I: FLO to JHO, Sept. 28, Dec. 10, 1843; JO journal, Apr. 15, 1844; FLO, "A Voice from the Sea," 526–29.

Lessons of the Land

1. PFLO I: JO journal, Oct. 30, 1844, Mar. 1, 21, 1847; FLO to FJK, May 18, 1894; FLO to JHO, May 27, 1845.

2. PFLO I: FJK sketch to CLB; FLO to CLB, July 30, 1846.

3. PFLO I: 213; FLO to JHO, June 18, 1845.

4. *Forty Years* 1:71; PFLO I: FLO to FJK, July 14, 1846.

5. PFLO I: FLO to JHO, June 23, 1845; FLO to Elizabeth Baldwin Whitney, Dec. 16, 1890.

6. PFLO I: FLO to FJK, June 12, 1846.

7. PFLO I: FLO to CLB, June 22, 1845.

8. Fairmount, the Geddes farm, was located near Camillus, on the south side of the north branch of the Seneca Turnpike at the corner of the old military road that ran from Onondaga Hill to Oswego, later New York State Routes 5 and 173.

9. PFLO I: FLO to JHO, June 12, 1846.

10. *Forty Years* 1:78.

11. PFLO I: FLO to JO, Sept. 25, 1848; JHO to JO, Mar. 19, 1855.

12. PFLO I: Autobiographical Fragment B; *Forty Years* 1:79–80.

13. PFLO I: FLO, flyer "Appeal to the Citizens of Staten Island," Dec. 1849.

14. PFLO I: Autobiographical Fragment B; FLO to FJK, Dec. 21, 1850; *Forty Years* 1:79–81.

15. *Forty Years* 1:63, 85–86; PFLO I: FLO to FJK, Oct. 14, 1848; Boyle-Cullen; DAB, Vanderbilt, William Henry.

16. DAB, Downing, Andrew Jackson; *Forty Years* 1:80–82, 88–93; PFLO I: Autobiographical Fragment B; FLO to JO, Mar. 14, 1850, Nov. 6, 1851.

17. A sketch of the house, attributed to Olmsted, suggests a simple structure of pleasant proportions, with strong lines and good, square corners.

18. FLO, *Walks and Talks* 1:1–2; PFLO I: FLO to JO [Mar. 1], 1850; JHO to FJK, Mar. 16, 1850.

19. PFLO I: JO journal, Apr. 30, Oct. 24, 1850.

20. His itinerary took him through London, Liverpool, Birkenhead, and Chester; into Wales; to Shrewsbury, Ludlow, Leominster, and Hereford; on to Bristol, Bath, Warminster, Salisbury, Winchester, and Portsmouth; to the Isle of Wight and back to Portsmouth and London.

21. FLO, *Walks and Talks* 1:87.

22. PFLO I: FLO to JO, Mar. 1, 1850.

23. FLO, *Walks and Talks* 1:135.

24. Ibid., 1:213–14, 99–109.

25. Ibid., 1:213–14.

26. Ibid., 1:79.

27. Ibid., 1:133.

28. Ibid., 1:213–24.

An Important Man

1. PFLO I: FLO to CLB, Nov. 12, 1850; FLO to FJK, Dec. 21, 1850.

2. PFLO I: JHO to FJK, Apr. 27, 1851; FLO to FJK, Aug. 5, 1851; JHO to FJK, Oct. 12, 1851.

3. PFLO I: FLO to CLB, Aug. 4, 1844.

4. PFLO I: FLO to CLB, Jan. 11, 1851.

5. PFLO I: JHO to FJK, Sept. 12, 1851; FLO to CLB, May 27, 1851; FLO to FJK, Aug. 5, 1851.

6. PFLO I: JHO to FJK, Sept. 12, 1851.

7. PFLO I: FLO to FJK, Apr. 27, 1851; FLO to FJK, Aug. 5, 1851; JHO to FJK, Oct. 12, 1851.

8. FLO, *Walks and Talks* 1:14–49.

9. PFLO I: FLO to JO, Feb. 24, 1852; "Reviews," *Horticulturist* 7, no. 3 (Mar. 1852): 135–41.

10. FLO, *Walks and Talks* 1:221.

11. PFLO I: FLO to Letitia Brace, Jan. 22, 1892, typed copy; LC: *New York Daily Times*, April 15, May 3, June 9, 1852; FLO, *Walks and Talks* 2:105–6.

12. PFLO I: FLO to CLB, Jan. 11, 1850.

13. PFLO I: FLO to Letitia Brace, Jan. 22, 1892, typed copy; LC: *New York Daily Times*, Feb. 13, 1853.

14. FLO, *A Journey in the Seaboard Slave States*, 1, 16, 307–9, 546, 602–7, 620; PFLO II: FLO to FJK, Feb. 26, 1853; PFLO II: "Yeoman" [FLO], "The South: Letters on the Production, Industry, and Resources of the Slave States; Number Forty-Four," *New York Daily Times*, Nov. 21, 1853, p. 2; JO journal, Apr. 8, 1853.

15. FLO, *Journey in . . . Slave States*, 249.

16. PFLO II: FLO to *New York Daily Times*, Mar. 17, 1853.

17. Ibid.

18. PFLO II: FLO to *New York Daily Times*, Apr. 28, 1853.

19. PFLO II: FLO to CLB and Charles Wyllys Elliott, Dec. 1, 1853.

20. FLO, *Journey through Texas*, 113, 142.

21. PFLO II: FLO to JO, Nov. 8, 1855.

22. PFLO II: FLO to JO, Dec. 9, 1855.

23. PFLO II: JHO to Bertha Olmsted, May 6, 1855; FLO to CLB and Charles Wyllys Elliott, Dec. 1, 1853; memorandum of agreement between Dix and Edwards and Olmsted, Apr. 2, 1855; JHO to JO, Mar. 19, 1855; Roper, " 'Mr. Law.' "

24. Roper, " 'Mr. Law' "; Miller, 336.

25. PFLO II: FLO to JO, Nov. 23, 1855; FLO to Olmsted Jr., Aug. 15, 1891; FLO to JO, July 7, 1855; DAB, Botta, Anne Charlotte Lynch.

26. FLO gave JHO permission to use the text from his journal of the trip "with free scope of expression and personality" (FLO, *Journey through Texas*).

Central Park, the Beginning

1. Charles Wyllis Elliott, secretary of the first Board of Commissioners of Central Park.

2. PFLO III: FLO to president of the Commissioners of Central Park, Aug. 12, 1857.

3. PFLO III: FLO to JHO, Sept. 11, 1857; *Forty Years* 2: 34–35.

4. PFLO III: FLO to JHO, Sept. 11, 1857; *Forty Years* 2: 37–38.

5. *Forty Years* 1:120; 2:31–36.

6. Ibid., 2:30–33.

7. PFLO III: FLO to JHO, Sept. 11, 1857.

8. *Forty Years* 2:33, 39–40.

9. Ibid., 2:36, 38–40; PFLO III: FLO to CLB, Dec. 8, 1860.

10. *Forty Years* 2: 22–29.

11. PFLO III: JHO to FLO, Nov. 13, 1857.

12. PFLO III: JO to FLO, Nov. 28, 1857.

13. *Forty Years* 2:32, 41–44.

14. FLO to Mariana Griswold Van Rensselaer, June 11, 1893; *Forty Years* 2:42–44.

15. *Forty Years* 2:45–48, 188, 217–19.

16. Ibid., 1:197; FLO, *Walks and Talks* 1:67, 75–84; 2:258–59.

17. FLO to Parke Goodwin, Aug. 1, 1858, in Bryant-Goodwin Papers, Manuscript Division, New York Public Library.

18. *Forty Years* 2:49–50, 238, 554–62.

19. PFLO III: FLO to William Augustus Stiles, Mar. 10, 1859; *Forty Years* 2:238–39.

20. Roper, *FLO*, 140.

21. PFLO III: JHO to FLO, Nov. 13, 1857.

22. Ibid.

23. *Forty Years* 1:7; 2:51–52, 55, 534.

24. PFLO III: CV to FLO, Sept. 29, 1859.

25. Giedion, 544–52; *Forty Years* 2:56.

26. *Forty Years* 2:57, 60–61.

27. DAB, Green, Andrew Haswell; *Forty Years* 2:65, 70–73; FLO to JO, Mar. 22, 1861; 2:534.

Civil War, Civil Servant

1. PFLO IV: Censer, 3–4.

2. PFLO III, FLO to CLB, Dec. 8, 1860.

3. PFLO III, FLO to the Board of Commissioners of the Central Park, Jan. 22, 1861.

4. Gerteis, 11–16; PFLO IV, FLO to HWB, June 1, 1861.

5. PFLO IV: FLO to JO, Mar. 22, 1861; FLO to JO, Apr. 17, 1861; Maxwell, 338–41.

6. Bremner, 37–46; Maxwell, 4–9; See also Stille, *History of the United States Sanitary Commission.*

7. Maxwell, 339.

8. PFLO IV: FLO to JHO, June 26, 1861; Strong, 3:159–60, 160n.

9. PFLO IV: FLO to MPO, June 28, 1861.

10. Frederickson, 23–35, 98–112.

11. PFLO III: FLO wrote to CV on Nov. 26, 1863: "I have taken more interest in it, given more thought to it, had greater satisfaction in it than in all else together."

12. PFLO IV: HWB to FLO, ca. June 19, 1861; MPO to FLO, June 2, 1861; FLO to JO, June 26, 1861; Stille, 476, 478–80, 490.

13. Maxwell, 339.

14. PFLO IV: FLO to William Cullen Bryant, July 31, 1861.

15. PFLO IV: FLO to JO, Aug. 3, 1861.

16. PFLO IV: FLO to MPO, Sept. 18, 1861.

17. PFLO IV: Steiner, *A Sketch of the History, Plans of Organization, and Operations of the U.S. Sanitary Commission,* 8.

18. PFLO IV: FLO to Lewis H. Steiner, Aug. 12, 1861.

19. PFLO IV: Censer, 10, citing Alfred D. Chandler Jr., *The Visible Hand: The Managerial Revolution in American Business* (Cambridge, Mass.: Harvard University Press, 1977), 79–121, points out that railroads had pioneered in management theories and practices in

the 1850s, but thinks it more likely that Olmsted, though arriving at most of his ideas about administration out of specific needs at Central Park and in the Sanitary Commission, may have been influenced by other masters of the subject, Quartermaster General Montgomery C. Meigs and Surgeon General William Hammond.

20. PFLO IV: FLO to MPO, Sept. 28, 1861; FLO to Mary Bull Olmsted, Feb. 3, 1862, in the possession of Terry Niles Smith, cited by Censer.

21. PFLO IV: Censer, 12.

22. PFLO IV: FLO to MPO, July 29, 1861.

23. FLO, "Introduction," *Englishman in Kansas*, 28–30, 405–24; PFLO IV: FLO to MPO, Sept. 28, 1861.

24. PFLO IV: Censer, 15.

25. PFLO IV: FLO to JO, Sept. 12, 1861; Maxwell, 96–97.

26. PFLO IV: FLO to HWB, Sept. 29, 1861.

27. PFLO IV: FLO to HWB, Aug. 16, 1861.

28. Maxwell, 109–10; Strong 3:197.

29. Maxwell, 113–15; Strong 3:226.

30. PFLO IV: Censer, 18.

31. PFLO IV: FLO to Thomas A. Scott, Dec. 9, 1861; FLO to HWB, Jan. 18, 1862.

32. PFLO IV: FLO to HWB, Sept. 1, 1863.

33. Maxwell, 137–38.

34. Ibid., 238–47.

35. PFLO IV: FLO to HWB, Dec. 20 and 21, 1861.

36. PFLO IV: Censer, 8; FLO to MPO, July 2, 1861.

37. Maxwell, 339, 341, 349–50; FLO, *Hospital Transports*, 23, 139–42.

38. PFLO IV, Censer; Roper, *FLO*, 190–205.

39. PFLO IV: Censer, 28.

40. Milne, 112–13; Roper, "Olmsted and the Port Royal Experiment," 272–84.

41. PFLO IV: FLO to Salmon P. Chase, Mar. 15, 1862.

42. *Forty Years*, 125–26.

43. PFLO IV: FLO to Manton M. Marble, Feb. 16, 1862; FLO to Edwin M. Stanton, [April 13, 1862].

44. Rose, 17–44.

45. PFLO IV: Censer, 21; FLO to Bertha Olmsted, Jan. 28, 1862; FLO to Lafayette S. Foster, Feb. 3, 1862.

46. PFLO IV: Censer, 22; U.S. Congress, Senate, *Index to Bills and Resolutions of the Senate of the United States, for the Thirty-Seventh Congress. 1861–62–63* (Washington, D.C., 1863).

47. PFLO IV: FLO to James R. Spalding, Feb. 15, 1862.

48. *New York World*, Feb. 19, 1862, 4; PFLO IV: FLO to JO, Feb. 19, 1862; FLO to Manton M. Marble, Feb. 16, 1862.

49. PFLO IV: FLO to HWB, Feb. 25, 1862.

50. PFLO II: 6–8, 13–16, 29–30.

51. PFLO IV: Censer, 24, citing FLO to F. G. Shaw, May 5, 1864; William P. Palmer Papers, Western Reserve Historical Society, Cleveland, Ohio.

52. PFLO IV: Censer, 24, citing Edwin L. Godkin to FLO, Apr. 1865, and FLO to Edwin L. Godkin, [ca. May 1, 1889], 1865, Edwin Lawrence Godkin Papers, Houghton Library, Harvard University, Cambridge, Mass.

53. PFLO IV: FLO to Edwin M. Stanton, [Apr. 13, 1862]; "The South no. 48."

54. McFeely, 99, 105, 146.

55. PFLO IV: Censer, 24, citing FLO, "Testimony before the Special Inquiry Commission," Apr. 22, 1863.

56. Somewhat earlier a similar club had been formed in Philadelphia, but the New York Union League Club — as it was to be known — was an independent organization initially, only later

becoming part of the national group of the same name.

57. PFLO IV: FLO to CLB, Aug. 25, Sept. 20, and Oct. 4, 1862.

58. Roper, *FLO*, 215.

59. PFLO IV: Censer, 39.

60. PFLO IV: FLO to Oliver W. Gibbs, Jan. 31, 1863.

61. PFLO IV: Censer, 40.

62. PFLO IV: FLO to JO, July 25, 1862; FLO to JFJ, Aug. 6, 1862; FLO to JSN, Aug. 21, 1862.

63. PFLO IV: FLO to MPO, Aug. 30, 1862; FLO to John Foster Jenkins, Aug. 31, 1862; FLO to JSN, Aug. 21, 1862.

64. PFLO IV: FLO to MPO, Sept. 21, 1862.

65. PFLO IV: FLO to HWB, Nov. [24], 1862.

66. PFLO IV: Censer, 35.

67. PFLO IV: FLO to JSN, Oct. 11, 1862.

68. PFLO IV: Censer, 37.

69. PFLO IV: FLO to HWB, Oct. 3, 1862.

70. Ibid.

71. PFLO IV: FLO to HWB, Dec. 10, 1862.

72. PFLO IV: FLO to JSN, Nov. 5; FLO to HWB, Dec. 17, 1862.

73. PFLO IV: FLO to HWB, Dec. 27, 1862.

74. PFLO IV: FLO to MPO, Oct. 11, 1862.

75. Beveridge, 404–7; PFLO IV: FLO to MPO, July 7, 1863.

76. PFLO IV: Censer, 8.

77. British writers William Howard Russell and Anthony Trollope had recently published reports on their travels in America. Olmsted believed that neither man did the subject justice.

78. PFLO IV: "Journey in the West, Cincinnati," Mar. 1, 1863; "Journey in the West, Nashville to Murfreesboro," Mar. 7, 1863; "Journey in the West, Memphis to Young's Point," Mar. 16–24, 1863; "Journey in the West, Louisville toward Cairo," Mar. 13, 1863; "Journey in the West, St. Louis, Chicago," Apr. 4–11, 1863.

79. PFLO IV: "Journey in the West, Cincinnati," Mar. 1, 1863.

80. PFLO IV: FLO to MPO, Sept. 28, 1861.

81. Strong 3:291, 304–5.

82. PFLO IV: FLO to HWB, Apr. 25, 1863.

83. Strong 3:160.

84. Ibid., 183–85.

85. Ibid., 211–13.

86. Ibid., 243.

87. Ibid., 276.

88. Ibid., 291.

89. Ibid., 303.

90. Ibid., 304.

91. Ibid., 327.

92. Ibid., 329.

93. Ibid., 502.

94. PFLO IV: FLO to CV, Feb. 16, 1863; PFLO III: CV and FLO to the Board of Commissioners of the Central Park, May 12, 1862.

95. PFLO II: FLO, "Plan of Weekly Magazine"; PFLO IV: FLO to MPO, July 2, 1863; FLO to Edwin L. Godkin, July 19, 1863.

96. PFLO IV: FLO to MPO, July 7, 1863; Maxwell, p. 220.

97. PFLO IV: FLO to HWB, July 25, 1863.

Nature, Barbarity, and Civilization

1. PFLO V: Ranney, 7–9.

2. PFLO V: FLO to MPO, Sept. 25, 1863.

3. PFLO V: FLO to MPO, Oct. 13, 1863.

4. PFLO V: FLO to MPO, Oct. 14–15, 1863.

5. Ibid.

6. PFLO V: FLO to James Hoy, Oct. 19, 1863.

7. Ibid.

8. PFLO V: FLO to JO, Nov. 27, 1863; FLO to MPO, Nov. 20, 1863.

9. PFLO V: FLO to JO, Oct. 30, 1863.

10. LC: FLO to George W. Farlee, Nov. 17, 1863, in Mariposa Letter Book.

11. Olmsted worked on the book at least until 1870, but never achieved a first draft. He established chapter headings, sorted material, collected observations and newspaper clippings.

12. Olmsted's "History of Civilization" — notes and fragments, Olmsted papers, LC R 41 — consists of newspaper clippings and other materials, as well as random jottings and observations recorded by FLO while traveling and reflecting on "communicativeness," sources of and influences on civilization.

13. PFLO V: FLO to MPO, Nov. 20, 1863.

14. FLO to HWB, Mar. 5, 1864, cited in Roper, *FLO*, 508n.

15. PFLO V: FLO to CV, Nov. 26, 1863.

16. Ibid.

17. PFLO V: FLO to CV, Mar. 25, 1864.

18. PFLO V: FLO to JO, June 25, 1864.

19. LC: MPO, Olmsted, Reel 41, undated passage.

20. LC: FLO, "Pioneer Community of the Present Day."

21. FLO, "The Yosemite Valley and the Mariposa Big Trees: A Preliminary Report (1865)," with an introductory note by Laura Wood Roper, *Landscape Architecture* 43 (Oct. 1952): 16. Olmsted's report, one of the most important documents in the history of the national park movement, was lost for many years. Laura Wood Roper, one of his biographers, located an imperfect copy in the Olmsted office in Brookline in 1952, reconstructed and published it.

22. PFLO V: FLO to JO, Aug. 1864.

23. PFLO V: FLO to JO, Sept. 14, 1864.

24. Huth, 52.

25. Roper, *FLO*, 285.

26. FLO, "The Yosemite Valley," 16.

27. Russell, 149.

28. It is sometimes claimed that Olmsted was the philosopher behind the preservation of Yosemite, but there is no evidence that he participated in preliminary discussions with Conness or had any influence on the drafting of the legislation. See Sax, 61, 59–60.

29. Roper, *FLO*, 287.

30. Sax, 71, 64–65.

31. FLO, "The Yosemite Valley," 13–25.

32. PFLO I: McLaughlin, 32.

33. Stevenson, 288.

34. Ibid., 288, 392–93.

35. Roper, *FLO*, 510: FLO to Edwin L. Godkin, Jan. 10, 1865.

36. PFLO V: FLO to JO, Feb. 11, 1865.

37. PFLO V: FLO to CV, Mar. 12, 1865

38. PFLO V: FLO to MPO, Apr. 16, 1865.

A Civilized Man Professes Landscape Architecture

1. PFLO I: FLO, "Passages in the Life of an Unpractical Man"; PFLO VI: FLO to Frederick Knapp, Oct. 8, 1866.

2. PFLO VI: FLO, "On Recreation and Common School Education," [ca. 1868–69].

3. PFLO I: FLO to JHO, June 23, 1845.

4. PFLO VI: FLO to Frederick N. Knapp, Oct. 8, 1866; Olmsted, Vaux and Co., "Architect's Report to the Board of Trustees of the College of Agriculture, and the Mechanic Arts, of the State of Maine," Jan. 22, 1867.

5. LC: FLO to Charles Eliot Norton, Apr. 26, 1866, typed copy. Original in Charles Eliot Norton Papers, LC.

6. Olmsted, Vaux, "Report for San Francisco," 4–5.

7. Ibid., 6–7.

8. Ibid.

9. Roper, *FLO*, 309.

10. PFLO IV: FLO to D. Waldo Lincoln, July 3, 1866.

11. PFLO IV: Olmsted, Vaux, "Preliminary Report Upon a Plan for the General Arrangement of the Premises of the Massachusetts Agricultural College," 1866, n.p. Expanded and published as "A Few Things to be Thought of Before Proceeding to Plan Buildings for the National Agricultural Colleges," Dec. 1866.

12 Ibid.

13. Ibid.

14. Ibid.

15. Ibid.

16. Roper, *FLO*, 309–11.

17. Olmsted, Vaux, "Architect's Report to the Board of Trustees of the College of Agriculture, and the Mechanic Arts, of the State of Maine," Jan. 22, 1867.

18. Roper, *FLO*, 309–11.

19. PFLO VI: Olmsted, Vaux to EMG, July 14, 1866.

20. PFLO VI: FLO to EMG, July 14, 1866.

21. Ibid.

22. PFLO VI: FLO to Andrew Dickson White, June 13, 1867.

23. PFLO VI: FLO to William W. Folwell, June 18, 1870; FLO to William A. Stearns, Apr. 5, 1870.

24. PFLO VI: FLO to Abner Jackson, May 25, 1872.

25. PFLO VI: FLO to Henry B. Rogers, Dec. 13, 1872.

26. PFLO IV: FLO to Edward Bright, Feb. 1, 1867.

27. PFLO VI: FLO, "Public Parks and the Enlargement of Towns," *Journal of Social Science* 3 (1871): 1–36.

Olmsted and Vaux, Partners Again

1. Fein, *Landscape into Cityscape*, 98.

2. Roper, *FLO*, 322.

3. Murray, 166.

4. Sutton, 214.

5. PFLO III: FLO to Parke Godwin, Aug. 1, 1858.

Community Design: Suburban and Urban

1. In 1869, Potter gave the cottage to President Grant for use as his summer cottage.

2. PFLO VI: FLO to CV, Aug. 19, 1868.

3. PFLO VI: Olmsted Vaux, *Preliminary Report upon the Proposed Suburban Village at Riverside, Near Chicago*, Sept. 1, 1868.

4. Ibid.

5. Olmsted held the stocks, paying their cash value to his former partners when Olmsted, Vaux & Company was dissolved. The Tarrytown Heights Land Company declared bankruptcy in 1873.

6. FLO, Elisha Harris, J. M. Trowbridge, and H. H. Richardson, *Report to the Staten Island Improvement Commission of a Preliminary Scheme of Improvement* (New York: n.p., 1871).

7. Roper, *FLO*, 368, from Theodora Kimball.

8. Hitchcock, 167; FLO, Leopold Eidlitz, Henry Hobson Richardson, *Report of the New Capitol Commission Relative to the Plans Submitted by Messrs. Frederick Law Olmstead [sic], Leopold Eidlitz and H. H. Richardson*, no. 49 (State of New York, Senate, March 3, 1876), 4.

9. Schuyler, 161–78; Roper, *FLO*, 367–68.

10. Roper, *FLO*, 367–68.

11. Van Rensselaer, *Richardson*, 22.

12. Ibid.

13. Hitchcock, 118–19; PFLO VI: H. H. Richardson to FLO, Dec. 6, 1874.

14. "New Capitol," 6, 14–15.

15. Roper, *FLO*, 369; PFLO VI: FLO to Charles Eliot Norton, Apr. 22, 1876.

16. "New Capitol," 6, 14–15; Schuyler, 161–78.

17. *American Architect and Building News* 1 (Apr. 1, 1876): 114.

18. Van Rensselaer, *Richardson*, 75; PFLO VI: FLO to William M. Hunt, Apr. 4, 1876.

19. *American Architect and Building News* 2 (Mar. 17, 1877): 85.

20. FLO, memorandum on Albany Capitol, n.d., cited by Roper, *FLO*, 371.

21. Roper, *FLO*, 370–71; Schuyler, p. 166.

22. Hitchcock, 169–70.

23. Schuyler, 167–69.

24. *American Architect and Building News*, 29.

25. *Architects' and Mechanics' Journal* 3 (February 1861), 233.

26. Roper, *FLO*, 373.

27. John Nolen, "Frederick Law Olmsted and His Work. II: The Terraces and Landscape Work of the United States Capitol at Washington," *House and Garden* 9 (Mar. 1906): 117–28; *Annual Report of the Architect of the United States Capitol for the Fiscal Year Ending June 30, 1882, Edward Clark, Architect, with a Paper Relating to the Trees, Shrubs and Plants in the United States Capitol Ground, Together with Some Observations upon the Planting and Care of Trees in the District of Columbia by Frederick Law Olmsted, Landscape Architect* (Washington, D.C.: Government Printing Office, 1882), 13.

28. *Annual Report . . . 1882*, 13–14.

29. Ibid, 14–15.

30. PFLO VI: Albert Henry Olmsted to FLO, May 28, 1873.

31. Frary, 307.

32. Roper, *FLO*, 375.

33. LC: FLO to William Hammond Hall, Mar. 28, 1874.

34. *Annual Report . . . 1882*, 15–16.

35. Ibid.

36. PFLO VI: FLO to George E. Waring Jr., July 19, 1874.

37. Roper, *FLO*, 377.

38. *New York Tribune*, Nov. 18, 1874.

39. Charles C. McLaughlin, "The Capitol in Peril? The West Front Controversy from Walter to Stewart," *Records of the Columbia Historical Society of Washington, D.C., 1969–70* (Washington, D.C., 1971), 241–46; *Annual Report of the Architect of the United States Capitol*, 14–15.

40. Roper, *FLO*, 378, 399.

41. LC: FLO to F. H. Cobb, June 11, 1878.

42. Collection of the Corcoran Museum, Washington, D.C.

43. Dow, 9.

44. Fein, *American Environmental Tradition*, 42.

45. Sax, 64.

46. Huth, 150.

47. Van Rensselaer, *Richardson*, 118.

48. FLO, *Government Preservation of Natural Scenery*, Brookline, Mass., Mar. 8, 1890.

49. Dow, 10–11.

50. Ibid.

51. Ibid.

52. Ibid.

53. *Special Report of the New York State Survey on the Preservation of the Scenery of Niagara Falls, and Fourth Annual Report on the Triangulation of the State. For the Year 1879. James T. Gardner, Director* (Albany, N.Y.: Charles Van Benthuysen & Sons, 1880), 7.

54. Roper, *FLO*, 381.

55. *Special Report of the New York State Survey*, 31–39.

56. Ibid.

57. Roper, *FLO*, 381.

58. LC: FLO to Howard Potter, July 4, 1881.

59. Roper, *FLO*, 382, 395.

60. Ibid., 396.

61. Todd, 152; Jonathan Baxter Harrison, "Charles Eliot Norton and Niagara Falls," Charles Eliot Norton Papers, LC.62. Roper, *FLO*, 397.

62. Roper, *FLO*, 397.

63. FLO, "Governmental Preservation of Natural Scenery."

64. Sax, 78–79.

The "Unpractical" Man

1. PFLO VI: FLO to FJK, Jan. 28, 1873.

2. Ibid.

3. PFLO VI: FLO to CLB, Apr. 20, 1871.

4. LC: MPO, July 16, 1920.

5. PFLO VI: FLO to Samuel Bowles, May 7, 1872.

6. PFLO VI: Samuel Bowles to FLO, May 14, 1872.

7. Ibid.

8. LC: MPO, July 16, 1879.

9. FLO, *City of Newport, Improvement of Easton's Beach, Preliminary Report* (Boston: Franklin Press, 1883).

10. Roper, *FLO*, 406, interview with FLO Jr.

11. PFLO VI: FLO to Charles Eliot, July 20, 1886.

12. Roper, *FLO*, 407, citing FLO, "Letter of Professor Olmsted. Relative to the General Duties of Park Commissioners and Incidental Matters," *Fourth Annual Report of the Board of Park Commissioners of the City of Minneapolis for the Year Ending March 14, 1887* (Minneapolis: Tribune Job Printing Co., 1887), 15–25.

13. Clark, 401–3.

14. *Garden and Forest: A Journal of Horticulture, Landscape Art, and Forestry* 1 (Dec. 9, 1888):507.

15. PFLO VI: FLO to JCO, Sept. 29, 1886; FLO to JCO, Sept. 24, 1886.

16. LC: FLO to LS, Nov. 27, 1886.

17. Ibid.

18. Bancroft, 117.

19. McGuire, 349; Roper, *FLO*, 412–14.

20. Roper, *FLO*, 411.

21. Ibid., 412, cites FLO letter to Mariana Griswold Van Rennselaer, May 17, 1887.

22. Ibid.

23. McGuire, 349.

24. Roper, *FLO*, 412.

25. LC: Henry S. Codman to FLO, Mar. 20, 1880.

26. LC: FLO to LS, Mar. 16, 1889.

27. Roper, *FLO*, 415, cites FLO to Ariel Lathrop, July 7, 1890.

28. LC: FLO to LS, Aug. 7, 1890.

29. Roper, *FLO*, 415, based on interviews with FLO Jr.

30. Stevenson, 382.

31. LC: FLO to FJK, Jan. 20, 1891.

32. Roper, *FLO*, 419.

33. LC: FLO to FJK, Jan. 20, 1891.

34. Newton, 339–46.

35. LC: FLO to Richard Morris Hunt, Mar. 2, 1889.

36. FLO to Charles McNamee, May 31, 1889.

37. LC: FLO to GWV, July 12, 1889.

38. LC: FLO to FJK, Jan. 20, 1891.

39. Ibid.

40. FLO, evidently to instruct GWV in the scientific nature of forestry, sent him two pamphlets: Cleveland's *The Cultivation and Management of Our Native Forests for Development as Timber or Ornamental Wood*, and his own and J. B. Harrison's *Observations on the Treatment of Public Plantations, More Especially Relating to the Use of the Axe.*

41. LC: FLO to GWV, July 12, 1889.

42. Pinchot, *Breaking New Ground*, 15.

43. Pinchot, *Diary*, Feb. 1, 1891.

44. Ibid., Oct. 14, Nov. 12, 1891; Pinchot, *Breaking New Ground*, 48–49.

45. LC: FLO to GWV, July 12, 1889.

46. Ibid.

47. Ibid.

48. *New York Sun*, June 19, 1890.

49. LC: FLO to his partners, Nov. 1, 1893.

50. Roper, *FLO*, 423, cites FLO to FLO Jr., Sept. 5, 1890.

51. Stevenson, 389; Newton, 351.

52. Giedion, 209.

53. Ibid., 210.

54. Andrews, *Architecture, Ambition, and Americans*, 214.

55. LC: FLO to W. A. Stiles, Mar. 10, 1895.

56. Newton, 362–63.

57. Fabos, Milde, and Weinmayr, 91.

58. LC: FLO to John Charles Olmsted, Nov. 24, 1890.

59. Newton, 360.

60. LC: FLO to Henry van Brunt, Jan. 22, 1891.

61. Tunnard, *City of Man*, 304.

62. Moore 1:47.

63. Newton, 359.

64. LC: FLO to FJK, Jan. 20, 1891.

65. LC: FLO to Henry S. Codman, Nov. 4, 1891.

66. Stevenson, 398.

67. Roper, *FLO*, 429, "Memorandum as to What is to be Aimed at in the Planting of the Lagoon District of the Chicago Exposition, as Proposed March, 1891," *American Florist* 11 (Jan. 11, 1896).

68. Roper, *FLO*, "Report upon the Landscape Architecture," 14.

69. LC: FLO to Daniel H. Burnham, Dec. 23, 28, 1891.

70. LC: FLO to partners, July 17, 1892.

71. Ranney, *Olmsted in Chicago*, 37–38.

72. Roper, *FLO*, 426n.

73. "Landscape Gardening at the Columbian Fair," 501.

74. Moore 1:74.

75. LC: FLO to Daniel H. Burnham, June 20, 1893.

76. Heckscher, *Open Spaces*, 19–24.

77. Roper, *FLO*, 383.

78. FLO, "The Future of New York," *New York Tribune*, December 28, 1879.

79. LC: FLO to Edouard André, July 29, 1878.

80. Stevenson, 353–54.

81. LC: FLO to C. F. Ware, Nov. 1, 1881.

82. LC: FLO to C. H. Cobb (architect, Capitol, Washington, D.C.), Nov. 22, 1881.

83. Stevenson, 356.

84. Ibid.

85. Roper, *FLO*, 383.

86. LC: FLO to CLB, Mar. 7, 1882.

87. Sutton, 56.

88. Ibid., 65.

89. Ibid., 78.

90. Ibid., 80.

91. Fabos, Milde, and Weinmayr, 57–58.

92. Newton, 295–96.

93. Ibid., 298.

94. Ibid., 299.

95. Fabos, Milde, and Weinmayr, 58–59.

96. Blodgett, "FLO": 883–85.

97. LC: FLO to his partners, Oct. 28, 1893.

98. Newton, 301, 304.

The End of a Career

1. LC: "Decoration Day," 1884.

2. Ibid.

3. FLO to John Charles Olmsted, Oct. 9, 1886.

4. Ibid.

5. Stevenson, 376.

6. Ibid., 357.

7. Ibid.

8. Roper, *FLO*, 401.

9. LC: FLO to CLB, Nov. 1, 1884.

10. Ibid.

11. LC: FLO to CLB, Mar. 15, 1887.

12. LC: FLO to CLB, Jan. 18, 1890.

13. Stevenson, 367.

14. LC: FLO to FJK, Jan. 20, 1891.

15. Roper, *FLO*, 419–21.

16. Ibid.

17. Ibid., 469.

Epilogue

1. Barlow and Alex, *FLO's New York*, 54, 56.

2. Smithson, "FLO and the Dialectical Landscape," 65.

3. Huxtable, "It Isn't Green Cheese," 25.

4. Roper, *FLO*, 398.

Bibliography

Olmsted's Papers and Collections

Olmsted, Frederick Law. Archives and photographs. Olmsted Associates, Brookline, Mass.

———. Papers and related materials. Manuscript Division, Library of Congress, Washington, D.C.

Works by Olmsted

Olmsted, Frederick Law. *The Cotton Kingdom*. Ed. Arthur M. Schlesinger. New York: Alfred A. Knopf, 1953.

———. Introduction to *The Englishman in Kansas, or, Squatter Life and Border Warfare*, by Thomas H. Gladstone. New York: Miller and Co., 1857.

———. *A Journey in the Back Country*. New York: Mason Brothers, 1860.

———. *A Journey in the Back Country*. With an introduction by Clement Eaton. New York: Schocken Books, 1970.

———. *A Journey in the Seaboard Slave States, with Remarks on Their Economy*. New York: Dix and Edwards, 1856.

———. *A Journey through Texas; or, a Saddle-Trip on the Southwestern Frontier*. New York: Dix and Edwards, 1857.

———. *Walks and Talks of an American Farmer in England*. 2 vols. New York: G. P. Putnam, 1852.

———. *Walks and Talks of an American Farmer in England*. With an introduction by Alex L. Murray. Ann Arbor: University of Michigan Press, 1967.

The Papers of Frederick Law Olmsted: I, The Formative Years. Ed. Charles Capen McLaughlin. Baltimore: Johns Hopkins Press, 1977

The Papers of Frederick Law Olmsted: II, Slavery and the South. Ed. Charles Beveridge and Charles Capen McLaughlin. Baltimore: Johns Hopkins Press, 1981.

The Papers of Frederick Law Olmsted: III, Creating Central Park. Ed. Charles E. Beveridge and David Schuyler. Baltimore: Johns Hopkins Press, 1983.

The Papers of Frederick Law Olmsted: IV, Defending the Union. Ed. Jane Turner Censer and Gerard J. Rauluk. Baltimore: Johns Hopkins Press, 1986.

The Papers of Frederick Law Olmsted: V, The California Frontier. Ed. Victoria Post Ranney. Baltimore: Johns Hopkins Press, 1990.

The Papers of Frederick Law Olmsted: VI, The Years of Olmsted, Vaux & Company. Ed. David Schuyler and Jane Turner Censer. Baltimore: Johns Hopkins Press, 1992.

Books about Olmsted and His Times

Adams, George Washington. *Doctors in Blue: The Medical History of the Union Army in the Civil War*. New York: H. Schuman, 1952.

Andrews, Wayne. *Architecture, Ambition, and Americans: A Social History of American Architecture*. Rev. ed. New York: Free Press, 1978.

———. *Architecture in America: A Photographic History from the Colonial Period to the Present*. New York: Atheneum Press, 1960.

———. *The Vanderbilt Legend: The Story of the Vanderbilt Family, 1794–1940*. New York: Harcourt, Brace and Co., 1941.

Bade, William F. *The Life and Letters of John Muir.* 2 vols. Boston: Houghton Mifflin, 1924.

Bancroft, Hubert Howe. *History of the Life of Leland Stanford: A Character Study.* Oakland, Calif.: Biobooks, 1952.

Barlow, Elizabeth, and William Alex. *Frederick Law Olmsted's New York.* New York: Praeger, 1972.

Bender, Thomas. *Toward an Urban Vision.* Lexington: University of Kentucky Press, 1975.

Bowles, Samuel. *Across the Continent: A Stage Ride over the Plains, to the Rocky Mountains, the Mormons, and the Pacific States, in the Summer of 1865, with Speaker Colfax.* New York: Hurd and Houghton, 1869.

Brace, Emma, ed. *Life of Charles Loring Brace, Chiefly Told in His Own Letters.* New York: Charles Scribner's Sons, 1894.

Bremner, Robert H. *The Public Good: Philanthropy and Welfare in the Civil War Era.* New York: Knopf, 1980.

Cecil, William A. V. *Biltmore: The Vision and Reality of George W. Vanderbilt, Richard Morris Hunt, and Frederick Law Olmsted.* Asheville, N.C.: Biltmore Estate, 1972.

Clark, George T. *Leland Stanford, War Governor of California, Railroad Builder and Founder of Stanford University.* Stanford, Calif.: Stanford University Press, 1931.

Cranz, Galen. *The Politics of Park Design: A History of Urban Parks in America.* Cambridge, Mass.: MIT Press, 1982.

Dow, Charles M. *The State Reservation at Niagara, a History.* Albany, N.Y.: J. B. Lyon, 1914.

Downing, Andrew Jackson. *The Architecture of Country Houses, Including Designs for Cottages, Farm Houses, and Villas.* New York: D. Appleton and Co., 1850.

———. *Rural Essays.* New York: George P. Putnam and Co., 1953.

———. *A Treatise on the Theory and Practice of Landscape Gardening, Adapted to North America, with a View to the Improvement of Country Residences.* New York: George P. Putnam and Co., 1853.

Fabos, Julius G.; Gordon T. Milde; and V. Michael Weinmayr. *Frederick Law Olmsted, Sr.: Founder of Landscape Architecture in America.* Amherst: University of Massachusetts Press, 1968.

Fein, Albert. "The American City: The Ideal and the Real." In *The Rise of an American Architecture,* by Henry-Russell Hitchcock et al. New York: Praeger, 1970.

———. *Frederick Law Olmsted and the American Environmental Tradition.* New York: George Braziller, 1972.

———. *Landscape into Cityscape: Frederick Law Olmsted's Plans for a Greater New York City.* Ithaca, N.Y.: Cornell University Press, 1967.

Fitch, James M. *Architecture and the Esthetics of Plenty.* New York: Columbia University Press, 1961.

Fogel, Robert William, and Stanley L. Engerman. *Time on the Cross: The Economics of American Negro Slavery.* Boston: Little, Brown and Co., 1974.

Frary, Ihna Thayer. *They Built the Capitol.* Richmond, Va.: Garrett and Massie, 1940.

Frederickson, George M. *The Inner Civil War: Northern Intellectuals and the Crisis of the Union.* New York: Harper & Row, 1965.

Gerteis, Louis S. *From Contraband to Freedman: Federal Policy toward Southern Blacks, 1861–1865.* Westport, Conn.: 1973.

Giedion, Sigfried. *Space, Time, and Architecture: The Growth of a New Tradition.* Cambridge, Mass.: Harvard University Press, 1949.

Heckscher, August. *Alive in the City: Memoir of an Ex-Commissioner.* New York: Charles Scribner's Sons, 1974.

———. *Open Spaces: The Life of American Cities.* New York: 1977.

Hines, Thomas S. *Burnham of Chicago, Architect and Planner.* New York: Oxford University Press, 1974.

Hitchcock, Henry-Russell. *The Architecture of Henry Hobson Richardson.* Hamden, Conn.: Archon Books, 1961.

Hoffman, Donald. *The Architecture of John Wellborn Root.* Baltimore: Johns Hopkins Press, 1968.

Huth, Hans. *Nature and the American: Three Centuries of Chang-*

ing Attitudes. Lincoln, Neb.: University of Nebraska Press, 1972.

Johnson, Allen, and Dumas Malone, eds. *Dictionary of American Biography.* New York: Charles Scribner's Sons, 1928–36.

Johnson, Philip. "Why We Want Our Cities Ugly." In *The Fitness of Man's Environment.* Smithsonian Annual II. Washington, D.C.: Smithsonian Institution Press, 1968.

Kimball, Theodora, and Frederick Law Olmsted Jr., eds. *Forty Years of Landscape Architecture: Frederick Law Olmsted, Sr.* 2 vols. New York: B. Blom, 1970.

Lynes, Russell. *The Art Makers of Nineteenth-Century America.* New York: Atheneum Press, 1970.

McFeely, William W. *Frederick Douglass.* New York: W. W. Norton and Company, 1991.

Mandelbaum, Seymour J. *Boss Tweed's New York.* New York: John Wiley, 1965.

Marx, Leo. *The Machine in the Garden.* New York: Oxford University Press, 1964.

Maxwell, William Quentin. *Lincoln's Fifth Wheel: The Political History of the United States Sanitary Commission.* New York: 1956.

Merriam, George S. *The Life and Times of Samuel Bowles.* 2 vols. New York: Century, 1885.

Miller, Perry G. *The Raven and the Whale: The War of Words and Wits in the Era of Poe and Melville.* New York: 1956.

Milne, Gordon. *George William Curtis and the Genteel Tradition.* Bloomington, Ind.: Indiana University Press, 1956.

Mitchell, Broadus. *Frederick Law Olmsted, a Critic of the Old South.* Baltimore: Johns Hopkins Press, 1924.

Moore, Charles. *Daniel Hudson Burnham, Architect, Planner of Cities.* Boston: Houghton Mifflin, 1921.

Mumford, Lewis. *The Culture of Cities.* New York: Harcourt, Brace and Co., 1938.

———. *The Myth of the Machine: The Pentagon of Power.* New York: Harcourt, Brace and Co., 1964.

———. *The Urban Prospect.* New York: Harcourt, Brace and World, 1968.

Mumford, Lewis, and Walter Muir Whitehill. *Back Bay Boston: The City as a Work of Art.* Publication accompanying an exhibition at the Museum of Fine Arts, Boston, Nov. 1, 1969–Jan. 11, 1970.

Nash, Roderick. *Wilderness and the American Mind.* New Haven, Conn.: Yale University Press, 1967.

Nevins, Allan. *The Emergence of Modern America, 1865–78.* New York: Macmillan, 1927.

———. *Frémont: Pathmaker of the West.* New York: D. Appleton-Century, 1939.

Newton, Norman T. *Design on the Land: The Development of Landscape Architecture.* Cambridge: Harvard University Press, 1971.

Novak, Barbara. *American Painting of the Nineteenth Century: Realism, Idealism, and the American Experience.* New York: Praeger, 1969.

Noyes, Russell. *Wordsworth and the Art of Landscape.* Bloomington, Ind.: Indiana University Press, 1968.

Pevsner, Nikolaus. *Sources of Modern Architecture and Design.* London: Thames and Hudson, 1968.

Pinchot, Gifford. *Breaking New Ground.* New York: Harcourt, Brace and Co., 1947.

———. *Diary.* Pinchot Papers, Library of Congress.

Putnam, George Palmer. *A Memoir of George Palmer Putnam.* 2 vols. New York: G. P. Putnam's Sons, 1903.

Ranney, Victoria Post. *Olmsted in Chicago.* Chicago: R. R. Donnelley and Sons, 1972.

Reed Jr., Henry Hope, and Sophia Duckworth. *Central Park: A History and a Guide.* New York: Clarkson N. Potter, 1967.

Rode's New York City Directory for 1850–1851. New York, 1850.

Roper, Laura Wood. *FLO: A Biography of Frederick Law Olmsted.* Baltimore: Johns Hopkins Press, 1973.

Rose, Willie Lee. *Rehearsal for Reconstruction: The Port Royal Experiment.* Indianapolis: Bobbs Merrill, 1964.

Russell, Carl P. *One Hundred Years in Yosemite: The Story of a Great Park and Its Friends.* Berkeley, Calif.: University of California Press, 1947.

Saarinen, Aline B. *The Proud Possessors: The Lives, Times and Taste of Some Adventurous American Art Collectors.* New York: Random House, 1958.

Saint-Gaudens, Augustus. *Reminiscences.* Ed. Homer Saint-Gaudens. 2 vols. New York: Century, 1913.

Schmitt, Peter J. *Back to Nature: The Arcadian Myth in Urban America.* New York: Oxford University Press, 1969.

Shepherd, Paul. *Man in the Landscape.* New York: Alfred A. Knopf, 1967.

Silver, Nathan. *Lost New York.* Boston: Houghton Mifflin, 1967.

Stevenson, Elizabeth. *Park Maker: A Life of Frederick Law Olmsted.* New York: Macmillan, 1977.

Stille, Charles J. *History of the United States Sanitary Commission: Being the General Report of Its Work during the War of the Rebellion.* Philadelphia: J. B. Lippincott, 1866.

Strong, George Templeton. *The Diary of George Templeton Strong.* Ed. Allan Nevins and Milton Halsey Thomas. 4 vols. New York: Macmillan, 1952.

Sullivan, Louis. *The Autobiography of an Idea.* New York: A.I.A., 1924.

Sutton, S. B., ed. *Civilizing American Cities: A Selection of Frederick Law Olmsted's Writings on City Landscapes.* Cambridge: Harvard University Press, 1971.

Tharp, Louise Hall. *Saint-Gaudens and the Gilded Era.* Boston: Little, Brown and Co., 1963.

Tocqueville, Alexis de. *Democracy in America.* Ed. Phillips Bradley. New York: Alfred A. Knopf, 1945.

Todd, John Emerson. *Frederick Law Olmsted.* Boston: Twayne, 1982.

Tunnard, Christopher. *The City of Man.* New York: Charles Scribner's Sons, 1953.

Tunnard, Christopher, and Henry Hope Reed Jr. *American Skyline.* Boston: Houghton Mifflin, 1955.

Turner, Frederick Jackson. *The United States, 1830–50: The Nation and Its Sections.* New York: Henry Holt and Co., 1935.

Van Rensselaer, Mariana Griswold. *Henry Hobson Richardson and His Works.* Boston: Houghton Mifflin, 1888.

Wilson, Edmund. *Patriotic Gore: Studies in the Literature of the American Civil War.* New York: Oxford University Press, 1962.

Periodicals, Newspapers, and Dissertations

Beveridge, Charles Eliot. "Frederick Law Olmsted: The Formative Years, 1822–1865." Ph.D. diss., University of Wisconsin, 1966.

"Birthday of New York's Central Park." *Nation,* Aug. 1, 1953, 83.

Blodgett, Geoffrey. "Frederick Law Olmsted: Landscape Architecture as Conservative Reform." *Journal of American History* 62 (1976): 883–85.

Boyle-Cullen, Margaret. "The Woods of Arden House." Part 3. *Staten Island Historian* 15, no. 2 (Apr.–June 1954): 14.

"Cities and Parks." *Atlantic Monthly,* Apr. 1861, 416–29.

Garden and Forest: A Journal of Horticulture, Landscape Art, and Forestry 6 (May 3, 1893).

Harrington, Michael J. "Addition to the West Side of the Capitol." *Congressional Record,* Jan. 28, 1970, E415–18.

Heidrich, Robert W. "A Village in a Park: Riverside, Illinois." *Historic Preservation* 25, no. 2 (Apr.–June 1973).

Huxtable, Ada Louise. "It Isn't Green Cheese." *New York Times,* May 21, 1972, sec. 2, p. 25.

———. "Up in Central Park." *New York Times,* Mar. 19, 1967.

"Landscape Gardening at the Columbian Fair," *Garden and Forest: A Journal of Horticulture, Landscape Art, and Forestry* 6 (Dec. 6, 1893).

McGuire, Diane Kostal. "Early Site Planning on the West Coast: Frederick Law Olmsted's Plan for Stanford University." *Landscape Architecture* 47 (Jan. 1957).

Martin, J. S. "He Paints with Lakes and Wooded Slopes." *American Heritage* 15, no. 6 (Oct. 1964): 14–19.

Murray, A. L. "Frederick Law Olmsted and the Design of Mount Royal Park, Montreal." *Journal of the Society of Architectural Historians* 26 (1967): 166.

"The Present Planner." *Time*, Dec. 11, 1972.

Roper, Laura Wood. "Frederick Law Olmsted and the Port Royal Experiment." *Journal of Southern History* 31 (Aug. 1965): 272–84.

———. "Frederick Law Olmsted and the Western Texas Free-Soil Movement." *American Historical Review* 57 (Oct. 1950): 58–64.

———. "Frederick Law Olmsted in the 'Literary Republic.'" *Mississippi Valley Historical Review* 39, no. 3 (1952–1953), 459–82.

———. " 'Mr. Law' and *Putnam's Monthly Magazine*: A Note on a Phase in the Career of Frederick Law Olmsted." *American Literature* 26 (Mar. 1954): 89–90.

Sax, Joseph L. "America's National Parks: Their Principles, Purposes, and Prospects." *Natural History Special Supplement* (Oct. 1976).

Schickel, Richard. "Frederick Law Olmsted, Creator of 'The Central Park.' " *New York Times Magazine*, Dec. 31, 1972.

Schuyler, Montgomery. "The Capitol of New York." *Scribner's Monthly Magazine*, Dec. 1879, 161–78.

Smithson, Robert. "Frederick Law Olmsted and the Dialectical Landscape." *Artforum* 11 (1973): 65.

Tatum, George B. "The Emergence of an American School of Landscape Design." *Historic Preservation* 25, no. 2 (Apr.–June 1973).

Van Rensselaer, Mariana Griswold. "Frederick Law Olmsted." *Century Illustrated Monthly Magazine* 46, no. 6 (Oct. 1893): 860–67.

Index